TRANSBOUNDARY POLICY CHALLENGES
IN THE PACIFIC BORDER REGIONS
OF NORTH AMERICA

TRANSBOUNDARY
POLICY CHALLENGES
IN THE PACIFIC BORDER REGIONS OF NORTH AMERICA

edited by
**JAMES LOUCKY,
DONALD K. ALPER,
AND J. C. DAY**

UNIVERSITY OF
CALGARY
PRESS

University of Calgary Press
2500 University Drive NW
Calgary, Alberta
Canada T2N 1N4
www.uofcpress.com

LIBRARY AND ARCHIVES CANADA CATALOGUING IN PUBLICATION

Transboundary policy challenges in the Pacific border regions of North
America / edited by James Loucky, Donald K. Alper and J.C. Day.

Includes bibliographical references and index.
ISBN 978-1-55238-223-3

1. Environmental policy–North America–International cooperation. 2.
Environmental management–North America–International cooperation. 3.
Environmental protection–North America–International cooperation. I.
Loucky, James II. Alper, Donald K. III. Day, John C.
(John Chadwick), 1936–

GE190.N7T73 2007   363.7'0526   C2007-905579-6

The University of Calgary Press acknowledges the support of the Alberta
Foundation for the Arts for our publications. We acknowledge the financial
support of the Government of Canada through the Book Publishing Industry
Development Program (BPIDP) for our publishing activities. We acknowledge
the financial support of the Canada Council for the Arts for our publishing
program.

Printed and bound in Canada by AGMV Marquis
∞ This book is printed on FSC Silva Enviro paper

Cover photo top: Twin border roads, British Columbia/Washington State, set
against Mount Baker, WA (photo by J.C. Day, August 2007).

Cover photo bottom: Border barriers between Tijuana and Otay Mesa, San
Diego (photo by James Loucky, November 2001).

Cover design, page design and typesetting by Melina Cusano

Contents

Acknowledgments

The magnitude of contemporary global economic developments and the gravity of environmental dilemmas underline how the capacity and health of natural systems are increasingly linked to the priorities and institutional arrangements of human communities. People are compelled to think and act in new ways, including through engaging more actively in international research and civic activities. Emerging from this sense of urgency as well as optimism about the potential synergies of cross-border efforts, this book represents a collaboration among scholars in the three countries of North America. Seeds for this book were nurtured further through a workshop on "Border Bio-Regions and Coastal Corridors" held in Bellingham, Washington, and Vancouver, British Columbia, in October 2001. Critical support was provided by a trinational grant awarded by the Bureau of Educational and Cultural Affairs, of the U.S. Department of State, to Western Washington University, Simon Fraser University, and El Colegio de la Frontera Norte (COLEF).

Many people contributed to the success of the transboundary activities reported in this book and to the book itself. The initial spark was set by Jorge Bustamante, founder of COLEF, who envisioned a time when cross-border and trinational knowledge would become standard for preparing new policy researchers in the countries of North America. We are grateful for the consistent support provided by Maria Urbina of the Bureau of Educational and Cultural Affairs, U.S. Department of State. Viva Barnes, Administrative Services Manager in the Department of Anthropology at Western Washington University, has been invaluable throughout the course of our efforts. We are also grateful to

Chuck Hart, Emma Spenner Norman, Marty Hitchcock, Jean Webster, and Alison Lesure for their dedicated assistance. Jose Luis Castro-Ruiz and Carlos de la Parra of El Colegio de la Frontera Norte were both instrumental in helping to make this initiative a reality. Thanks also go to Paul DeGrace of Simon Fraser University for the cartography.

1

POLICY CHALLENGES IN NORTH AMERICA'S PACIFIC BORDER REGIONS: AN OVERVIEW

J.C. Day, James Loucky, and Donald K. Alper

Border regions, which were once peripheral to growth and development, are now primary areas for economic and social transformations, which in turn engender significant changes elsewhere within countries. The accelerated flows of people, products, and pollutants associated with global integration also make border regions particularly vulnerable to environmental degradation. In North America, increasing evidence of substantial environmental problems has provoked an upsurge of concern on both sides of the Canada–United States and Mexico–United States borders. Nonetheless, efforts to confront problems posed by growth and by past environmental neglect continue to be constrained by nation-centred policy processes, distinctive institutional structures, and lack of trained specialists capable of working across cultures.

Rising awareness of deepening environmental problems and of the complexities entailed in wise development decisions, particularly in high-growth border areas, has spurred recognition that new realities require innovative responses. Critical for effective environmental protection, restoration, and education is a sharing of information and efforts across borders. Currently, as with many maps, knowledge of environmental, social, and economic issues and of local and

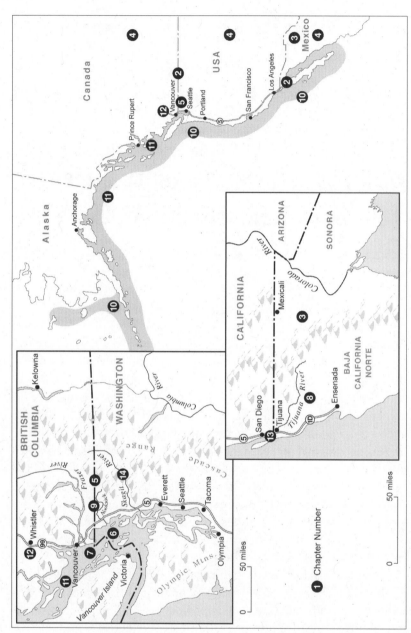

Figure 1.1   Study areas in this volume identified by chapter.

J.C. Day, James Loucky, and Donald K. Alper

educational responses often stops at borders. Comprehensive strategies to deal with these problems are still largely incipient. But there is growing agreement regarding the need for binational and trinational cooperation in adopting comprehensive environmental and economic management systems for effective environmental protection and sustainable development across North America.

This volume responds to a heightening interest in borderlands environmental policy by reporting on significant transboundary research and practice being undertaken within and across the Pacific border regions of North America. The interconnections between ecosystems management and urban and social policy formation are complex, particularly within the fast-growing border areas of the continent. The goal of this book is to advance transborder environmental research along with sensible policy directions, particularly in the most critical areas of international concern and engagement: land and water planning, regional growth management, trade and transportation corridors, environmental education, and travel and tourism. Coverage encompasses both North American borders, principally along the Pacific coast, as well as a wider region where border events are significant (fig. 1.1). In undertaking this assessment, multidisciplinary expertise is drawn from institutions in all three countries.

The critical relationship between growth and environmental health in border bioregions is a central underlying theme. The seeds for this book emerged following a conference on border bioregions and Pacific coastal corridors of North America held at Western Washington University (WWU) and Simon Fraser University (SFU), British Columbia, in October 2001. This meeting involved participants in a multiyear trinational project involving universities in all three North American countries (WWU, SFU, and El Colegio de la Frontera Norte). Contributors to this book also include a select number of invitees from other Pacific border institutions and agencies. Beyond the knowledge generated through each case, the book identifies policy concerns common to the two North American border regions as well as critical issues requiring further interdisciplinary, cross-border effort.

Methodologically, the book draws together empirical case studies that, in most instances, have a comparative or cross-border dimension. Each also explicitly addresses environmental, social, or economic policy concerns as well as implications for longer-term regional and multinational frameworks for cooperation and reform. These cases allow the examination of crucial aspects of similar problems set in different sociopolitical contexts.

The range of cross-border interactions on the Pacific coast is extremely complex and the web of institutional responsibility to monitor and control these interactions are equally complex. Movements occur at a variety of spatial scales, at varying speeds, some predominantly in one direction and others with balanced movement. Some of these movements are largely restricted to, or in close proximity to, a narrow border region while others are continental in scale.

While there are obvious differences between the U.S.-Mexico border and the U.S.-Canada border in terms of ecological character, the two main west coast human corridors – Vancouver-Seattle and San Diego–Tijuana – have much in common. In the introductory chapter, Loucky and Alper examine these commonalities, which include rapid growth, urbanization, and accelerated transborder linkages. Both borders are also characterized by serious environmental vulnerability. These similarities provide a valuable opportunity for sharing knowledge of environmental and growth management approaches between, as well as across, each border.

The demographic growth that is fundamental to the profound changes in the Pacific border regions of North America is examined in chapter 3. Mendoza and Loucky analyze recent U.S.-Mexican border demographic trends in an effort to determine if there is a unique border region in sociodemographic terms, and whether the international line deters spatial diffusion or influences regional environmental impacts. The chapter concludes that striking differences persist on both sides of the border in terms of population distribution and growth, as well as age profiles, and questions whether a unified region exists in demographic terms along the Mexican-U.S. border.

The crucial relationship between energy use and economic growth in the Mexico–United States and the Canada–United States Pacific border regions is elaborated by Díaz-Bautista, Alper, and Martinez in chapter 4. Growing energy demands driven by more users and higher economic activity have direct impacts on the environment, including increased air pollution. The emerging energy crises in North America appear most obvious in Mexico and California. But energy flows, national economic and environmental regulations, and policy prospects only make sense when viewed from a continental frame of reference. Currently, energy movements for electricity, gas, and oil – which are continental in scale – are well established along the west coast of North America, largely from Canada and Mexico to the United States. Challenges associated with natural gas demands, oil import vulnerability, refinery capacity, and energy needs require transnational approaches, as do successful responses to international movement of pollutants, migration of species, and protection of habitats.

The interrelationships of transportation, land use, and sustainability in the booming western Canadian and U.S. border corridor extending south to Oregon are given much-needed focus by Schiller in chapter 5. Current public policy discussions highlight the role of the region's major cities in influencing the overall development of the area, as well as heightened security concerns associated with cross-border transportation of people and freight. The author recommends that policy discussions focus on how to transform current patterns of transportation, land use, and commerce to ensure that they are more environmentally and socially sustainable. Much of the automobile, long-distance truck traffic, and commercial aviation travel within the region, for example, might be diverted to rail to enhance the sustainability of the region's transportation system and to reduce the burden of transportation on the binational environment. These movements vary in scale from national to short- or long-haul international shipments of goods and people.

The Georgia Basin–Puget Sound, shared by the United States and Canada and lying at the centre of the growing Pacific border region, is examined in the next two chapters. In chapter 6, Fraser traces the evolution, design, and function of transboundary institutional arrangement in this shared bioregion. Focusing on the complexities and limitations of existing transboundary ecosystem-based management mechanisms, the author concludes that close attention is required to address complicated binational policy issues regarding institutional design and function to limit detrimental effects on water-quality degradation in one country on the other.

In chapter 7, Day and Calbick analyze institutional arrangements for controlling water pollution following the identification of widespread pollution in the Puget Sound–Strait of Georgia basin in the mid-1970s. Drawing on a variety of progressive environmental management institutions elsewhere in North America, comparatively they assess the effectiveness and efficiency of institutional arrangements for sustainable water and environmental quality management in British Columbia and Washington State. Legislation, agency roles and personnel, funding, and public involvement at federal, provincial-state, regional, and local governmental levels form the basic structure for water quality and environmental protection in both jurisdictions. Unlike the situation in Washington State, Canada and British Columbia have lagged in stabilizing and remediating water quality in the Canadian section of the binational basin. This result is related to the failure to create effective legislation, in which standards for fresh and marine waters are established. There also continues to be a need to publish ambient environmental water quality conditions on the British Columbia side of the shared waters on a regular basis as well as a need for opportunities for civic participation and continuing public involvement in ambient water quality management in that province.

Water – increasingly viewed as the single most critical resource of the twenty-first century – is the focus of the next two chapters. On the Mexico-U.S. border, in chapter 8, Cástro-Ruíz and Sánchez-Munguía examine problems related to the availability of water in an area where its scarcity clashes with a surge of human habitation and economic activity, especially on the Mexican side of the border. Despite the proximity of fourteen pairs of binational cities across the shared border, the economic, social, and political asymmetries between the two countries impede cooperative planning and management at local and regional levels. Using the most dynamic urban complex – the San Diego–Tijuana Region – as a case study, comparison of the management systems in both countries reveals how critical water supply problems are in both countries and how essential improved binational policies are for shared water management. Generally, border Mexican cities have limited financial resources with which to create infrastructure for their rapidly increasing populations. In spite of binational environmental initiatives along the shared border, the environment has improved only slowly. Fundamental differences in the systems of governance in each country complicate collaboration in water planning and management within the binational region.

A promising example of the ability of organizations, working at different geopolitical scales, to reduce pollution is the study of binational groundwater management contiguous to the Canadian-U.S. border by Norman and Melious in chapter 9. The Abbotsford-Sumas aquifer, to the east of Vancouver and Bellingham, has been the site of coordinated management initiatives by a number of organizations. Using an index system that ranks groups according to their institutional capacity, the authors conclude that community-based success was largely contingent on supporting scientific research on specific questions by senior government agencies in both countries. This new knowledge has allowed local stakeholders to reach consensus on what problems needed to be resolved so that mutually acceptable binational solutions to environmental problems were attainable.

Gray whale watching is a highly visible and useful means of achieving wildlife conservation objectives in Mexico, the United States, and Canada, the geographical range through which these mammals migrate twice annually. Focusing largely on the Bahia Magdelena Region of Baja California Sur, Mexico, in chapter 10, Knowler, Williams, and Garcia-Martinez suggest the need to limit the growth of this industry to avoid adverse impacts on the whale population. However, the creation of sustainable community ecotourism requires a better understanding of the dynamic links between tourism, whale ecology, and biology, not only in Mexico but also throughout the ecosystems used by these animals. The study contributes to the few extant studies of gray whale economics and helps fill a gap in our understanding of the ecological and economic benefits of the whale watching industry to coastal communities in Mexico. The authors outline how bioeconomic modelling and valuation techniques contribute to informed resource management decisions concerning a level of whale watching that is sustainable from both biological and tourism management perspectives. They recommend that parallel research be undertaken on the ecological needs of whales throughout their range and that coordinated policies be adopted to integrate management practices from Mexico, throughout the United States and Canada, to Alaska in the north.

The next two chapters focus on the environmental implication of large-scale tourism in and around Vancouver, Canada's western economic and cultural metropolis and one of the great ports of the Pacific. In chapter 11, Munro and Gill investigate transnational policy issues in the fourth largest global cruise market – to Alaska, principally from Vancouver, with fewer sailings from Seattle and San Francisco. Within this market, certain regional facilities and access to regional natural and cultural resources are fundamental to the success of the product. Passengers augment on-board interests with touristic activities in various Alaskan ports and with on-shore travel in British Columbia, Alberta, and Washington State. This complex international milieu generates a host of transnational policy challenges involving shared economic impacts, environmental monitoring and regulation, and national maritime policy.

North of Vancouver, Whistler is a thriving community and leading four-season mountain resort. It is poised for the international spotlight of the 2010 Winter Olympics, while attempting to direct development and tourism in accordance with well-developed sustainability criteria. In chapter 12, O'Reilly and Symko explore the evolution of Whistler's initiatives focusing on local, regional, and international collaboration. Though there have been several early successes, Whistler's experience has not been without challenges. Cross-boundary collaboration requires accommodating different sets of values and associated political priorities. Creative solutions result in aligning actions with a common vision for a shared international region. The Cascadia Mayors Council, for example, has succeeded in large part because of its ability to work collectively on a regional, binational scale. Similarly, the work of the Pacific Northwest Economic Region in promoting the concept of a "Two Nation Vacation" has focused attention on the value of regional approaches to tourism and environmental well-being. With nearly 5 million annual foreign visitors, Whistler has the potential for global leadership in championing sustainability principles in an innovative, binational tourism effort.

Environmental education is a critical factor in achieving long-term balance between environmental health and the resource and space needs of growing human populations. The two final chapters explore initiatives in the southern and northern border regions. Medina's study, chapter 13, is set in the contiguous San Diego and Tijuana urban metropolitan areas, the largest conurbation on the U.S.-Mexico border which consists of two of the fastest growing cities in their respective countries. Because of vastly different socioeconomic conditions and financial resources, the environmental issues facing Tijuana diverge greatly from those in San Diego. North of the

J.C. Day, James Loucky, and Donald K. Alper

border, San Diego has more resources to direct to socially desirable and economically viable environment policies, whereas the urgent need in Tijuana is to educate decision makers on best practices for urban environmental management. The author presents Ecoparque, where neighbourhood-generated wastewater is recaptured to create a visible green urban park, as a small but replicable example of successful public, research, and governmental collaboration.

On a larger scale to the north, Miles argues in chapter 14 that, although environmental education occurs widely in both British Columbia and Washington State, there is little sharing of knowledge across the boundary. He points out impediments to cross-border collaboration while identifying the potential for more transborder education in the Cascadian transborder mountain region. Miles also describes a promising agreement for mitigating environmental degradation through education and highlights an institution that promotes cooperation that enables a relatively small transboundary watershed, the Skagit, to be managed as a unified natural system.

Clearly there is growing awareness of the need for more effective environmental management in border regions. The issues covered in this volume reveal how intricate and interrelated social, economic, and environmental concerns have become, particularly along borders, as North American nations collectively search for sustainable solutions. The breadth and complexity of Pacific border issues currently confronted by the three countries are reflected in this volume. As growth and resource utilization, environmental degradation, and social impacts accelerate where Canada and Mexico edge together with the United States, it is increasingly apparent that current institutional arrangements adopted to manage both borders are severely challenged. This book, of course, presents only a small microcosm of the critical issues that Canada, Mexico, and the United States confront in working toward more harmonious national, binational, and trinational relations. And making sense of border regions is far more than just an academic matter. To do so, a greater range of political, disciplinary, and civic expertise – and a long-term commitment across multiple borders – is needed to effectively confront mounting challenges. Given the heightened human problems emergent along and across increasingly populated borders, finding innovative and effective solutions is a vital public concern.

2

PACIFIC BORDERS, DISCORDANT BORDERS: WHERE NORTH AMERICA EDGES TOGETHER

James Loucky and Donald K. Alper

Abstract

The U.S.-Mexico border has drawn enormous, and often singular, attention from Americans; by contrast, while the U.S.-Canada border figures prominently in the psyche of Canadians, people in the United States strain to realize that it even exists. The reasons for this dissimilarity emerge through comparative consideration of both borders along the Pacific. Despite obvious differences in ecological character, with the northern bioregion comprised of temperate rainforests and the south characterized by arid desert, the two main human corridors – Vancouver-Seattle and San Diego–Tijuana – have much in common in terms of rapid growth, urbanization, and accelerated transborder linkages. Both also are characterized by serious environmental vulnerability. This provides a valuable opportunity for sharing knowledge of environmental and growth management approaches between, as well as across, each border.

"Poor Mexico and poor United States! So far from God and so close to each other!" (Carlos Fuentes 1996: 159)

"It is physically invisible, geographically illogical, militarily indefensible, and emotionally inescapable." (Canadian diplomat Hugh Keenleyside, on the Canada-U.S. border, in 1929)

Introduction

Just as visions of a seamless, borderless world were beginning to be seriously contemplated, the calamitous events of September 11, 2001, resurrected sudden and powerful reassertion of the security role of national borders. Linear demarcations again appear bold. Rhetoric of exclusion drowns out calls for integration. And yet persistent uncertainties and widening economic asymmetries continue to spur people from peripheral economies to move. National boundaries can hardly constrain the desire for better conditions and comforts, knowledge about them gained through myriad new forms of telecommunications, or organized responses to obtain such goals. So despite renewed emphasis on protecting those within while keeping others out, the reality remains that borders are simultaneously sites of nexus and convergence as well as lines of delineation and disjunction. They are alternately flexible and fixed, open and closed zones of transition as much as institutional settings. As places where people both, exchange and change, the areas adjoining borders are as prone to hybridization as they are to separation and polarization.

In the case of the United States, the defensive assertion of the right to control our borders has in the past essentially been equated with the southern border. The U.S.-Mexico border has drawn enormous attention – indeed it has long been the only border in North America meriting media attention. By contrast, the U.S.-Canada border has figured prominently only in the psyche of Canadians. In the United States, people strain to realize that it even exists.

This chapter argues that the borders and border regions of North America are increasingly significant in an era of heightened security. Borders are where the people, products, and pollutants of the three nations come into first contact, while cross-border regions, and especially north-south corridors, are where cultural, political, and economic interaction occur and play out through inevitable integration as well as separation. These regions are set within a larger continental and global context as well, buffeted by the asymmetries between neighbouring nations, forces of neoliberal economics, and the influences of external events. The borders are themselves also a matter of perception insofar as political, economic, and cultural actors imagine north-south institutions and border-crossing strategies affecting all countries.

The comparative approach adopted in this volume provides an invaluable perspective for examining the evolving nature and functions of borders and border regions. This is especially the case today as national security imperatives in the United States have increasingly dominated discourse. This has been to the detriment of historic evidence of practical interactions among the three nations as well as contemporary knowledge of emerging transboundary interdependencies, interactions, and collaboration. Understanding the contrasts as well as commonalities between the borders that the United States shares with Canada and with Mexico enjoins us to examine and compare the distinctive histories as well as contemporary nature of each binational relationship.

Similarities in the northern and southern border regions include a long history of cross-border population movement, ever-increasing economic exchange, and overlapping ecological spaces in which species, marine waters, rivers, and mountain ranges are intermingled. Although these factors exist across the length of both the U.S.-Canadian and the U.S.-Mexican borders, the demographic and physiographic make-up of the continent has created particularly active corridors in spatially discrete transboundary areas. Our primary focus is on the transboundary areas commonly known as the Seattle-Vancouver and San Diego–Tijuana border corridors. These north-south corridors, so named because of the natural flows of people, trade, ideas, and pollutants, overlay broader bioregional spaces. Despite obvious differences in the ecological characteristics of the northern and southern border bioregions, one comprised of temperate rainforests and the other of arid desert, the two corridors have much in common in terms of rapid growth, urbanization, and accelerated transborder linkages. Both are characterized by serious environmental vulnerability that has stimulated a variety of cooperative remediation efforts by public and private actors. More recently, both are also facing similar security challenges as all three North American governments attempt to adapt to a new national security paradigm without undermining economic vitality.

These two border regions represent a valuable opportunity for sharing knowledge of north-south environmental, economic, and security interdependencies. The economic and strategic significance of the burgeoning Tijuana-San Diego and Seattle-Vancouver regions, their comparable size, and the attendant land-use, water-allocation, and air-quality issues make these ideal locations for highlighting the implications of growing human populations in borderlands. There has been considerable attention to transboundary approaches to environmental and growth management in the San Diego–Tijuana corridor (Ganster 1996; Herzog 1999, 2000b; Spalding 2000a; Fernandez and Carson 2002). Of late, there have also been notable advances in transboundary approaches to environmental and urban planning in the Seattle-Vancouver corridor to the north (Blatter 2000, 2001; Alper 2004; Smith 2004), as well as the beginning of comparative work that simultaneously considers both borders (Kiy and Wirth 1998; Pfau 2001; Andreas and Biersteker 2003).

North American Border Regions: North and South

Canada and the United States are conjoined along an 8,895-kilometre border, the longest shared border between two countries in the world. Canada is also the largest country in the world that borders a single nation. The countries have the largest volume of global binational trade, in excess of US$1 billion each day. Thirty-eight American states have Canada as their largest trading partner. The Province of Ontario alone has more trade with the United States than does Mexico or Japan, the second and third major trade partners of the United States. Nearly 90 per cent of Canadians live within 150 miles of the United States. The country's orientation is to the south, economically, culturally, and environmentally. This is the central fact in the Canadian psyche. For Canadians, the border's principal meaning has been its formal delineation of sovereignty between two very similar countries. This meaning is all the more important because of the enormous economic "pull" exerted by the powerful economy to the south. For Americans, the border has seemed almost nonexistent, more like a border between American states. Although the U.S. economy is more intertwined with Canada than any other country in the world, the Canadian reality hardly registers on the U.S. political agenda. At the same time, there is frustration in Canada with the seeming unilateralism exhibited by the United States in matters such as border security and disputed jurisdiction in the Arctic north.

By contrast, the 3141-kilometre border between Mexico and the United States has figured prominently in American politics, press, and even public parlance. Significant trade and tourism does not automatically translate into deeper knowledge of underlying relationships, however. In light of persisting misperceptions, a better way to understand the evolving nature and functions of the U.S.-Canada and U.S.-Mexico borders is to use as starting points of comparison those characteristics which have been identified as keys to understanding the U.S.-Mexico border.

Economic asymmetries are perhaps the clearest set of differences characterizing the Canada-U.S. and U.S.-Mexico borders. The ambiguous and contentious nature of the U.S.-Mexico border is profoundly associated with the fact that this is the most dramatic case in the world where developed and developing countries directly meet. Some have argued that the two sides have drawn apart during the twentieth century, although others foresee the North American Free Trade Agreement (NAFTA) as mitigating that growing differentiation. By comparison, Canada and the United States are not now widely differentiated, nor were they before. The two countries have similar levels of economic development, wage levels, types of products produced, and levels of consumption, as well as other symmetries in culture and values such as language (except in Quebec), literacy, media, lifestyles, and environmental consciousness. Perhaps the major differentiation between the two nations currently is the comparative wealth of natural resources, renewable and nonrenewable energy, and water in Canada and the comparative advantage in climate, and related support of settlement and agriculture in the United States. Clearly, the key economic issue is not one of closing the gap between a rich and poor country, but that of managing the largest and perhaps most complex bilateral economic relationships in the world.

A second difference between the two borders is that the U.S.-Mexico border was born of bitter conflict. It emerged amid polarization and convulsions associated with rapid capitalist expansion, dominance of Anglo-American racism, and continuing systematic discrimination. The U.S.-Canada boundary, on the other hand, emerged in 1846 as a measured extension of the forty-ninth parallel to the Strait of Georgia, in line with an 1818 agreement that reached from the Lake of the Woods to the Rocky Mountains. Several hundred troops did confront each other once, in 1857, following disputes over which channel marked the boundary through the islands lying between the mainland of what is now Washington State and Vancouver Island. However, in the end the only casualty was an American pig, which had made the mistake of rooting out potatoes in a British garden.

The porosity of both borders is a third significant characteristic, cited repeatedly in debates over immigration, drugs, and terrorism. In the case of Mexico, this porosity is evident in the fact that only since late in the twentieth century has the border been perceived as a problem. Prior to that point, there was nearly always a constant shift back and forth of residents, workers, money, and goods. For much of the century, in fact, citizenship posed little barrier to entry or work. The northern border is equally porous, with few natural barriers; even the Great Lakes and St. Lawrence River serve to facilitate as much as to hinder crossing. However, while drugs and entry of terrorists have become concerns along the northern border in recent years, there is little comparable labour mobility as in the south. Free flow of people has long been encouraged between Canada and the United States, with openness considered conducive to strengthening business relations, but significant cross-border human movement between the two countries occurs mainly in tourism.

Fourth, the two borders are also distinctive in terms of intended and real control functions. For the past two decades in the minds of many in the United States, the southern border has become synonymous with a "final barricade" against unauthorized people and unwanted products. The result has been substantial militarization, along with its unfortunate implications – further endangerment of those who seek to cross as well as continuing antipathies between Mexico and the United States. By contrast, the U.S.-Canada border is often no more than a ditch or country road, if demarcated at all. From the U.S. perspective, until recently the northern border has been largely inconsequential, a back door which hardly merits attention. But that status is changing rapidly as both countries have adopted more assiduous programs to monitor and control illicit border traffic. With Canada, undergoing a new kind of intense political scrutiny and media attention since 9/11, the border is experiencing a form of politicization that has led some to see growing "Mexicanization" of the U.S.-Canada border and cross-border relations (Andreas 2005).

For Canadians the border is central to identity. There is substantial concern over the influence of the United States on virtually every aspect of Canadian life. Many of Canada's largest industries are headquartered and controlled in the United States. American broadcasting, publishing, film, and sports are integral to the Canadian way of life. A long-standing and pervasive concern among Canadians – perhaps angst is a better word – is the weakening of Canadian identity as a result of American influence. Thus, the border is viewed, somewhat optimistically, as a necessary if insufficient protective shield to help maintain Canadian sovereignty. Just as federal legislation requires that 60 per cent of media content in daily prime time scheduling be "Canadian," the border serves, in the minds of many Canadians, to maintain the distinctiveness of Canada. However, regionalism and continentalism are as much territorial realities as is nationalism. The strong sense of awareness of this reality has for generations helped shape a unique Canadian nationalism. This nationalism is based on Canada as "not the United States." As one writer puts it, "Canada is unthinkable without its border with the U.S.A." (New 1998: 6).

On the United States side, there has been almost no concern over sovereignty since Canada has represented no conceivable threat. Until terrorism became such an operative concern, the border was largely insignificant in the minds of most Americans. However, interest by Americans in the northern border seems to have been growing substantially even before 9/11, most likely the result of a combination of increased trade associated with NAFTA, more media attention paid to unauthorized entries, and greater interest and activism by citizens in border communities in making the border work more effectively (Papademetriou and Meyers 2001).

A fifth difference between the two borders relates to their cultural distinctiveness from the nations at large. The U.S.-Mexico border has a distinctive nature, a "border culture" that has been the subject of considerable academic research and much literary expression. Great debate has ensued regarding what defines border culture, how far north or south it extends, and the powerful dynamics associated with burgeoning Mexican and Latin American immigrant populations. In the northern United States and in southern Canada, on the other hand, the border is not an area of uniqueness. The demographic concentration of the vast majority of Canadians along the border means that not only is there no border culture per se, effectively all of Canada is a border society. Canada is also one of the most urbanized countries in the world, with most citizens concentrated in cities within a narrow band thousands of miles long. However, even this band is diverse, insofar as Canada's immense size and small population contributes to a discontinuous settlement pattern. The result is strong community and regional isolates marked by distinctive border-adjacent provinces (excluding Prince Edward Island and Newfoundland) and large cities contiguous to the border but far from one another. Geographically, the population zone of cities and provinces is strung in a kind of east-west "island archipelago" (Widdis 1997).

Finally, while the northern and southern border regions may not seem to have much in common in terms of geography or environmental matters, they actually share many similarities. These include numerous problems associated with rapid urban growth, pressures on species that cross international borders such as salmon, whales, owls, and caribou, and effects of pollutants and industrial wastes. As in the case of sewage from Victoria as well as Tijuana, environmental concerns also frequently cross-sect north and south across the international borders.

Environmental Correlates of the North-South Orientation of North America

While the two major borders of North America run mainly east-west, sometimes in straight lines for hundreds of kilometres, economic and demographic flows run more naturally north-south. These correspond to what some observers have noted as the natural grain of North America, with obvious reference to mountain ranges, river valleys, agricultural zones, and transportation corridors. Just as connectivity in terrestrial environments depends on corridors, so to does much human activity in the continent. Nowhere is this more apparent than along the Pacific coast.

The north-south corridors that bisect both the U.S.-Canada and U.S.-Mexico borders are characterized by intense flows of people, products, and pollutants. The forces of global integration and NAFTA's trade-expanding mandate have focused increased pressure on border-spanning corridors and made them especially vulnerable to environmental degradation. Areas once peripheral are now primary zones of growth and development, crucibles for economic and social transformations that in turn engender changes in the interiors of countries.

In the rapidly growing north-south border corridor that links Seattle and Vancouver, which embraces the Georgia Basin–Puget Sound bioregion, managed and sustainable growth are priorities of numerous public and private groups. Yet little progress has been made in developing truly collaborative approaches for dealing with transboundary environmental issues such as water contamination, air pollution, forest depletion, and urban sprawl. For example, it took years for regional and national authorities to bring peace to the endemic conflict over the harvesting of salmon, a resource that symbolizes how environmental realities rarely correspond to international boundaries.

Problems on the U.S.-Mexico border, so acutely visible in the San Diego–Tijuana area, are even more serious because of their direct impact on human health and life expectancies. This borderland has the fastest demographic growth in both countries; with over-concentration of population in large cities, aquifers and surface waters have come under intense pressure from overuse. Enormous levels of toxins are produced by industrial activity as well agricultural operations. Infrastructure to address these problems is at best weak, and some even argue that anticipation of reduction, rather than strengthening, of environmental standards was key to the political coalitions that formed to push for free trade.

Increasing awareness of deepening environmental problems has provoked an upsurge of environmental concern on both sides of both the Canada-U.S. and the Mexico-U.S. borders. However, efforts to grapple with problems posed by growth as well as past environmental neglect are constrained by overlapping political jurisdictions, nation-centred policy processes, and the absence of trained specialists capable of working across national cultures. While shared environmental threats and commonalities in strategies for confronting them are increasingly acknowledged, distinct loyalties, ignorance of differing systems of governance, and xenophobic suspicions continue to hinder cross-border environmental cooperation. Residents and communities in both North American border regions also find themselves distant from, and having different priorities than, centralized national authority. They suffer inordinate environmental impacts stemming from intensive demographic and economic growth, yet those changes far outpace capacity of government to meet demands.

Such sobering environmental realities require responses characterized by cross-border arrangements, practical problem-solving, and new and more innovative forms of involvement of various governmental and nongovernmental actors. Growing momentum for transboundary environmental management in North America is strongly associated with shared perception of environmental stress, emergence of the environment as a potent political issue – especially for constituencies in border communities – and new binational and trinational institutional frameworks for addressing shared environmental matters (Hufbauer et al. 2000; Kiy and Wirth 1998).

In the two sections that follow, we examine the two Pacific regions in comparative, transboundary perspective. Given the scope and complexity of these environmental issues, we advocate an ecosystems approach that includes: 1) anthropological knowledge of local practices, which encompass a variety of successful models of resource management; and 2) an understanding of political ecology, which directs our attention to the social and cultural contexts of environmental behaviours and policies, and particularly to how contests over control of natural resources shape human influences on, and interactions with, the environment (Escobar 1996).

Two Californias: The Political Ecology of the U.S.-Mexico Pacific Corridor

The nearly 2,000-mile border between Mexico and the United States brings together two distinctly different cultures and countries that are at vastly different stages of economic development. The northern side of the border is the setting of substantial economic and demographic growth, processes that are rapidly transforming landscapes as well as regional and national concentrations of power. To the south, Mexico's long history of economic dependence on its northern neighbour is underscored by the prevalence of immigration and assembly plants (*maquiladoras*), both of which are driven by opportunities created by proximity to the United States. The border development context of both countries entails major shifts in population; the current population of 12 million in contiguous counties and communities within fifty miles north and south of the international boundary is projected to double by the year 2020, the vast majority urban (Herzog 2000a). The combination of growth and juxtaposition of such socioeconomic asymmetries lies at the core of U.S.-Mexican border relations.

For more than fifty years, Mexico emphasized rapid growth as the key to economic development. The Border Industrialization Program instituted in the 1960s was designed to bring Mexico into the modern era by generating high employment along with foreign earnings through establishment of export-processing assembly plants, which currently employ over 630,000 workers in over two thousand factories (Ruiz 2000). Population growth has been accompanied by great increases in cross-border trade, especially following implementation of NAFTA in 1994. Together, population and trade place significant stress on water, energy, and other resources. In addition to water shortages, poorer air quality, inadequate sewage and solid waste disposal, and attendant human health effects, other problems include loss of habitat and considerable traffic congestion. Despite growth in bilateral trade, persistence of relatively low wages on both sides of the border has led to the observation that the border has experienced far more economic growth than real economic development (Ganster et al. 2000).

Because Mexico and the United States meet in an arid frontier zone, water is the most critical resource that must be shared. The current situation is one in which all surface waters are fully allocated, while groundwater deposits are severely limited if not overused. In addition, air-borne particulates and ozone are frequently at very unhealthy levels. Long vehicular delays at the border add to declining air quality. The depletion of natural resources is accompanied by widespread use and haphazard disposal of toxic chemicals in many assembly plants, as well as use of dozens of pesticides in Mexican agriculture that are banned in the United States.

The U.S.-Mexico case shows the daunting challenges facing city and state governments on both sides of the border. As population and trade increase, the limited fiscal base of many border communities and lack of basic information hinder environmental accords and sustainable development efforts. Mexican border cities, in particular, are ill-prepared to meet the needs associated with economic growth and exploding populations. Most face significant problems relating to inadequate infrastructure, including in poor neighbourhoods with few services.

Despite these challenges, rising alarm over the serious nature of border ecological problems is creating a proliferation of networks and nongovernmental organizations with a focus on environmental impacts of national development strategies and of growth in general. Within Mexico, where environmental mobilization has long been weak and nongovernmental organizations marginalized (Simonian 1996), there is growing political awareness and realignments. These range from the "Group of 100," composed of some of the country's most prominent intellectuals, to cross-border coalitions seeking safeguards under NAFTA and preservation of significant areas of biodiversity. Efforts to address border environmental problems include nongovernmental organizations (Zabin 1997) and coalitions of community leaders, such as through the Border Institute I, convened in 1998 to address transborder spillover effects in the human and natural environments (Herzog 2000a). The Border Environmental Cooperation Commission (BECC) and the North American Development Bank (NADBank), both spawned by NAFTA, have a history of funding public water and sewage plants along the border with a mix of U.S. and Mexican funds.

However, much more could be done if NADBank's funding could be substantially increased. Hufbauer and Schott (2004) contend that the NADBank's capital base should be increased to at least $10 billion (from $4.5 billion) and rather than a 50/50 split between the U.S. and Mexico, the division should be 75/25.

Other programs, such as the Environmental Protection Agency's Border XXI, have been initiated to promote sustainable development, ecological democracy, and long-term vision of living within ecological limits. Although many observers criticize these and other border institutions for not doing enough, border region researchers acknowledge that these institutional structures have increased public participation, improved cooperative efforts among different levels of governments, and helped to infuse stronger support for sustainability values in public and private institutions (Spalding 2000b; Hufbauer et al. 2000).

The San Diego–Tijuana corridor, with nearly 5 million people, accounts for approximately 40 per cent of the border population. As the most heavily populated border subregion, and the most economically polarized as well, San Diego–Tijuana represents a setting for substantial challenges to cross-border cooperation. It remains to be seen whether such different cities, one affluent and post-industrial and the other encompassing migrant neighbourhoods and assembly plants, along with their respective states of California and Baja California, can effectively plan for the region's long-term environmental management (Herzog 1999). The historical inertia of the region has been determined by outside economic forces, making it difficult for state and local governments to become responsible for their own future. While population growth in and of itself is an environmental concern, the quality of that growth exacerbates environmental degradation (Ganster 1999). Continuing to have transborder metropolitan growth dependent on the automobile will exacerbate existing problems such as congestion, air pollution, and increased social isolation. On the U.S. side, new development patterns, such as tract housing and the loss of unique neighbourhoods, cause sprawling suburbanization into environmentally sensitive areas and farmlands as well as a diminished sense of place.

The urban development of this Pacific corridor highlights the intimate connection between population, development, and environmental issues. While a new consciousness about long-term quality of life and environmental issues has come to the fore, pressures of population growth, the historical precedent of poor infrastructure planning, and inadequate funding for NAFTA-generated institutions continue to stress the carrying capacity of the landscape. Recognizing the binational nature of these concerns is essential to developing an effective regional planning and regulatory climate that considers the nature of growth as well as its connections to social justice, economic viability, and environmental health. If nothing else, the institutional context created by NAFTA has induced increased social partnerships involving volunteer and community groups. Lara's study (2000) on transboundary networks in the San Diego–Tijuana region suggests that many innovative integrative approaches at the regional level are emerging involving public-private partnerships, exchanges of scientific expertise, and the rapid growth of volunteer organizations.

Cascadia: The Political Ecology of the U.S.-Canada Pacific Corridor

On the Canada-U.S. border in the Pacific west, environmental issues are an outgrowth of geography and the proximity of most Canadian population centres to the border. Unlike the U.S.-Mexico border, where enormous asymmetry in economic opportunity pulls Mexicans northward, the U.S.-Canada border is far less a magnet. On the Canadian side there are few discernible differences between Canadian population centres and border communities, while on the U.S. side most Americans live far away from the border and pay little attention to their Canadian neighbours. Conversely, for Canadians, the border looms large because the U.S. has such a strong presence in all aspects of Canadian life. Gibbins (1996) uses the term "borderlands society" to refer to the country's proximity to the United States and the pervasive influence of American culture and business in Canada.

Given this geopolitical reality, one might expect that the border regions between Canada and the U.S. would be the subject of considerable research. In general, however, borderlands have not attracted a great deal of interest (Blatter and Clement 2000). Scholars have for the most part focused on specific border disputes involving fish, water diversions, and pollutants, but most attention has been focused on the broader relationship between the two countries as it is affected by conditions of dependence and interdependence. Such issues as North American defence, bilateral trade, acid rain, and American cultural influence have been the mainstay of academic research and public policy discourse. And, of course, since September 2001, both academic interest and government involvement in border security have greatly increased.

The study of Canada-U.S. borderlands is most commonly approached through the lens of regionalism. Much of this is due to the growing activity of provinces and states in transnational activity (Abgrall 2004). In part, such activity is an attempt to track cross-border "coalition strategies" to pursue regional economic interests (Groen 1994; Brown 1993). Similarly, transboundary cooperation strategies have also been devised to deal with particular issues that defy national boundaries such as environmental pollution and public health. Much of this activity is facilitated by the two nations' federal political systems where subnational governments have the competence and capacity to engage in their own forms of "paradiplomacy" (Mouafo 2004; Duchacek 1990). Provinces are not peripheral actors in the Canadian system. Many would argue that they have become the most powerful level of government. It is no longer an exaggeration to say that provinces engage in foreign policy. In the case of British Columbia, one of its priority areas of external relations is cross-border environmental and economic linkages with the Pacific Northwest states (Guttieri 1997).

Against a background of deepening trade integration between Canada and the United States, cross-border regions have become central economic and environmental players. The role of regional actors in both national and continental contexts is controversial

(Tomblin 2004), yet there is little doubt that regions have become central economic and environmental players. Although the trajectory of international agreements such as NAFTA and the WTO are toward bringing national economies into greater alignment, global trends are, if not favouring, certainly encouraging the regionalization of economic activity characterized by regional economic strategies and a "pan-jurisdictional" environmentalism marked by bioregionalism. Yet the economic integration accelerated by NAFTA does not necessarily lead to cross-border public institutional cooperation because local and regional governments compete to develop their own economic and tax bases (Brunet-Jailly 2000).

In the Pacific west, where there is the greatest degree of remoteness from the national centres of power, various coalitions have formed to encourage economic and environmental integration. On the economic side, the most ambitious of these is the Pacific Northwest Economic Region (PNWER), formed to bring together public and private sector leaders from Washington, Oregon, Idaho, Montana, Alaska, British Columbia, Alberta, and the Yukon to engage in regional economic cooperation. At the subregional level an organization called the Cascadia Project formed in the late 1980s to institute a framework for cooperating on issues ranging from tourism to transportation. "Cascadia" has become the adopted name of the heavily populated north-south corridor running from Portland, Oregon, to north of Vancouver, B.C. This also is the "main street" of a region that contains more old growth forest than any other part of North America and more temperate rain forest than anywhere in the world. The rich environmental quality of the region is why Joel Garreau, in *The Nine Nations of North America*, called the area "Ecotopia" (Garreau 1981).

Cascadians have been successful in drawing attention to the need for thinking in regional terms in order to tackle high-profile issues such as efficient transportation, growth management, joint approaches to environmental protection, and cooperative business relationships. Although Cascadia as a movement suffers from lack of institutional coherence and political support, it has helped to define a new spatial context for regional action (Clarke 2001). Most Cascadian projects are aimed at facilitating infrastructure such as rail, ports, freeways, and border crossings with the aim of encouraging shared economic development. Further, the Cascadia regional movement has spawned an ambitious West Coast Corridor Coalition, which is an alliance of states, cities, business groups, and freight and transportation advocacy organizations from British Columbia to Baja.

Environmental mobilization in Cascadia has been steady, but only recently has such activity been translated into cross-border linkages. The impetus for joint action came in 1987 when Puget Sound was listed as a priority estuary of concern under the United States Environmental Protection Agency's National Estuary Program (NEP). While the focus was mostly on the U.S. side of the border, the NEP mandated a system-level management regime that implied a region-wide approach involving governments and community groups on both sides of the border (Hildebrand et al. 1997). On the Canadian side, the B.C. Roundtable on the Environment and the Economy was mandated in 1992 to consider ways to manage the Georgia Basin as a whole – including ways of working with other levels of government in the United States and Canada. Increasingly, the term "transboundary shared waters" was used and a proliferation of cross-border linkages occurred. These take the form of informal associations linking academics and scientists across the border, NGO alliances which focus on the marine environment, wilderness areas, and local issues such as protecting ground water and battling against the siting of energy-generation plants in border communities, and intergovernmental environmental agreements, including ones on oil spills, growth management, and Pacific salmon.

Transboundary institutional frameworks are harder to come by, and those that exist are largely the result of problem-solving efforts by local and regional elites. At the regional level, the most important is the British Columbia-Washington Environmental Cooperation Council, created in 1992, to improve bilateral cooperation in dealing with marine, air, and fresh water issues in the border region spanning British Columbia and the state of Washington (Alley 1998). This body brings together high level government officials, scientists, and NGOs from both sides of the border to prioritize and address key transboundary issues relating to shared marine waters, air quality, and fresh water issues that are confounded by the border. However, the council is limited in what it can do jointly because it lacks policy-making and implementation authority.

At the federal level, the Environmental Protection Agency has been an active partner, and major funder, of many cross-border efforts for increasing cooperation on environmental matters. In 2000, the EPA joined with its Canadian counterpart, Environment Canada, and signed a Joint Statement of Cooperation on the Georgia Basin–Puget Sound Ecosystem pledging closer environmental cooperation across all jurisdictions throughout the region. In Canada, transboundary governance mechanisms were given a boost in 1998 when federal and B.C. agencies aligned themselves in the Georgia Basin Ecosystem Initiative, which is intended to coordinate the work of federal agencies with the B.C. government in promoting sustainability in the shared Fraser Basin–Georgia Basin–Puget Sound bioregion.

Although the shared waters of the Georgia Basin–Puget Sound bioregion have received the greatest amount of attention, it has not led to equivalent levels of pollution-control infrastructure in British Columbia vis-à-vis Washington State. Cross-border coalitions have also extended to wilderness and land use. In 1994, the Cascades International Alliance was formed as a consortium of thirteen environmental organizations in Canada and the United States "who share a common goal of seeking protection for the North Cascades ecosystem" (Cascades International Alliance 1994). Perhaps the most prominent transnational network to promote terrestrial corridors is the ambitious Yukon to Yellowstone (Y2Y) project engaged in by a large coalition of wilderness groups in the United States and Canada. However, to date it has not achieved much public recognition, particularly on the Canadian side of the border.

Energy issues, relatively unexamined in the northern Pacific corridor, could become the economic and environmental issue of the future, especially given current concerns about North American energy independence. The Pacific Northwest is the largest market for B.C. natural gas, and Canada now exports more oil to the United States than any other country. Within the Georgia Basin–Puget Sound are thousands of miles of electric transmission lines and natural gas and oil pipelines that crisscross the region. The fact that many gas pipelines in the region are at capacity (Cascadia Institute 2002), coupled with perceived environmental damage wrought by new and expanded energy infrastructure, ensures that transboundary energy issues will be front and centre in the region in years to come. The recent proposed siting of the SE-2 gas-fired energy plant at Sumas,

Washington, within a mile of the Canadian border, led to strong protests from downwind Canadian residents in the Fraser Valley and concerned citizens on both sides of the border, even though the plant would have produced far lower levels of greenhouse gases than existing natural gas plants in the lower mainland of B.C.

Today, environmentalist perspectives on the region are expressed in a variety of ways. Environmental websites such as *Cascadia Planet* and *Ecotrust* advocate and communicate bioregional visions through borderless ecosystem maps and daily news stories and communiqués about environmental threats. Scientists at the major universities in the region share information through sophisticated computer programs focused on land use, resource depletion, and habitat destruction. A number of transboundary conferences and symposia link scholars, activists, policy officials, and the media.

Some analysts contend that the dominant Cascadian vision that privileges economic regionalism could in the end do more harm than good to the goal of ecological sustainability in the transboundary region. Sparke (2000) makes a strong case that Cascadians represent the front line of a "geo-economic" movement that wishes to entrench at the regional level the kinds of policy shifts toward neoliberalism that free trade regimes have introduced at the supranational level. This kind of regional economic integration, with the attendant pressures to rationalize and harmonize business practices and markets, could very well set back, rather than move forward, an agenda for greater ecological well being. Whether or not, and to what extent, ecological and economic regional integration are compatible is a fundamental question that needs to inform future research in both Pacific corridors, north and south.

Conclusion

Border corridors are especially important because they represent points of contact where cultures, economic forces, political systems, and pollutants intermingle, often with uncertain and even tragic consequences. The fact that both the U.S.-Canada and U.S.-Mexico corridors are major points of convergence among the three national economies, and are overlaid by sensitive transboundary bioregions, adds to the urgency for addressing serious environmental problems while underscoring the importance of cross-border approaches.

Cross-border discourse, and cross-border linkages in general – whether community, government, or corporate – are hampered by the extraordinary pace of border economic growth, differing political and jurisdictional systems, and continuing asymmetries between respective countries (Kiy and Wirth 1998; del Castillo 2001; Barry and Sims 1994). This has been further complicated by new security imperatives. Different sociopolitical contexts bear on the development and implementation of effective solutions to transboundary environmental problems. Environmental and economic policy in the three countries reflects distinct historical traditions, cultural influences, political practices, and variations in valuation placed on environmental considerations. The role of subnational governments vis-à-vis national governments varies considerably, with Canada being the most decentralized federation, a factor that provides provinces incentive, capacity, and opportunities for a stronger and more systematic approach to cross-border cooperation (Blatter 1997). Mexico's higher degree of centralization may impede flexibility and innovation at the local and regional level, where policies tend to strongly reflect national priorities and programs. The nations also differ in their respective commitments of political capital and resources for addressing environmental problems. Legal and administrative remedies differ, as do the relative influence of anti-environmental interest groups and levels of grassroots mobilization and participation. Public participation is often still relatively weak in places where it involves more risk-taking and where economic constraints limit the availability of economic resources for environmental protection.

There is also a disconnection between our understanding of bioregions and corridors. Bioregions are treated as zones of ecological integrity, areas of integrated components such as species, and interrelationships involving growing human populations. By contrast, corridors have emerged largely in context of linear connections, lines of flow between urban centres in an expanding global economic system. Both the Seattle-Vancouver and San Diego–Tijuana corridors overlay bioregions that are experiencing common growth problems.

James Loucky and Donald K. Alper

The environment is a primary economic generator in both border regions, as reflected in the growth of sectors relying on watershed, marine, visual landscape, forestry, and tourism resources in the north, and solar, marine, and tourism resources in the south.

Furthermore, while bioregions and corridors connote spatial connectivity, functionality, and interactive flows, borders represent linearity, disjunction, and artificial constraints. The "edging" together that occurs in border regions, with their inherent intertwining of ecological, demographic, and economic futures, can be intentionally overshadowed by the "edginess" implicit in nationalism, particularly in a security age. Creative imagination is essential to affirm a regional imperative, so that policy decisions about whether to nationalize can occur without ruining the vital, natural, north-south flows that help keep the border regions healthy and in turn all three North American countries.

In light of the crucial interface between national borderlines of political and cultural demarcation, and the regional spaces of "natural" interaction involving people, commerce, and ecologies, the implications for policy research are both rich and timely. First, both Pacific borderlands have much in common, including contending with border-control systems that both confound and challenge the historic patterns of contact and interaction that mark the binational and trinational reality of North America. The impetus for challenging conventional notions of border control is not just a transformed security environment, but also a long-overdue response to the evolution of commercial and social patterns of interaction in North America that have made continental relationships more dynamic, organic, and integrated (Flynn 2003). To this end, shared social psychology as residents of border regions (Pfau 2001), transborder environmental research, and both binational and trinational environmental policy frameworks are as necessary as they remain infrequent (Sanchez-Rodriguez et al. 1998).

Second, academic institutions need to rise to the challenge of addressing from a trinational perspective the changing meaning of borders and boundaries in North America. Our experience – first through advocating that border educational institutions serve as centres for transboundary linkages and synergy including student field study in border regions in all three countries, and more recently through surveying existing as well as neglected areas of research

– reveals how much can be gained on either border from examining the approaches and knowledge generated on the other (Nelson et al. 2003). Effective trinational learning requires wide sharing of efforts and understandings across international, disciplinary, and academic-nonacademic borders. Now, more than ever, there is need for a new generation of policy professionals competent to work in all three countries. Despite the magnitude of problems, we believe that comparative and collaborative efforts have the best chance of deepening understanding of the complex interconnections between ecosystems management, population growth, and urban planning in the Pacific border corridors of North America and beyond.

Finally, we must reaffirm that borders are fundamentally about relationships and that these are fluid and dynamic. How we define and speak of borders matters to how we conceptualize the continent and imagine possibilities for a "new continental community" (Kiy and Wirth 1998: 3; Tomkins 2005). Some of the most promising directions for "thinking globally, acting locally" are emerging in transborder corridor regions, and the habits, lessons, and experiences being developed there are both cumulative and consequential for North America as a whole.

References

Abgrall, Jean-François. 2004. "The Regional Dynamics of Province-State Relations." *Policy Research Initiative* 7(1); http://policyresearch. gc.ca/page.asp?pagenm=v7n1_art_09.

Alley, Jamie. 1998. "The British Columbia-Washington Environmental Cooperation Council," pp. 53–71. In *Environmental Management on North America's Borders*, eds. Richard Kiy and John D. Wirth. College Station: Texas A&M Press.

Alper, Donald. 2004. "Emerging Collaborative Frameworks for Environmental Governance in the Georgia Basin-Puget Sound Ecosystem." *Journal of Borderland Studies: Special Issue, The Canadian-American Border, Toward a Transparent Border?* 19(1): 79–98.

James Loucky and Donald K. Alper

Andreas, Peter. 2005. "The Mexicanization of the US-Canada Border: Asymmetric Interdependence in a Changing Security Context." *International Journal* 60(2): 449–62.

Andreas, Peter, and Thomas J. Biersteker, eds. 2003. *The Rebordering of North America: Integration and Exclusion in a New Security Context*. New York: Routledge.

Barry, Tom, and Beth Sims. 1994. *The Challenge of Cross-Border Environmentalism: The U.S.-Mexico Case*. Albuquerque: Interhemispheric Resource Center.

Blatter, Joachim. 1997. "Explaining Cross-border Cooperation: A Border-Focused and Border External Approach." *Journal of Borderlands Studies* 12(1&2): 151–74.

———. 2000. "Emerging Cross-border Regions as a Step Towards Sustainable Development: Experiences and Considerations from Examples in Europe and North America." *International Journal of Economic Development* 2/3: 402–409.

———. 2001. "Active Cross-Border Regions: International Dynamics and Institution Building," pp. 257–83. In *Gaining Advantage from Open Borders*, eds. Marina Van Geenhuizen and Remigio Ratti. Aldershot, UK: Ashgate.

Blatter, Joachim, and Norris Clement. 2000. "Cross Border Cooperation in Europe: Historical Development, Institutionalization, and Contrasts with North America." *Journal of Borderlands Studies* 15(1): 15–53.

Brown, Douglas M. 1993. "The Evolving Role of the Provinces in Canada-U.S. Trade Relations," pp. 93–144. In *States and Provinces in the International Economy*, eds. Douglas M. Brown and Earl H. Fry. Berkeley: Institute of Intergovernmental Relations, University of California Press.

Brunet-Jailly, Emmanuel. 2000. "Globalization, Integration and Cross-Border Relations in the Metropolitan Area of Detroit and Windsor." *International Journal of Economic Development* 2: 479–501.

Cascades International Alliance. 1994. "Nature Has No Borders." *The Newsletter for Cascades International Alliance* I (Spring).

Cascadia Institute. 2002. "Report on the Activities, Results and Recommendations of the BC-Washington Corridor Task Force." Vancouver, BC: Cascadia Institute.

Clarke, Susan E. 2001. "Regional and Transnational Discourse: The Politics of Ideas and Economic Development in Cascadia." *International Journal of Economic Development*, 2(3): 5–22.

del Castillo V., Gustavo. 2001. "Between Order and Chaos: Management of the Westernmost Border Between Mexico and the United States," pp. 117–161. In *Caught in the Middle: Border Communities in an Era of Globalization*, eds. Demetrios G. Papademetriou and Deborah Waller Meyers. Washington: Carnegie Endowment for International Peace.

Duchacek, Ivo D. 1990. "Perforated Sovereignties: Toward a Typology of New Actors in International Relations," pp. 1–32. In *Federalism and International Relations: The Role of Subnational Units*, eds. Hans J. Michelmann and Panayotis Soldatos. Oxford: Clarendon Press.

Escobar, Arturo. 1996. "Constructing Nature: Elements for a Poststructural Political Ecology." *Liberation Ecologies: Environment, Development, Social Movements*. London: Routledge.

Fernandez, Linda, and Richard T. Carson. 2002. *Both Sides of the Border: Transboundary Environmental Management Issues Facing Mexico and the United States*. Boston: Kluwer.

Flynn, Stephen. 2003. "The False Conundrum: Continental Integration Versus Homeland Security," pp. 110–27. In *The Rebordering of North America: Integration and Exclusion in a New Security Context*, eds. Peter Andreas and Thomas J. Biersteker. New York: Routledge.

Fuentes, Carlos. 1996. *A New Time for Mexico*. New York: Farrar, Straus, and Giroux.

Ganster, Paul. 1996. *Environmental Issues of the California-Baja California Border Region*. Border Environment Research Reports No. 1. San Diego, CA: Institute for Regional Studies of the Californias, San Diego State University.

———. 1999. "The Environmental Implications of Population Growth in the San Diego-Tijuana Region," pp. 35–56. In *Sustainable Development in San Diego-Tijuana*, ed. Mark J. Spalding. La Jolla: Center for U.S.-Mexican Studies, University of California, San Diego.

Ganster, Paul, Alan Sweedler, and Norris Clement. 2000. "Development, Growth, and the Future of the Border Environment," pp. 73–103. In *The U.S.-Mexican Border Environment: A Road Map to a Sustainable 2020*, ed. Paul Ganster. San Diego: San Diego State University.

Garreau, Joel. 1981. *The Nine Nations of North America*. New York: Avon.

Gibbins, Roger. 1996. "Meaning and Significance of the Canadian-American Border," pp. 227–37. In *Border Regions in Functional Transition: European and North American Perspectives on Transboundary Interaction*. Report no. 9. Berlin: Institute for Regional Development and Structural Planning.

Groen, James P. 1994. "British Columbia's International Relations: Consolidating a Coalition Building Strategy." *BC Studies* 102 (Summer): 54–82.

Guttieri, Karen. 1997. "British Columbia's Foreign Policy." Paper presented at the British Columbia Political Science Association Annual Meeting, North Vancouver, B.C.

Herzog, Lawrence A. 1999. "Urban Planning and Sustainability in the Transfrontier Metropolis: The Tijuana-San Diego Region," pp. 1–15. In *Sustainable Development in San Diego-Tijuana*, ed. Mark J. Spalding. La Jolla: Center for U.S.-Mexican Studies, University of California, San Diego.

Herzog, Lawrence A., ed. 2000a. "Cross-Border Planning and Cooperation," pp. 139–61. In *The U.S.-Mexican Border Environment: A Road Map to a Sustainable 2020*, ed. Paul Ganster. SCERP Monograph No. 1. San Diego: San Diego State University Press.

———. 2000b. *Shared Space: Rethinking the U.S.-Mexico Border Environment*. La Jolla: Center for U.S.-Mexican Studies, University of California, San Diego.

Hildebrand, Larry, Victoria Pebbles, and Holly S. Ross, et al. 1997. *Cooperative Ecosystem Management Canada and U.S.: Approaches and Experiences of Programs in the Gulf of Maine, Great Lakes and Puget Sound/ Georgia Basin*. A Report, Coastal Zone 97 Meeting, Boston, MA.

Hufbauer, Gary, Daniel C. Esty, Diana Orejas, Luis Rubio, and Jeffrey J. Schott. 2000. *NAFTA and the Environment: Seven Years Later*. Washington, D.C.: Institute for International Economics, No. 61 (October).

Hufbauer, Gary, and Jeffrey J. Schott. 2004. The Prospects for Deeper North American Economic Integration: A U.S. Perspective. Toronto: C.D. Howe Institute *Commentary* No. 195. The Border Papers (January).

Kiy, Richard, and John D. Wirth, eds. 1998. *Environmental Management on North America's Borders*. College Station: Texas A&M Press.

Lara, Franscisco. 2000. "Transboundary Networks for Environmental Management in the San Diego-Tijuana Border Region," pp. 155–84. *In Shared Space: Rethinking the US-Mexico Border Environment*, ed. Lawrence A. Herzog. La Jolla: Center for U.S.-Mexican Studies, University of California, San Diego.

Mouafo, Dieudonne. 2004. "Regional Dynamics in Canada-United States Relations." Paper presented at the annual meeting of Canadian Political Science Association, Winnipeg: Manitoba (June 3).

Nelson, J.G., J. Chadwick Day, Lucy Sportza, James Loucky, and Carlos Israel Vasquez, eds. 2003. *Protected Areas and the Regional Planning Imperative in North America*. Calgary: University of Calgary Press.

New, W. H. 1998. *Borderlands: How We Talk About Canada*. Vancouver: UBC Press.

Papademetriou, Demetrios G., and Deborah W. Meyers. 2001. *Caught in the Middle: Border Communities in an Era of Globalization*. Washington: Carnegie Endowment for International Peace.

Pfau, Michael R. 2001. "Looking Forward: A Survey of Cross-Border Impression Formation in the Tijuana-San Diego and Seattle-Vancouver Border Corridors." *Journal of Borderlands Studies* 16: 1–13.

Ruiz, Ramón Eduardo. 2000. *On the Rim of Mexico: Encounters of the Rich and Poor*. Boulder, CO: Westview.

Sanchez-Rodriguez, Roberto A., Konrad von Moltke, Stephen Mumme, John Kirton, and Donald Munton. 1998. "The Dynamics of Transboundary Environmental Agreements in North America: Discussion of Preliminary Findings," pp. 32–52. In *Environmental Management on North America's Borders*, eds. Richard Kiy and John D. Wirth. College Station: Texas A&M University Press.

Simonian, Lane. 1996. *Defending the Land of the Jaguar: A History of Conservation in Mexico*. Austin: University of Texas Press.

Smith, Patrick. 2004. "Transboundary Cascadia: Opportunities and Obstacles." *Journal of Borderlands Studies: Special Issue, The Canadian American Border, Toward a Transparent Border?* 19(1): 99–122.

Spalding, Mark. 2000a. "Addressing Border Environmental Problems Now and in the Future: Border XXI and Related Efforts," pp. 105–37. In *The U.S.-Mexican Border Environment: A Road Map to a Sustainable 2020*, ed. Paul Ganster. San Diego: San Diego State University Press.

———. 2000b. "The NAFTA Environmental Institutions and Sustainable Development on the U.S.-Mexican Border," pp. 75–100. In *Shared Space: Rethinking the U.S.-Mexican Border Environment*. La Jolla: Center for U.S.-Mexican Studies, University of California, San Diego.

Sparke, Matthew. 2000. "Excavating the Future in Cascadia: Geoeconomics and the Imagined Geographies of a Cross-Border Region." *BC Studies: The British Columbia Quarterly* 127 (Autumn): 5–44.

Tomblin, Stephen G. 2004. "Introduction and Overview: Comparative New England-Atlantic Policy Lessons," pp. 7–36. *In Regionalism in a Global Society: Persistence and Change in Atlantic Canada and New England*, eds. Stephen G. Tomblin and Charles S. Colgan. Peterborough, ON: Broadview Press.

Tomkins, Richard. 2005. "Analysis: A North American Community." (March 14), http://www.washingtontimes.com/upi-breaking/20050314-061236-1773r.htm.

Widdis, R. W. 1997. "Borders, Borderlands and Canadian Identity: A Canadian Perspective." *International Journal of Canadian Studies* 15 (Spring): 49–66.

Zabin, Carol. 1997. "Nongovernmental Organizations in Mexico's Northern Border." *Journal of Borderland Studies* 12(1–2): 41–65.

3

RECENT TRENDS IN MEXICO-U.S. BORDER DEMOGRAPHICS

Cristóbal Mendoza and James Loucky

Abstract

The extent to which there is a unique border region in sociodemographic terms carries strong implications for effective long-term planning and potential binational growth management strategies. The debate on demographics of the U.S.-Mexican border area has shifted from highlighting similarities across the border to emphasizing how trends in the border region follow respective national patterns rather than determining distinctive cross-border trends for the whole region. This chapter analyses recent Mexican and U.S. census data for the municipalities and counties in the large border region that encompass all or most of nine Mexican and five U.S. states. With the exception of migration, there is little evidence of a unified border region in demographic terms; rather there are striking differences in population distribution, density, and age profiles on both sides of the border, patterns which in turn impact use of resources and environmental health.

Introduction

The Mexico-U.S. borderlands are unique in many respects, and demography is no exception. Border populations within each country are often the result of long-distance migration from within Mexico and the United States, or from other countries. The international border milieu also connotes a geographic and cultural imprint on the population of the region, well documented in the literature and popularized in music and film. Reflecting how borders simultaneously integrate and separate, residents to a large extent share common characteristics associated with shared problems – such as versatility, transnational interactions, and accommodation (Martínez 1994) – at the same time that separateness and south-north symmetries prevail (Ruiz 2000). Still, conceptualizing and quantifying the border is difficult. This is in large part because cross-border statistical data are not often collected and because the census bureaus of Mexico and the United States conduct their respective surveys according to different interests and purposes. In addition, the bulk of border demographic studies have concentrated on one country or the other, with few exceptions (Weeks and Ham-Chande 1992; Howard 1994; Rubin-Kurtzman et al. 1996; Peach and Williams 2000). Nonetheless, it is possible to identify a number of comparable census variables across the border (Pick et al. 2000), in order to determine the extent to which there is a unique border region in sociodemographic terms.

In the last half century, the U.S.-Mexico border region has experienced some of the greatest population growth and economic expansion as anywhere in the world. In addition to consuming substantial amounts of natural resources, including water and energy, this dynamism causes serious pollution problems and overall deterioration of ecosystems. This chapter analyzes recent demographic trends on population distribution and growth, age structure, and migration in the U.S.-Mexico borderlands based on selected comparable census variables in each country. The objective is to identify the extent to which the international line demarcates demographically, as it does economically and politically, and conversely whether it is an effective deterrent to spatial diffusion in sociodemographic respects. These border demographic patterns in turn have significant implications for overall environmental impact or remediation in an extraordinary, and fragile, transnational region.

Early sociodemographic studies of northern Mexico focused on its particularities with respect to the close proximity to the United States (Bustamante 1981; Ham-Chande and Weeks 1988). The essence of the argument was that strong interaction effects of movements of people, capital, and goods across the international line influenced population patterns in the region. Even if explicitly stated, this literature considers diffusion effects from the U.S. to Mexico to be the basis for change. For example, an early demographic transition in northern Mexico compared to the rest of the country was attributed to spatial congruity of the two nations (Coubès 2000). In the 1990s, sociodemographic studies of northern Mexican states also began comparing trends in the region with those elsewhere in the country. These studies generally concentrated on single events, as Quilodrán (1998) did for marriage, and in general devoted little attention to interconnections between events in, or parts of, the region. An exception is the work of Estrella et al. (1999), which analyzes the impact of migration on fecundity and family patterns in northern Mexico.

In the United States, on the other hand, studies of the sociodemography of the Southwest concentrate on migration and ethnicity, with the flow of undocumented workers and the use of the Spanish language being the most popular topics (Bean et al. 1992), in addition to poverty (Betts and Slottje 1994; Ward 1995). While not always stated clearly in the debate on poverty, the interconnections of immigration and Mexican proximity to the U.S. are generally assumed. Certainly this coincides with popular views about migration in U.S. border towns (Vila 2000). Yet the debate on the relationship between poverty and migration goes beyond the border area. For instance, Sassen (1996) argued that structural conditions of urban labour markets, rather than characteristics of the labour force, are the fundamental reasons for the precariousness and downgrading of jobs in the United States.

The debate on border demographics has been influenced by parallel controversy regarding the definition and extent of the border region (Ham-Chande and Weeks 1988; Martínez 1994; Zenteno and Cruz 1992). Some authors (Bustamante 1989; Herzog 1990) assert the existence of a common U.S.-Mexico region contiguous to the international border, while others (such as Alegría 2000) criticize such conceptualizations as lacking a convincing theoretical base or empirical frame of reference. Resolution of the debate requires delineating and comparing the essential demographic features of this huge area, one that is situated north and south of an international border that extends nearly three thousand kilometres.

Population Distribution, Density, and Growth

In the extensive Mexico-U.S. border area, which covers all or part of nine Mexican and six U.S. states, population – and associated demand for available or imported resources, along with pollution – is heavily concentrated in binational corridors (figs. 3.1 and 3.2).

- *Californian cities along the Pacific coast.* The area from Los Angeles to Tijuana is a densely urbanized region (258.4 inhabitants/km^2), with a population of nearly 20.5 million people in 2000, twice the size of countries like Portugal or Cuba. With the exception of Tijuana, this area experienced lower annual growth in the 1990s than in the 1980s. However the area continues to grow rapidly in absolute numbers, with the regional population increasing by almost 4 million from 1980 to 1990, and by more than 2 million in the 1990–2000 period. San Diego and Tijuana represent the fastest growth of all. In the 1980s, San Diego experienced the highest increase in absolute numbers of any border city (636,170 people), though Tijuana grew fastest overall in relative terms (4.8%). Tijuana's growth accelerated still further in the 1990s, in both absolute numbers (526,859) and in relative terms (5.3%).
- *Texas–Tamaulipas–Nuevo León corridor.* The region extending from Dallas to Monterrey, and including Austin, San Antonio, and the two Laredos, had a population that rose from 7 million (7,238,570) in 1980 to 12 million (12,095,423) in 2000. While this corridor lacks the urban and geopolitical continuity that characterizes the

Cristóbal Mendoza and James Loucky

California coast, traditional economic relations between
Monterrey and the U.S. southwest justify considering
the cities along Interstate 35 in Texas and Route 84 in
Tamaulipas–Nuevo León as a unique region. Monterrey's
manufacturing growth has depended heavily on export
industries, and on migration and easy transportation links
between San Antonio and northern Mexico (Cerutti 2001).
Commensurate population growth is evident mainly in
the 1990s. Comparing urban areas in relative terms, the
Austin–San Marcos Metropolitan Area experienced the
highest annual growth rates in both periods (3.7% in the
1980s and 3.9% in the 1990s). For other metropolitan
areas (the Laredos, Killen-Temple, Dallas, Fort Worth–
Arlington, and San Antonio), growth was also more
pronounced in the 1990s than the 1980s.

- *Border cities.* Except in the case of the Californias
  and Ciudad Juárez–El Paso, border communities do
  not constitute extremely high-density zones, but they
  nonetheless significantly affect regional population as
  well as urbanization. The so-called "twin cities" of San
  Diego–Tijuana, Mexicali-Calexico, Ciudad Juárez–El
  Paso, Laredo–Nuevo Laredo, Reynosa-McAllen, and
  Matamoros-Brownsville had a combined population of
  almost 9 million people in 2000. In absolute numbers,
  these cities experienced similar annual growth rates in
  the 1980s and 1990s, of 2.9 per cent and 2.8 per cent
  respectively. All Mexican border cities gained more
  population in relative terms in the 1990s than in the 1980s,
  with Nuevo Laredo leading the way, accelerating from 0.8
  per cent annual growth in the 1980s to 3.5 per cent in the
  1990s. For U.S. border towns, east-west differences are
  evident, with relatively greater growth between San Diego
  and El Paso in the 1990s, compared to a slower rate of
  growth in the westerly Texas border towns in the 1990s.
  Other notable centres of population seen in figure 3.1 are
  the state capitals of Saltillo, Coahuila, and Chihuahua
  in northern Mexico, and Las Vegas, Tucson, Phoenix,
  Albuquerque, Corpus Christi, and Amarillo in the U.S.
  southwest.

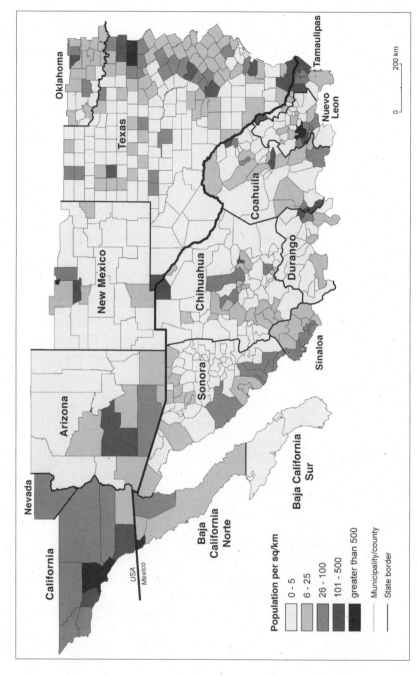

Figure 3.1 Population Density (1990)

Cristóbal Mendoza and James Loucky

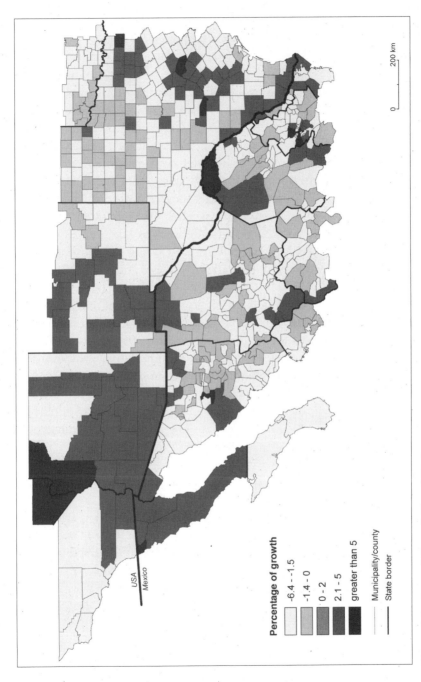

Figure 3.2 Annual Growth Rate (1990)

Percentage of growth

- -6.4 - -1.5
- -1.4 - 0
- 0 - 2
- 2.1 - 5
- greater than 5

Municipality/county

State border

0   200 km

USA
Mexico

Viewed conjointly, the populations of all border regions increased in both decades, though the trend was towards slower growth in the 1990s for some cities, especially in the west. Overall the region remains scarcely inhabited. Almost all New Mexican counties, northern Arizona, and most of western Texas had five or less inhabitants per km² in 2000. For northern Mexico, non-border inland Sonora, plus large parts of Chihuahua, Baja California Sur, Durango, and Coahuila exhibit the same pattern of low population density. The exceptions are zones of rapid rural-urban and urban-urban migration, where high densities place corresponding stress on limited resources such as water. Most notable are the municipalities of Tijuana and Monterrey, which had densities exceeding 500 inhabitants per km² in 2000, while in the U.S., densities reached as high as 500 inhabitants per km² in Los Angeles and Orange Counties on the California coast and two counties in the Dallas–Fort Worth Consolidated Metropolitan Area.

The polarization of population growth is evident in the fact that many border regions with low population densities experienced negative annual growth rates during the 1980–2000 study period (fig. 3.2). Sonora, for instance, displays high population growth along the Pacific coast and the border area, in contrast to inland areas of the state. Similarly, whereas west-Texas rural areas experienced depopulation in the 1990s, middle-sized cities such as Amarillo, the Dallas–San Antonio corridor, and the border towns gained new inhabitants.

By contrast, the areas with the fastest population growth are Tijuana and Las Vegas. Las Vegas, habitable only because of a huge draw on the Colorado River, had the largest annual growth of all counties and municipalities in the border. Clark County, where Las Vegas is located, almost doubled its population in both the 1980s (from 463,087 to 741,459 in 1990) and the 1990s (increasing by another 634,306); in relative terms this was an annual growth of 4.7 per cent for the 1980s and 6.2 per cent for the 1990s. Tijuana, a municipality whose irregular topography makes building difficult and which lacks the natural harbours of Ensenada to the south and San Diego to the north, experienced spectacular growth in both absolute and relative terms between 1980 and 2000. Clearly, population growth or decrease relates to factors other than traditional geographical conditions.

Age Structure and Migration

The age structure is dramatically different on the two sides of the border, with Mexicans being considerably younger than their American neighbours. For the United States, the proportion of population under five years is 10 per cent or lower throughout the region, with the exception of three border Texan counties, which have high immigration from Mexico (fig. 3.3). This contrasts sharply with Mexico, where this is the case only in small rural municipalities which are depopulating, such as in the Tarahumara mountains and the Chihuahua desert. This north-south contrast is also clear when viewing the population that is 65 and older (fig. 3.4). Those 65 and older constituted more than 5 per cent of the total population in every county in the U.S. southwest in 2000, with the exception of Denton County in the Dallas Metropolitan Area. Most counties have at least 10 per cent who are 65 or more, and many have over 20 per cent. In contrast, no municipality in the Mexican border region has 20 per cent of its population aged of 65 or more, and most have less than 10 per cent. For example, Baja California has no municipality with more than 5 per cent of people of this age.

Clearly, counties on both sides of the border are in different stages of the demographic transition. In Mexico, younger people move north for jobs, while the U.S. side attracts older persons, both those moving for employment as well as retirees, including so-called "snow birds" escaping to what has become known as the "sun belt."

Apart from these major cross-border differences, more subtle similarities regarding age structure patterns across the border are also evident. For example, areas with large indigenous populations, such as Navajo County in Arizona or Guadalupe y Calvo in Chihuahua, stand out as having higher percentages of children and fewer old people than the rest of the U.S. southwest and northern Mexico. This explains differences in age structures within the rugged Sierra Madre Occidental in Mexico. Population growth is negative toward the north, while the mountainous Baja Sierra Tarahumara in southern Chihuahua shows considerable positive population growth. This is associated with sizeable indigenous Tarahumara and Tepehuan communities, with shorter life expectancy, higher fertility, and low emigration combining to produce younger populations.

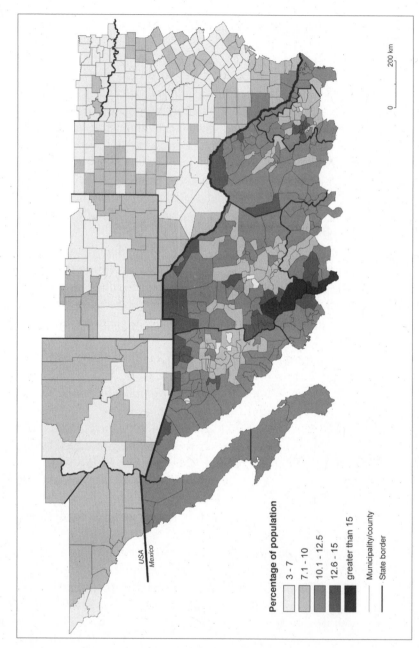

Percentage of population

- 3 - 7
- 7.1 - 10
- 10.1 - 12.5
- 12.6 - 15
- greater than 15

—— Municipality/county
—— State border

USA
Mexico

0   200 km

Figure 3.3   Population Less Than 5 Years Old (2000)

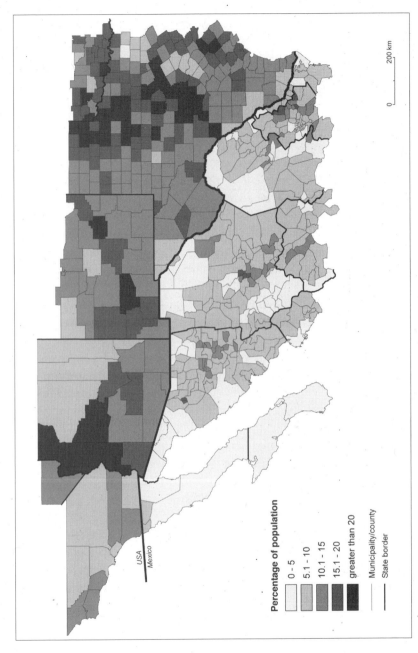

Figure 3.4 Population Greater Than 65 Years Old (2000)

Beyond national differences, then, variance in migration behaviour among "sending" communities is also critical to examine. Generally speaking, cities on both sides of the border have younger age components in their population structures than rural peripheries, though this is truer for the United States than for Mexico. Indeed differences are more striking between rural and urban areas in the U.S. southwest than in Mexico, where the pattern is less clear. This perhaps relates to dissimilarities in migration behaviour in the two countries. Although the trend seems to be changing (Marcelli and Cornelius 2001; Lozano 2002), men are still overrepresented in international out-flows from Mexico (Durand et al. 2001; Mendoza 2005). The relatively early age of marriage and childbearing in many rural areas also helps explain the younger age structure. On the other hand, migration does not completely break the complex network of extended families in Mexico. Indeed, many such arrangements actually cross the border, with multiple family and household arrangements easing and channeling migration and return migration. Flexible labour market practices on the Mexican border, in addition to growing insecurity in maquila or maquila-related jobs, also influence "flexible" patterns of migration and mobility. In other words, migration patterns in Mexico may be the primary reason for high percentages of children in the total population of rural Mexico, while small proportions of people 65 and older are a consequence of shorter life expectancy in rural Mexico compared with urban Mexico or the rural United States.

For the United States, by contrast, rural areas experience a more typical process of depopulation, with more young people leaving to cities and older people remaining to live our increasingly long life expectancies in rural areas. The great percentage of older people is also the consequence of internal patterns of migration, with retired people increasingly on the move today, including to locations like southern Arizona with their clear attraction of mild weather.

Here it has been suggested that younger populations are not necessarily associated with high immigration counties or municipalities (witness the immigration of retired people in the United States), while an older age structure is not always linked to emigration (because of patterns like early age for first child and union in Mexico). More localized analyses are required to separate out the determinant power of various factors (including immigration, emigration, and the characteristics and volume of flows) for explaining the different age structures in the two countries. Such demographic and social characteristics must, in turn, be considered in both macro- and micro-level analyses of the environmental correlates associated with population growth in the borderlands.

Ethnicity and Destinations

Censuses only give a rough approximation of migration, which is in fact the most difficult demographic phenomenon to measure. In both the United States and Mexico the census asks place of birth and residence, as well as ethnicity. But relations between ethnicity and migration are diffuse, and links to perceptions of environment and related patterns of resource consumption are even less straightforward. Focusing on the percentage of people born out of the state of residence in 1990 as a rough index of the sheer volume of immigrants (either from another state or abroad) reveals that for the United States nearly the entire border region is one of high immigration (fig. 3.5 and 3.6). This is especially the case for southern California, all of Arizona except counties with a strong indigenous presence, most of New Mexico except counties in the north (with high Hispanic non-Mexican populations), and many Texas counties, including Dallas. The highest rates are in Las Vegas Metropolitan Area (80.7% of the population of Clark County, around Las Vegas, was born outside Nevada). Similarly 83.8 per cent of the Mohave county population was born outside Arizona. In both cases, the bulk of immigrants are born in the U.S.A., since only 3.6 per cent of Mohave and 9.5 per cent of Clark are native of another country.

As a substantial portion of immigrants is not foreign-born and interstate movements are not recorded in these figures, differences of immigration rates between Texas and the other southwestern states may relate strongly to the size, shape, and internal population distribution of the areal units employed in migration analysis. These limitations can also be observed in northern Mexico. The largest border cities, Tijuana and Ciudad Juárez, have roughly the same population,

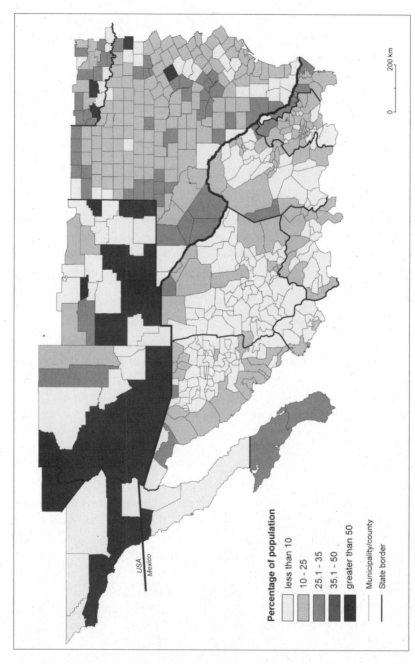

Percentage of population

less than 10
10 - 25
25.1 - 35
35.1 - 50
greater than 50

Municipality/county
State border

USA
Mexico

0   200 km

Figure 3.5   Population Born Out of State (1990)

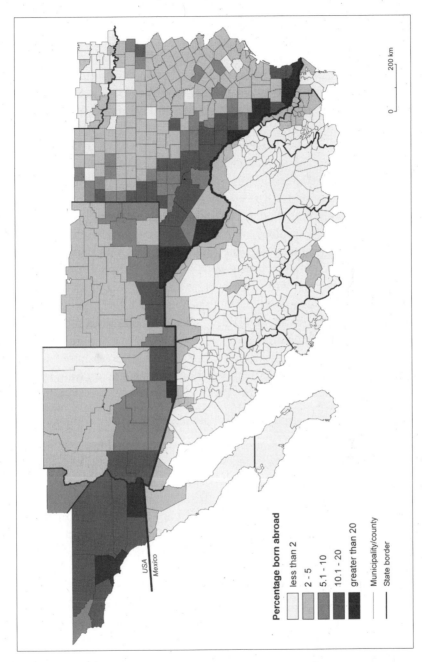

Figure 3.6 Population Born Abroad (1990)

Percentage born abroad

- less than 2
- 2 - 5
- 5.1 - 10
- 10.1 - 20
- greater than 20

Municipality/county
State border

USA
Mexico

200 km

but substantial differences in immigration numbers and rates (fig. 3.5). Tijuana, as well nearby Ensenada and Tecate, stands out with respect to percentage of people born outside of Baja California. In 1990, this was 57.3 per cent for Tijuana, in contrast to Juárez, which had only 31.7 per cent of its population from out of Chihuahua. Data on the most "recent" immigrants, in the period 1995–2000, reveal that Tijuana attracted more immigrants (163,194) compared to Juárez (128,967). Juárez, on the other hand, benefited from greater interstate movement, with 11.3 per cent of those (age five or more) who changed residence originating from another Chihuahua municipality, compared to only 3 per cent of Tijuana immigrants originating from elsewhere in Baja California (Mendoza 2001).

Besides sheer number of immigrants, environmental impacts also relate to asymmetries in settlement patterns. Many factors combine to enhance immigration as well as determine destinations. First, labour migration is derived from new economic activities set up in the region (particularly manufacturing and assembly industries in Mexico), together with established ones (such as leisure). Secondly, the older age structure on the U.S. side (fig. 3.4) suggests that migration unrelated to labour constitutes a remarkable share of new immigrants. This explains the position of Arizona as well as Las Vegas as significant new immigration areas in the 1990s. Finally, recent immigrants seem increasingly likely to migrate to more rural or medium-sized metropolitan areas. While Los Angeles County stands out as the highest immigration county in 1985–1990 (with an inflow of 1,058,836 new residents from outside California in that period), the decentralization process evident around Los Angeles shows signs of moving beyond the state. For Texas, immigration concentrates along the San Antonio–Austin–Dallas corridor, with the medium-sized metropolitan area of Killen-Temple standing out as the single most important immigration area, beyond the counties proximate to the border with Mexico itself.

As for Mexico, figure 3.5 shows clearly that northern Baja California is an immigration area. In 1990, 40 per cent or more of the population of three of its four municipalities (Tijuana, Tecate, and Ensenada) was born out of the state. Other border municipalities also stand out as immigration areas, including Ciudad Juárez, Nogales, and San Luis Colorado (all of which received more than 10 per cent of its 1990 population from out of state in the previous five years). In effect, border cities contrast with non-border cities within their respective states, which have had comparatively less capacity to attract immigrants of some medium-sized non-border cities in northern Mexico. High immigration into Mexican border towns in the 1980s and 1990s relates directly to economic cycles (Ruiz 2000). The devaluation of the peso, with devastating effects elsewhere in Mexico, had positive effects in the export-oriented industries of the border region, resulting in a peaking of migration inflows into border municipalities at a time of the most dramatic economic crisis (e.g., Coubès 1997). As NAFTA opens all of Mexico to free trade with the United States, and as cross-Pacific trade expands, more labour-intensive industries may shift elsewhere to take advantage of lower wages, and consequently have an impact on decreasing immigration to border towns. Still, border employment continues strong in places such as San Diego–Tijuana, where 7.6 per cent of the Tijuana labour force was employed in San Diego in the first trimester of 1999 (Mendoza 1999). Certainly, as Rubin-Kurtzman et al. (1996) pointed out, migration and transborder mobility are key elements to demographic behaviour such as population growth in the border region.

Particularities of the border region are also found in international immigration (fig. 3.6). With few exceptions, Mexican border municipalities are the only ones with more than 2 per cent of their populations being born abroad. This is a consequence of the number of Mexican-Americans, and to a lesser extent other Americans, who live in Mexico's border towns. Transnational families are increasingly frequent (see Ojeda and López 1994, for a Tijuana case study), while women residing in border towns sometimes also use facilities in the United States for giving birth (González 1992). There is also a border effect on the U.S. side, seen more clearly in the east, with the percentage of those born abroad decreasing as one moves further from the international border. A notable exception is San Diego, with its relatively low foreign-born population (at least compared to Orange–Los Angeles and Imperial Valley). The opposite tendency is observed in Texas non-border cities, with substantial numbers of people in San Antonio, Austin, Corpus Christi, and Dallas who were born outside the United States.

Certainly high volumes of migration seem to be a key demographic phenomenon in the border region. Yet migration flows have different characteristics, both internal and international in the

United States, and mainly internal movements in Mexico and labour-oriented flows in northern Mexico. Along with contrasting differences in age structure, the significant human movement on both sides of the border has both immediate and long-term environmental consequences that cannot be underestimated.

Conclusions

Population growth in the U.S. southwest and northern Mexico has two distinctive dynamics. From a demographic point of view, growth is less concentrated in the United States than in Mexico. To the north, some rural areas are gaining population (especially in Arizona and New Mexico, but not in Texas). This relates to both economic and non-economic reasons, such as the leisure industry in Las Vegas and the appeal of mild weather, respectively, as well as cultural considerations. Furthermore, rural life is traditionally idealized in the United States. Rural Mexico, by contrast, remains underdeveloped in both real and imaginary terms, and consequently is of little interest for urban dwellers. Extreme geographical conditions appear to have had less impact on settlement patterns in the United States (as the growth of Las Vegas demonstrates) than in Mexico, where deserts and mountains remain scarcely inhabited and in a process of depopulation (with the exception of indigenous areas). The border region is a notable exception to this, however, largely because of the presence of introduced manufacturing capacity to take advantage of cheap labour and proximity to supplies and markets to the north.

Similarly, age structures on both sides of the border are substantially different. Mexico's northern region is younger than the U.S. southwest as a consequence of differentials in fertility and mortality, which are particularly striking between rural areas on either side of the border. Migration dynamics also operate in different ways on both sides of the border. Urban-rural movement in the United States offsets migrations in the opposite direction, contributing to population growth as well as aging of rural populations. For Mexico, emigration effects in sending areas are masked by younger marriage and childbearing rates as well as the fact that children often remain with grandparents when parents migrate.

The only sociodemographic phenomenon for which there is not a clear north-south divide is migration. Certainly migration and mobility characterize the borderland to such extent that they are key to understanding most other trends in the region (Rubin-Kurtzman et al. 1996). However, whereas flows are internal of origin in Mexico, both internal and international movements are relevant in the U.S. southwest. The complexity of extended family practices, plus considerable flexibility in the labour market of Mexico's border towns, make it difficulty to clearly delimit how migration operates in Mexico. The difference between the two migration systems is clear, however, when observing places of destination for immigrants, with flows being channelled into both rural and urban areas in the United States but only to urban areas in Mexico.

In short, the international line that separates the United States and Mexico also separates two distinctive sociodemographic systems. The high volume of human migration and mobility is the single feature in common, but the characteristics of the flows are so different so as to seem even to reinforce the dissimilarities in the implications of migration on both sides of the border. Nonetheless, internal migration continues to be hardly seen as problematic in either country, despite the negative consequences it may imply for destination places. This is especially true for towns and cities on Mexico's northern border, where continuing internal in-flow cities have experienced dramatic impacts on housing and services in municipalities that can hardly manage current structural deficiencies in public services. As for the contentious issue of U.S.-Mexico migration, actors and factors obviously go far beyond the border itself. Besides labour requirements, relative earnings, and the vitality of various sectors in a globalizing economy, differentials in fertility and age structure between the two countries are also changing. Decreasing fertility in Mexico is reducing the size of the young population, suggesting that labour surpluses will continue to be less robust in the future, with a predictable decline in cross-border flows beyond what immigration policies devolve. The debate that swirls around immigration almost seems to spotlight the glaring absence of an equally significant need: for cohesive policy discourse about the close relationship between environmental and economic health.

In a setting where a fine ecological balance is precarious at best, rapid demographic growth undermines even the most well-intended environmental planning. Water, in particular, is key to survival. It has deteriorated seriously in both volume and quality, through haphazard sprawl, industrial and agricultural pollutants, and rampant exploitation of rivers as well as ground water (including for high users like suburban lawns, golf courses, and hospitals). By virtue of its economic and settlement attractiveness – and as long as such logic remains unchecked – the region will inevitably experience even more profound ecological problems (Blake and Steinhart 1994; Ganster et al. 2000; Herzog 2000; Ruiz 2000). Demographic change, fuelled by growth and demand for retirement amenities in the north, and growth and continuing socioeconomic needs in the south, necessitates cross-border cooperation in research and policy formulation as well as effective and innovative infrastructure, especially in high-density border corridors where environmental impacts are most severe.

References

Alegría, Tito. 2000. "Juntos, pero no revueltos." *Revista Mexicana de Sociología* 62(2): 89–107.

Bean, Frank B., W. Parker Frisbie, Edward Telles, and B. Lindsay Lowell. 1992. "The Economic Impact of Undocumented Workers in the Southwest of the United States," pp. 219–29. In *Demographic Dynamics of the U.S.-Mexico Border*, ed. J.R. Weeks and R. Ham-Chande. El Paso: Texas Western Press.

Betts, Dianne C., and Daniel J. Slottje. 1994. *Crisis on the Rio Grande: Poverty, Unemployment, and Economic Development on the Texas-Mexico Border.* Boulder, CO: Westview.

Blake, Tupper Ansel, and Peter Steinhart. 1994. *Two Eagles/Dos Aguilas: A Natural History of the United States-Mexico Borderlands.* Berkeley: University of California Press.

Bustamante, Jorge. 1989. "Frontera México-Estados Unidos: Reflexiones para un marco teórico." *Frontera Norte* 1(1): 7–24.

———. 1981. "La interacción social en la frontera México-Estados Unidos: Un marco conceptual para la investigación," pp. 26–45. In *La Frontera del Norte: Integración y Desarrollo*, ed. R. González. Ciudad de México: El Colegio de México,

Cerutti, Mario. 2001. *Espacios de Frontera, Empresariado, y Desarrollo Regional: La Experiencia de Monterrey*. Paper presented in the Conference "The U.S.-Mexico Border Economy in the 21st Century." El Colegio de la Frontera Norte, 22–23 June. Tijuana, B.C.

Coubès, Marie-Laure. 1997. *Les Différentiations par sexe dans l'emploi à la frontière nord du Mexique*. PhD thesis, X-Nanterre. Paris: Université de Paris.

———. 2000. "Demografía fronteriza: cambio en las perspectivas de análisis de la población en la frontera México-Estados Unidos." *Revista Mexicana de Sociología* 62(2): 109–23.

Durand, Jorge, Douglas S. Massey, and René M. Zenteno. 2001. "Mexican Immigration to the United States: Continuties and Changes," *Latin American Research Review*, 36: 107–27.

Estrella, Gabriel, Alejandro Canales, and María Eugenia Zavala de Cosío. 1999. *Ciudades de la Frontera Norte: Migración y Fecundidad*. Mexicali: Universidad Autónoma de Baja California.

Ganster, Paul, Alan Sweedler, and Norris Clement. 2000. "Development, Growth, and the Future of the Border Environment," pp. 73–103. In *The U.S.-Mexican Border Environment: A Road Map to a Sustainable 2020*, ed. Paul Ganster. San Diego: San Diego State University.

González, Raúl. 1992. *Fecundidad en la Frontera Norte de México*. Tijuana: El Colegio de la Frontera Norte.

Ham-Chande, Roberto, and John Weeks. 1988. "Resumen del simposio binacional de población en la frontera México-Estados Unidos." *Cuadernos de Trabajo de El Colegio de la Frontera Norte*, 18. Tijuana: COLEF.

Herzog, Lawrence. 1990. *Where North Meets South: Cities, Space and Politics on U.S.-Mexico Border*. Austin: Center for Mexican American Studies, University of Texas at Austin.

———. 2000. *Shared Space: Rethinking the U.S.-Mexico Border Environment*. San Diego: Center for U.S.-Mexican Studies, University of California.

Howard, Cheryl. 1994. "Demography of the U.S.-Mexico Border Region," pp. 197–206. In *Sociological Explorations: Focus on the Southwest*, eds. Howard C. Daudistel and Cheryl A. Howard. Minneapolis: West.

Lozano, Fernando. 2002. "Migrantes de las ciudades: Nuevos modelos de la migración mexicana a Estados Unidos," pp. 241–59. In *Población y*

Sociedad al Inicio del Siglo XXI, ed. García B. Ciudad de México: El Colegio de México.

Marcelli, Enrico A., and Wayne Cornelius. 2001. "The Changing Profile of Mexican Migrants to the United States: New evidence from California and Mexico." *Latin American Research Review* 36: 105–31.

Martínez, Oscar J. 1994. *Border People: Life and Society in the U.S.-Mexico Borderlands*. Tucson: University of Arizona Press.

Mendoza, Cristóbal. 1999. *Migración y Mercados de Trabajo en el Norte de México*. Paper presented in "Workshop on Mexico-U.S. Border Demographics." El Colegio de la Frontera Norte, 21–22 October. Tijuana, B.C.

———. 2001. "Sociodemografía de la región fronteriza México-Estados Unidos: Tendencias recientes. *Papeles de Población*" 30: 31–63.

———. 2005. "La migración femenina en el contexto de cambio de patrón migratorio México-Estados Unidos: Aportes de cuatro encuestas mexicanas de los noventa. Paper presented in the Workshop "Mobilités en feminine," Tanger, Morocco, 16–19 November.

Ojeda, Norma, and Silvia López. 1994. *Familias Transfronterizas en Tijuana: Dos Estudios Complementarios*. Tijuana: El Colegio de la Frontera Norte.

Peach, James, and James Williams. 2000. "Population and Economic Dynamics on the U.S.-Mexican Border: Past, Present, and Future," pp. 37–72. In *The U.S.-Mexican Border Environment: A Road Map to a Sustainable 2020*, ed. Paul Ganster. San Diego: San Diego State University.

Pick, James B., Naska K. Viswanathan, James Hettrick, and Tim Turley. 2000. *A Study of the Urban Structure and Extent of Socioeconomic Commonality in the Twin Metropolitan Areas of Ciudad Juárez, México, and El Paso, Texas*. Paper presented in VI Meeting of Sociedad Mexicana de Demografía. Ciudad de México, 31 July–4 August 2000.

Quilodrán, Julieta. 1998. *Le Mariage au Mexique: Évolution national et typologie régionale*. Louvain la Neuve: Bruylant Academia/ L'Harmattan.

Rubin-Kurtzman, Jane R., Roberto Ham-Chande, and M. R. Van Arsdol. 1996. "Population in Trans-border Regions: The Southern California-Baja California Urban System." *International Migration Review* 30(4): 1020–1045.

Ruiz, Ramón Eduardo. 2000. *On the Rim of Mexico: Encounters of the Rich and Poor*. Boulder, CO: Westview.

Sassen, Saskia. 1996. "New Employment Regimens in Cities: The Impact of Immigrant Workers." *New Community* 22: 579–94.

Vila, Pablo. 2000. *Crossing Borders, Reinforcing Borders: Social Categories, Metaphors, and Narrative Identities on the U.S.-Mexico Frontier.* Austin: University of Texas Press.

Ward, Peter. 1995. *Colonias and Public Policy in Texas and Mexico: Urbanization by Stealth.* Austin: University of Texas Press.

Weeks, John R., and Roberto Ham-Chande, eds. 1992. *Demographic Dynamics of the U.S.-Mexico Border.* El Paso: Texas Western Press.

Zenteno, René, and Rodolfo Cruz. 1992. "A Geodemographic Definition of the Northern Border of Mexico," pp. 29–42. In *Demographic Dynamics of the U.S.-Mexico Border,* ed. R. Weeks and R. Ham-Chande. El Paso: Texas Western Press.

4

ENERGY POLICY AND ECONOMIC GROWTH IN THE PACIFIC BORDER REGIONS OF NORTH AMERICA

Alejandro Díaz-Bautista, Donald K. Alper, and Krista Martinez

Abstract

North American energy supply is intricately tied to the economy, through the energy demand of users, as well as to the environment, primarily through air pollution related to energy use and the impact of hydroelectricity on hydrological systems. This chapter describes and analyzes major features of North American energy flows as they relate to economic growth and environmental well being. The focus is on energy and environmental interdependencies in cross-border bioregions in the Pacific west of North America. By focusing on these regions – where geography, resource wealth, and concentrated populations have led to interconnected political economies – the possibilities of promoting sustainable energy programs and consumption can be assessed in the context of increasing continental economic integration.

Introduction

As the North American border regions experience accelerated economic and population growth, expanding requirements of burgeoning metropolitan areas are putting increased pressure on energy resources and existing intra-national and international supply networks. This creates a critical need for research and policy that addresses the relationship between energy and economic demands and resource supply and environmental health. Close cross-border cooperation in both research and policy is essential because of the ecological and economic interdependence of the three countries. Although there is no North American energy policy, energy interdependence is growing, and the momentum of continental integration has spilled over into the border regions where proximity of supply and demand result in significant challenges, but also mutual benefits. Because they are magnets for growth, the Pacific border regions are especially affected by the complex challenges of ecosystem management and development of economic and social policy. The experiences of these binational regions are important in revealing the problems and potential solutions in reconciling increased consumption with protection of environmental health.

Sustainable Development and Energy Use

Sustainable development is based on the premise that population and per capita consumption operate within the ability of the ecosystem to respond to current needs without jeopardizing the needs of future generations (World Commission on Environmental Development 1987). Population effects vary widely due to vast regional differences in ecosystem characteristics and sensitivities. While large populations exert considerable stress on their ecosystems, small populations with high rates of consumption can eclipse the effect of larger populations operating at lower rates of consumption.

Alejandro Díaz-Bautista, Donald K. Alper, and Krista Martinez

World population growth and consumption have become major topics in the sustainable development discourse, including the Rio Declaration of 1992 and Agenda 12. The latter proposes to incorporate demographic trends in the global analysis of environmental and development issues in order to promote patterns of consumption and production that reduce environmental stress while meeting basic human needs. The threat that heavily populated developing countries pose to the world environment has been a major concern, even though developed countries have far higher per capita levels of consumption than developing countries. Although the majority of North America is highly developed, any prospects for sustainable development require that population and consumption are taken into account as well as the asymmetry between the prosperous north (Canada and the United States) and the developing south (Mexico).

Within a sustainability framework, the concept of bioregion is particularly useful since it regards territory as defined by a combination of interrelated social, environmental, and geographic criteria, rather than solely by geopolitical considerations (Frankel 1994; Sale 1985). A bioregional perspective holds considerable promise for confronting the North American energy dilemma insofar as it locates people in the natural world and helps to focus attention on how economies affect, and are affected by, the availability and development of energy resources. A focus on the north-south bioregions regions anchored by the metropolitan centres of San Diego/Tijuana and Seattle/Vancouver, where capital and resources are cycled within each region, enables us to see more clearly the critical links between economic and energy needs.

North American Energy Use and Economic Growth

Just as increased energy use does not generate much economic growth unless accompanied by increased use of capital and labour, increase in capital and labour is futile unless increase in energy use also occurs; otherwise little gain in a nation's output can be expected. Innovations that increased energy supply at the beginning of the Industrial Revolution removed limitations that had constrained economic growth prior to that time. In North America, the relatively smooth expansion of energy supply and its rising quality has been essential to maintaining economic growth during much of the last century.

The countries of North America consume and produce more energy than all other countries of the Americas combined (tables 4.1 and 4.2). The United States, Canada, and Mexico make extensive use of abundant domestic resources. Consumption of natural gas and coal, which is greater than petroleum, is concentrated almost exclusively in the United States and Canada. The United States and Canada also provide virtually universal access to electric power for their populations, while Mexico's level of access is close to 95 per cent. In Mexico, most electricity is delivered by two state-owned energy conglomerates: Comisión Federal de Electricidad (CFE) and Luz y Fuerza del Centro (LFC). In the United States, about one third of electricity is delivered from public power sources (U.S. Department of Energy. Energy Information Administration 2004; hereafter cited as U.S. EIA).

Table 4.1 Energy Consumption Per Capita in North America.

	POPULATION	PER CAPITA ENERGY CONSUMPTION
Canada	32.5 million	418 million Btu*
Mexico	102.4 million	65 million Btu
United States	293 million	339.1 million Btu

*Btu (British thermal units). **Source:** U.S. EIA 2004.

Table 4.2 North American Energy Consumption Statistics.

	2002 TOTAL ELECTRICITY CONSUMPTION	2002 ENERGY-RELATED CO$_2$ EMISSIONS	2003 OIL CONSUMPTION
Canada	487.3 Bkwh*	592 Mmt† of CO$_2$ (2.4% of world total)	2.30 bbl/d‡
Mexico	186.7 Bkwh	362.5 Mmt of CO$_2$ (1.5% of World Total)	2.02 bbl/d
United States	3,641 Bkwh	5,796 Mmt of CO$_2$ (24% of World Total)	20.00 bbl/d

*Bkwh (billion kilowatt hours). †Mmt (million metric tons). ‡bbl/d (barrels per day).
Source: U.S. EIA 2004.

The primary driver of energy consumption in North America is the rate of economic growth, which, as measured in real gross domestic product (GDP), is forecast to be about 2.3 per cent per year through 2020 (U.S. EIA 1999). Economic development is proceeding much more rapidly in coastal and urban areas than in the rural hinterland, while also widening regional economic disparities. Although GDP per person provides some indication of the level of development in each country, a more significant indicator is the human development index (HDI). According to the United Nations Human Development Programme 2004 Report, Canada had the fourth highest HDI, the United States was eighth, and Mexico was ranked 53 out of 177 countries evaluated (United Nations Development Programme 2004; hereafter cited as UNDP). This index takes into account GDP per person along with life expectancy at birth, level of school attendance, and literacy rates. The GDP per capita in 2002 for Mexico was US$8,970 using the purchasing power parity method, while the Canadian GDP per capita was a US$29,480, and the United States had a GDP per capita of US$35,750 (UNDP 2004). In terms of per capita carbon emissions, Mexico produces 3.5 metric tons per person per year, compared to 19.8 in the United States and 18.2 in Canada (U.S. EIA 2004). It is apparent that as economic conditions improve, and Mexico aspires to have a higher level of human development, we can expect corresponding growth in greenhouse-gas emissions from Mexico unless renewable sources and sustainability principles gain priority.

Energy Use and Economic Growth in Canada

Canada is a significant energy exporter, and a major part of recent Canadian economic growth is high world energy prices. Canada's energy abundance has encouraged the development of a highly fuel-intensive economy based on natural resource extraction and processing. Only recently, however, has this heavy reliance on energy-intensive industries led to serious environmental concerns, primarily regarding air pollution and climate change related to the Kyoto Protocol Agreement of 1997.

Before the end of the twentieth century, Canada had already become the fifth-largest energy producer in the world – behind the United States, Russia, China, and Saudi Arabia – as well as the world's sixth-largest energy consumer. In 1999, about 36 per cent of Canada's primary energy production was natural gas, followed by oil (23%), hydropower (20%), coal (11%), and nuclear power (4%) (World Energy Council 2001; hereafter cited as WEC). Canada has also become a significant net energy supplier, exporting about 30 per cent of its energy production in 1999. The United States is by far the main customer. Canada is the top supplier of U.S. oil imports. Over 75 per cent of oil production is based in the province of Alberta (Canada. Natural Resources Canada 2002). Integration of U.S. and Canadian markets is seen in the cross-border web of infrastructure: more than 35 cross-border natural gas lines, 22 oil and petroleum product pipelines, 55 cross-border electric transmission lines. Recently, China invested heavily in the development of large oil sand deposits in Alberta. It is likely that the emerging China energy market will absorb increasing amounts of Canadian oil, thus complicating the north-south export market with the United States.

Canada has about 56.1-trillion cubic feet (Tcf) of proven natural gas reserves, and its 2002 production was 6.6 Tcf (U.S. EIA 2005a) of natural gas per year. Thus Canada is the world's third largest gas producer after the United States and Russia, and the second largest gas exporter after Russia (WEC 2001). Canada's gas exports go almost exclusively to the United States. In 2003, Canadian natural gas accounted for 100 per cent of U.S. gas imports by pipeline and over 14 per cent of U.S. gas consumption (Gaul 2004). Canadian gas consumption is projected to grow significantly in coming decades, largely for use in electricity generation. As natural gas production and infrastructure grow, there is a potential for emergence of a unified North American natural gas market. Recent expansion of gas interconnections between Canada and the United States is seen in the Northern Border Pipeline, which came onstream in late 1999, connecting Chicago through the upper Midwest.

Canada is also a major coal producer and consumer, with an estimated 1999 production of 72,497 thousand metric tons, consumption of 60,500 thousand metric tons, and proved recoverable reserves of 6,578 million metric tons (WEC 2001). Fifty-seven per cent of Canadian coal exports go to Asia (Downing and Store 2005).

Canada is the world's largest producer of hydropower (WEC 2001). Nationally, hydropower accounts for about 60 per cent of electricity generation, compared with about 26 per cent through conventional thermal power (oil, gas, and coal), 12.4 per cent from nuclear generation, and 1 per cent derived from renewable sources (Canada. National Energy Board 2003). Trends in coming years are expected to favour thermal power generation, mainly from natural gas.

Canada is a major electricity exporter to the United States. More than thirty states are recipients of Canadian electricity. The preponderance of energy exports from Quebec, Ontario, and New Brunswick go to the New England states and New York state. Smaller volumes from British Columbia and Manitoba go to the states of Washington, California, Oregon, and Minnesota. There is considerable reciprocity between the Canadian and U.S. border power markets, as the United States also exports smaller volumes of electricity to Canada. Natural-gas-fired power plant construction is increasing in Canada, with a three-fold increase in gas power generation anticipated in the next decade.

In most Canadian provinces, generation, transmission, and distribution of electricity are provided by a few dominant utilities. Although some of these utilities are privately owned, most are owned provincially, such as BC Hydro. There is also limited independent power producer (IPP) generation, mostly for sales to the larger utilities. Alberta and Ontario have introduced legislation to deregulate their power sectors, though Alberta is much further along in the deregulation process. In 1995, Alberta was the first province to introduce privatization legislation, and a 1998 amendment to the original legislation allowed retail customers to choose their electricity suppliers beginning in January 2001. Ontario introduced privatization legislation in 1998, but deregulation originally scheduled for November 2000 has been postponed indefinitely. Quebec and British Columbia allow third party access to their electricity grids as the result of trade agreements with the United States, but neither province plans to break up its utility monopoly.

In 2002, Canada's per capita energy consumption was second only to the United States among G-8 nations (Ménard 2005). The same year, Canada's per capita carbon emissions ranked third among OECD countries (Organisation for Economic Co-operation and Development 2005). Canada's total energy consumption increased by 23 per cent, from 8,549 petajoules to 10,477 petajoules, during the period between 1990 and 2003. One petajoule is roughly equivalent to the energy needed to fill one million automobile gas tanks (Ménard 2005). Canada's energy consumption per capita is more than six times as much as Mexico's (U.S. EIA 2005a).

Energy Use and Economic Growth in the United States

The mammoth U.S. gross domestic product (GDP), which has exceeded $10 trillion/year since 2001, is sustained through major trading relationships with Canada, Japan, the European Union, Mexico, and beyond, as well as through significant consumption of energy from both domestic and international sources. The United States had 21.9-billion barrels of proved oil reserves as of 1 January 2005, over 80 per cent concentrated in Texas (23%, including the state's reserves in the Gulf of Mexico), Louisiana (22%, including Gulf reserves), Alaska (20%), and California (18%) (U.S. EIA 2005b). However, proven oil reserves declined about 17 per cent since 1990, while total oil production declined sharply (26%) from 1985 to 2003 (U.S. EIA 2005b).

In the past two decades, the structure of the natural gas market has also changed dramatically, shifting from a market relying almost exclusively on price regulation to one where prices are determined by the balance of supply and demand, subject to the regulatory oversight of the Federal Energy Regulatory Commission (FERC). Augmented by imports, mainly from Canada, natural gas production is likely to increase sharply in response to strong demand, abundant reserves, and improved unconventional and offshore recovery technology. Natural gas consumption in the United States increased by about 15 per cent from 1990 through 2003, although consumption fell by 5 per cent in 2003 due to high prices (U.S. EIA 2005b). Lower costs resulting from greater competition and deregulation in the gas industry, and an expanding transmission and distribution network, also contributed to its use. U.S. natural gas is used mainly in the industrial sector (37%), followed by electric utility (23%), residential (22%), and commercial (14%) sectors (U.S. EIA 2005b).

North American natural gas import/export and consumption rates are expected to expand substantially through 2020. The fastest volumetric growth is attributable to additional gas-fired electric power plants. In particular, new combined-cycle facilities furnished with more efficient gas turbines have lowered the cost of gas-generated electricity to levels competitive with coal-fired plants. Increased consumption of natural gas in the United States will require expansion of gas pipeline and storage capacity.

Electric utilities account for about 90 per cent of U.S. coal consumption (U.S. EIA 2005b). This pattern is expected to continue through 2020 at least, with coal maintaining a fuel cost advantage over oil and natural gas. In 2003, the United States generated 3,848 billion kilowatt hours (kWh) of electricity. For utilities, coal-fired plants accounted for 53 per cent of generation, nuclear 21 per cent, natural gas 7 per cent, hydroelectricity 8 per cent, oil 3 per cent, geothermal and other 1 per cent (U.S. EIA 2005b). Electricity prices in the United States fell every year between 1993 and 1999, but this trend has reversed in recent years (U.S. EIA 2005b).

In 2002, estimated electricity consumption in the United States was 3,641-billion kilowatt hours, compared to 186.7-billion kilowatt hours in Mexico (U.S. EIA 2004). The U.S. power demand is predicted to increase at a 1.8 per cent average annual growth in sales through 2020. This increase will require a significant addition in generating capacity. Many new power plants will be needed within the next twenty years; the majority will most likely be powered by natural gas.

At the December 1997 global warming summit in Kyoto, Japan, the U.S. delegation agreed to reduce U.S. carbon emissions 7 per cent from 1990 levels by 2008–2012. In 2001, President Bush declared that his administration would not seek to regulate power plants' emissions of carbon dioxide, citing an Energy Information Administration (EIA) study that regulating these emissions could result in higher electricity prices. The Bush administration also declared that the United States would not ratify the Kyoto Treaty, saying it would be too harmful to the U.S. economy, and that the nation would pursue other ways of addressing the problem of climate change. Increasingly, individual states and cities have taken proactive climate change actions (Selin and Vandeveer 2005).

Energy Use and Economic Growth in Mexico

In 2000, President Vicente Fox and the Partido Acción Nacional (PAN) won a historic presidential election, ending seventy-one consecutive years of the *Partido Revolucionario Institucional* (PRI) rule. Fox had an ambitious plan to restructure and modernize the Mexican government and industry, especially the energy sector, although privatization of the state-owned Comisión Federal de Electricidad (CFE), the state power company, and Petróleos Mexicanos (Pemex), the state oil company, was ruled out of bounds as politically infeasible. The stated commitment was to make the country less financially reliant on oil exports, which generate about one-third of government revenues.

Mexico has the second largest proven crude oil reserves in the western hemisphere after Venezuela. In 2003, Mexico produced about 3.8-million barrels per day (bbl/d) of oil, with net oil exports of roughly 1.78-million bbl/d, making Mexico the world's fifth-largest oil producer (U.S. EIA 2004). In 2001, 1.6-million bbl/d went to the United States (U.S. EIA 2004). The value of Mexican oil exports increased from US$6.4 billion in 1998 to US$13.2 billion in 2004, accounting for about a third of the government's annual budget (U.S. EIA 2004). Mexico produces three grades of crude oil: heavy

Maya-22, which accounts for more than half of total production; light, low-sulphur Isthmus-34, accounting for less than one-third of total production; and extra-light Olmeca-39, which is about one-fifth of total production. About three-quarters of Mexican production come from Campeche Bay in the Gulf of Mexico. Production at the largest field, Cantarell, located off the Yucatan coast, is steadily increasing, and recent investment in the oil sector continues to focus more on enhancing production at existing fields than exploration for new fields.

The Mexican oil industry was nationalized in 1938. Pemex is one of the world's largest oil companies, the single most important entity in the Mexican economy, and a symbol of Mexican sovereignty and independence. Pemex is the only company in the Mexican oil market, upstream and downstream. Pemex is upgrading its oil transport infrastructure. Currently, there are nearly three thousand miles of crude oil pipelines and more than five thousand miles of oil product pipelines. A seven-hundred-mile pipeline currently under construction will connect production from offshore Veracruz to refineries. Mexico's downstream oil sector was nationalized in the 1950s, and privatization is not planned.

Although Mexico is one of the world's largest oil producers, about a quarter of gasoline consumption is imported due to insufficient refinery capacity. The country has six refineries, and controls 50 per cent of a refinery in Deer Park, Texas, with a total throughput capacity of 1.73-million bbl/d (U.S. EIA 2004). Major upgrades on the refineries, begun in 2001, aim to increase the percentage of gasoline and light products refined, allow refineries to process heavier crude such as Mexican Maya, meet clean fuel specifications, and increase overall refining capacity by 350,000 bbl/d (U.S. EIA 2004).

Mexico is a small net importer of U.S. natural gas, a trend that is expected to continue in coming decades. The tariff on Mexican imports of U.S. gas was eliminated in 1999, which should encourage growing volumes of imports in the future. Natural gas will also play a more important role in the future as demand rises quickly, especially in the power sector. In response to anticipated demand growth, Pemex plans to increase Mexican-U.S. border infrastructure and capacity and to focus more on gas exploration activities. The Burgos Field, located in northeastern Mexico, is expected to contain massive volumes of largely non-associated, recoverable natural gas resources. Cantarell holds significant gas reserves in association with oil deposits, most of which are flared.

Mexico's growing reliance on natural gas coincides with historically high price levels for the fuel in North America. The Mexican gas price was fixed to the Houston Ship Channel price in Texas in the early 1990s. As U.S. natural gas prices spiked in early 2001, Fox came under pressure from Mexican industry and labour unions, who claimed high prices were causing irreversible damage to Mexican industry. The natural gas industry is the most liberalized of Mexico's energy sectors. While upstream exploration and production are the sole domains of Pemex, the downstream gas market has been open to private investors since the passage of the 1995 *Natural Gas Law*. This legislation modified the constitution, allowing the involvement of private companies in gas transportation, storage, and distribution in Mexico, although it prohibits a company from ownership in more than one function within the industry. The legislation also liberalized natural gas trade and established the regulatory framework for building and expanding transmission and distribution pipelines. La Comisión Reguladora de Energía (CRE) regulates the gas industry and oversees the CFE. The CRE's powers include enforcement of regulations, inspections of facilities, issuance of permits, regulation of prices, overall supervision of the industry, promotion of competition, and elimination of cross-subsidies. Private-sector participation in these areas currently is subject to permits granted by CRE for thirty years, based on competitive bidding.

Mexico's electricity sector is at a crossroads. Although generation has increased rapidly over the past decade, supply is not expected to meet demand growth over the next two decades. In 2004, it was estimated that Mexico's power generation capacity was over 50.7 gigawatts (U.S. EIA 2004). The CFE's effective power generation capacity is constituted by 154 power plants, with 64 hydroelectric, 79 thermoelectric with fossil fuel consumption, 6 geothermal, 2 carbon-based plants, 1 nuclear plant, and 2 wind-based plants. In 2004, the combined installed capacity of this Mexican institution was 38,400 MW (México. Comisión Federal de Electricidad 2004). Given current grid capacity constraints, shortages could result, which could result in nationwide blackouts in coming years. The key to generating more electricity is the availability of gas. Thus the success of meeting electricity requirements is bound up with continuing investment in, and development of, gas resources (De la O 2002).

Independent power producers (IPPs) are permitted to build and own power generation facilities, and the power can be used at related industrial companies, or sold under long-term contracts to public utilities. These projects account for over 14 per cent of Mexico's electric generation capacity (U.S. EIA 2004). Of the twelve IPP projects in progress, ten are in northern Mexico; five of these are totally dependent on natural gas imports from the United States, while the other five are partially dependent on U.S. imports. Uncertainty regarding import sources could explain the low level of interest in new projects offered by the CFE. Subsidies paid to agricultural and residential electricity consumers and to LFC and the lack of an open power market are blamed for escalating industrial electricity costs, now above average international industrial electricity costs. Mexican industry has continually warned that these costs will make Mexican industry internationally uncompetitive.

Effects of NAFTA on Energy, the Environment, and the Economy

In 1994, the North American Free Trade Agreement (NAFTA) created the largest single free trade market in the world containing well over 360 million consumers at that time. The strength of this continental trade partnership is supported by the fact that Mexico and Canada account for approximately 60 per cent of the growth in total U.S. exports since 1994. The North America energy market is now bigger than that of the expanded European Union. The three countries' energy production accounts for almost one-quarter of all the energy on Earth.

The move toward energy interdependence and the emergence of a continent-wide market was stimulated by NAFTA, which eliminated tariff and non-tariff barriers to energy trade. At the same time, increased privatization of certain aspects of Mexican electricity and gas services, and the establishment of an independent body of energy regulators in Mexico, further enabled cross-border cooperative ventures. The trinational North American Energy Working Group (NAEWG), created in 2001, fostered new efficiency initiatives, performance requirements, and renewable programs that helped to increase confidence and cooperation among industry leaders and officials of the partner governments. Indeed, by 2005, one energy specialist referred to the increasingly integrated North American energy sector as "at long last, one continent" (Dukert 2005).

NAFTA also opened the discussion of continental environmental matters. The North American Agreement on Environmental Cooperation (NAAEC), the environmental side agreement to NAFTA, established the Council for Environmental Cooperation (CEC), which has important energy implications because of pollutants generated from energy operations. The NAFTA side agreement also created the North American Development Bank (NADBank) and the Border Environment Cooperation Commission (BECC). NADBank, a bilaterally funded organization capitalized and governed by the U.S. and Mexico, arranges financing for environmental infrastructure projects in the border region. Although freshwater supply and waste treatment form the core activities of the bank, assistance can also be provided in other areas such as air quality and clean energy. The BECC works with border states and local communities to develop and certify projects. The U.S.-Mexico Border XXI Program, established under BECC, sets five-year objectives for achieving and sustaining a clean border environment. Nine binational groups created through this program are working to reduce emissions at border crossings, tracking trans-boundary shipments of hazardous wastes, and operating a U.S.-Mexico Joint Response Team to minimize the risk of chemical accidents. NAAEC was created to enhance intergovernmental cooperation in addressing important environmental issues such as border pollution, trade in hazardous wastes, and climate change. One of NAAEC's main goals is to evaluate the environmental effects of increased electricity generation and overall energy trade.

Under the NAFTA agreement, the CEC does not have the power to enforce regulations against private companies. The CEC does, however, have the capability to publicize reviews of accused companies, with the intent that public exposure will lead to better compliance. The CEC also serves as a forum for public dialogue on issues of environmental concern. With increased energy production and trade under NAFTA, the need to cooperate is all the greater and thus the CEC process which emphasizes participation and transparency is increasingly important.

There are no formal dispute settlement mechanisms available under multinational environmental agreements (MEAs) should a member complain about trade sanctions taken against it because of the alleged lack of compliance with environmental obligations. The only legal recourse for countries is the dispute settlement mechanism available under the World Trade Organization (WTO). In 1995, the WTO Committee on Trade and the Environment (CTE) first convened. The WTO provisions are generally designed to ensure that measures are not disguised restrictions on trade, or unduly discriminatory. There have been no environmental disputes based on energy trade between NAFTA members brought before the CTE/WTO.

Despite the promise of greater trilateral environmental cooperation, NAFTA has done little to alleviate pollution impacts throughout North America. Increased population and an overall trend of rising per capita incomes in the western hemisphere have led to increased emissions in the transportation, industrial, and residential sectors. The result is higher levels of ozone, particulate matter, and carbon monoxide, often exceeding World Health Organization standards by wide margins (Council for Environmental Cooperation 2006).

In part, the problem is that in North America there is no common approach to monitoring and managing air pollution and even climate change. Each of the North American governments has developed independent domestic approaches to climate change (Betsill 2005). In the United States, the approach has been focused on reducing pollutants through voluntarism, scientific research (especially focused on cleaner technologies), and public awareness. In recent years many state governments have been the leaders in addressing climate change. In Canada, efforts have been directed at a Kyoto target (6% emissions reductions below 1990 levels by 2008–2012, equivalent to a 37% reduction), and public outreach focused on fostering more sophisticated and efficient energy consumption. As in the United States, the Canadian federal government has been reluctant to take actions that might offend industry, and provinces are now leading on this issue. Mexico ratified the Kyoto Protocol in 2000, but the Mexican emphasis has been on developing mitigation projects in the forest and energy sectors (Betsill 2005). Although the three NAFTA member states' approaches diverge, they do have common interests regarding energy pollution that could serve as a basis for a regional governance system based on effective management of emissions. Utilizing the offices of the CEC, a North American adaptation strategy, with an initial focus on the border regions could be developed and implemented. The overall goal would be a shared commitment to reducing air pollution in North America rather than a more global commitment to address climate change (Betsill 2005).

Reductions in carbon emissions and other pollutants in North America can be achieved through the conversion of coal-fired power plants to those fuelled by natural gas, increased use of renewable energy technologies, and improvements in energy efficiency. Agreements focusing on energy conservation and alternatives among the three countries are unlikely given very different domestic priorities and the imbalance between the developed and developing economies. Nevertheless, steady efforts to promote energy efficiency are evident with emphasis on coordination and equivalency of energy efficiency standards, elimination of barriers for adopting new technologies and establishment of a common system for labelling equipment. With a significant rise in oil prices in 2005–2006, these efforts have accelerated.

NAFTA has affected continental energy trade by fostering wider and deeper trade linkages among the three nations, of which energy is an important part. Trade liberalization has lessened government's role in the North American energy sector. This is not without controversy as both Canada and Mexico feel pressured to cede more and more control to the powerful U.S.-dominated industry and market (Cohen 2006). One of the issues in Canada is that there is significant debate – accelerated since 2000 with the presidency of George W. Bush – over the proper roles of state and market in the electricity sector (Gattinger 2005). Canadians also express unease about the security of domestic supply since NAFTA prohibits energy cutbacks to the U.S. market without proportionate actions at home.

In Mexico, NAFTA-driven economic growth has put pressure on successive governments to open up energy-related investment and service opportunities and therefore deepen North American energy integration. For example, natural gas imports from the United States to Mexico are tariff free and the United States and Canada are now able to invest in secondary petrochemicals in Mexico. NAFTA permits Mexico to issue import and export licences to reserve foreign

Alejandro Díaz-Bautista, Donald K. Alper, and Krista Martinez trade in certain goods to Pemex, in recognition of its monopoly position. These goods include virtually all refined petroleum products plus bitumen, oil shale, tar sands, and liquid petroleum gases.

The increasing demand for natural gas in Mexico, stimulated in part by NAFTA, and by greater emphasis on environmental quality by CFE, will encourage a further opening of Mexican markets and supply capabilities. With NAFTA, Mexico has become more receptive to proposals made in the past to develop Mexican gas resources. These include extension of a gas pipeline in northern Mexico to Tijuana and construction of a gas-fired desalination plant in the Baja California Peninsula. The Gulf of Cortez is an area known to contain natural gas, yet development has been precluded by Pemex budget restrictions. NAFTA provides a framework for some erosion of the Pemex tutelage and hence could allow more gas development projects to go forward.

Greater openness in the North American energy market is a thorny political issue. Critics in all three countries worry about a more integrated continental system dominated by large (mostly U.S.) corporations whose profit objectives could displace national values such as energy security, social equity, and regional development (Cohen 2006; Ross 2003; Dobbin 2002).

Western North America Bioregions and Energy Issues

The Canada-U.S. border region in the Pacific west, encompassing much of western Washington and Oregon and southwestern British Columbia, has gained an international reputation as a remarkably rich bioregion. This binational region contains vast watersheds of rivers that flow into the Pacific Ocean through North America's temperate rain forest zone. Within this zone are some of the fastest growing metropolitan areas of North America. The region is a leading centre for advanced technology in aerospace, computer software, electronics, medical equipment, and environmental engineering. A vibrant telecommunications sector, with extensive fibre optic corridors serving numerous commercial areas, has encouraged the growth of the technology sector, especially in the Seattle area.

During the 1990s, the region's population increased at nearly twice the North American rate. This rapid growth has challenged the region to reconcile economic development and environmental well being or risk erosion of the area's attractiveness and economic competitiveness. As seen in table 4.3, this rapid growth is expected to continue into the foreseeable future.

Table 4.3 Population in the San Diego–Tijuana and the Seattle-Vancouver Bioregions.

	GREATER SEATTLE AREA	GREATER VANCOUVER REGIONAL DISTRICT	GREATER SAN DIEGO REGION	GREATER TIJUANA REGION
2000	2,727,000	1,959,000	2,683,000	1,297,000
2005 (est.)	2,959,000	2,125,000	2,818,000	1,570,000
2010 (est.)	3,164,000	2,273,000	2,958,000	2,273,000

Source: United Nations (2003).

The fuel for regional growth has been a diversified and abundant energy supply. British Columbia has had the luxury of a secure supply of energy, although it may be jeopardized by future requirements and costs. Hydropower has been abundant; however, the province is no longer self-sufficient in electricity (BC Progress Board 2005a,b). Most refined petroleum products are imported from Alberta. The northeast of the province is the area of focus for increased gas production, but constraints include labour and equipment shortages and opposition to offshore drilling. Although still a small energy player in global terms, British Columbia is an important source of natural gas for the U.S. Pacific Northwest and coal for Asia, Europe, and the United States. Governments in the province have had the foresight to build a transportation system to efficiently move energy to market. This system includes an extensive electricity transmission network that moves power from generation in the Peace and Columbia rivers (in north central B.C.) to demand in the Lower Mainland and Pacific Northwest states. Natural gas is piped south to the United States.

Rail lines connect coal deposits in the Kootenays to the Pacific, via a coal super-port south of Vancouver, and within one kilometre of the Canada-U.S. border.

In Washington state, hydroelectricity is a major energy source and renewable energy is increasingly a factor in the region's overall requirements. Coal-fired thermal electricity is also important. The environmental impact of dams imposes a limit on the use and expansion of hydro power. As a result, the west coast of the United States also relies on energy transmitted from the states of Wyoming, Colorado, and Utah, but the majority of imported energy is from western Canada. The Pacific Northwest is the closest export market for British Columbia and Alberta.

The Pacific Northwest states and western Canada have an interdependent energy relationship, trading oil, natural gas, coal, and electricity. Determining how to ensure long-term, low-cost access to fuel in the Pacific Northwest region presents an ongoing challenge.

With interdependent electricity networks, regional and national cooperation is essential to ensure reliability of supply in the event of emergencies. Due to past problems, such as the 2000–2001 electricity crisis in California and the 2003 Northeast blackout, a bilateral international electric reliability organization was formed to enforce reliability standards for the entire North American bulk electric system (U.S. EIA 2005b). Hydroelectric power transmission infrastructure along the Peace and Columbia rivers in British Columbia and the Columbia in Washington state has provided electricity for the majority of the Lower Mainland, and remains the dominant mode of electrical energy supply for the Pacific Northwest Region. In 2005, 129.84-billion kilowatt hours in the Northwest Power Pool area (Washington, Idaho, Oregon, Utah, and parts of Montana, Nevada, and Wyoming), accounted for over 70 per cent of electric power generated (U.S. EIA 2006a). British Columbia's electricity consumption is predicted to increase at a rate of 2 per cent annually (BC Hydro 2004). Regional dependence on hydroelectric power is not sustainable in the long term because new and expanded generating capacity is limited by environmental concerns, the costs of new plants, and supply variability stemming from climatic conditions. With the prospect of little or no growth in generating capacity in future, other forms of energy will have to be brought into the mix.

Coal, natural gas, and possibly nuclear power will account for more and more of the region's electrical energy supply.

In addition to supplying hydroelectric power to the western states, British Columbia has provided approximately 50 per cent of the natural gas needs of the United States for more than fifty years. The traditional markets for B.C. natural gas are the province and the Pacific Northwest region. A 44,000-mile pipeline network delivers nearly 8 billion therms of natural gas annually to approximately 2.5 million residential, commercial, industrial, and electric power generation consumers in British Columbia, Idaho, Oregon, and Washington. Gas basins in B.C. and Alberta bring gas south to Sumas, Washington, where it connects with the Northwest pipeline that runs south near Seattle and Portland along the I-5 Corridor. Natural gas has become an important competitor in the energy market, mostly because of its abundance and its reputation as a cleaner fuel source than oil. However, forecasted volatility in natural gas prices could make coal and renewable energy sources more competitive in future.

Although rising prices have impacted consumer demand for natural gas (Canada. National Energy Board 2004), the EIA's long-term forecasts extending to 2030 indicate that the natural gas consumption average annual growth (includes residential, commercial, and industrial use) of the Pacific states of Washington, Oregon, and California is projected to be 0.3 per cent (U.S. EIA 2006a). Western Canada also expects an increase in demand for natural gas, with the industrial sector – especially in Alberta – being the driving force.

The supply of natural gas in Canada (97 per cent originates from western Canada) continues to be much greater than Canadian demand. Pipeline capacity for natural gas imports and exports between the United States and Canada is expected to remain "roughly sufficient" through 2012 (North American Energy Working Group 2005). After 2012, Canadian natural gas production is expected to decline (North American Energy Working Group 2005).

With energy demand projected to remain strong throughout the region, new steps will be necessary to ensure that growing residential and industry requirements are met. Although the region likely will become more attracted to unconventional supply methods, such as extraction of methane from coal beds and import of liquefied natural gas (LNG) from overseas, there is also considerable pressure to be self-sufficient. In British Columbia, many stakeholders are insisting that provincial requirements be given priority in the marketplace as booming economies in China, India, and elsewhere place heavier pressure on Canadian supplies. To ensure a B.C. advantage, recommendations have been made to increase exploration and development of natural gas resources in the northeastern portion of the province (BC Progress Board 2005a,b). In addition, many government and industry experts have called for increasing electricity production to meet the growing demand in B.C. and the Pacific Northwest. Overall, improved efficiency and alternatives are increasingly viewed as the best way to meet energy demand in the future. Greater energy efficiency, switching fuel sources, and combined heat and power efforts could reduce grid electricity demands in the Pacific Northwest by 12 per cent in 2010 and 24 per cent in 2020 (Northwest Energy Coalition 2002).

Many energy experts expect an increase in nuclear power plants to offset more expensive and exhaustible energy sources. This is extremely controversial in the B.C.-Pacific Northwest region. Washington has one nuclear power plant, the only one of five proposed commercial nuclear plants to ever reach completion in the state. The plant accounts for about 8 per cent of the electricity produced in Washington (Washington State. Energy Facility Site Evaluation Council 2003). Nuclear power has been rejected by B.C. as an option to meet its energy needs. In California, a state energy commission recommended in 2006 that a state moratorium on construction of nuclear plants be continued (Young 2006).

Alternative Energy Sources in British Columbia and the Pacific Northwest

Increasing demand for energy has resulted in the need to look to alternative sources. A RAND report (2002) determined that the Pacific Northwest could diversify its energy production to include more energy efficiency and renewable energy sources without harming the regional economy. There are numerous alternative energy initiatives underway in British Columbia and the Pacific Northwest region. Wind, biomass, biodiesel, geothermal, hydrogen fuel technology, and ethanol represent alternative, "cleaner" energy generation sources. Alternative energy and power technology is one of the largest growth sectors in B.C. In Greater Vancouver, more than a dozen municipalities are now using some form of biodiesel in the fleets (Constantine 2006). Power Smart, a BC Hydro program, focuses on energy efficiency initiatives to offset new demand for energy in the province. The goal is to make energy efficiency a way of life by providing financial incentives to businesses and homeowners to purchase energy-efficient products. Wind, geothermal, and biomass energy sources are highlighted in BC Hydro's 2004 *Integrated Energy Plan*. The costs of wind and geothermal production could be relatively high, but environmental impacts are low, whereas the use of biomass has relatively low costs but a slightly higher environmental impact due to emissions released from the burning of materials. Biomass energy in the Pacific Northwest is already widely used and there is great potential to expand production. Currently, solid waste landfills capture and burn methane to produce electricity in places like Eugene, Oregon, and Spokane, Washington, and there are possibilities for expansion to agriculture and logging sectors which produce vast residues. It is plausible that wind, biomass, and geothermal resources could account for as much as 35 per cent of future energy production in the Pacific Northwest (Northwest Energy Coalition 2002). Another alternative energy effort is B.C.'s Hydrogen Highway. a large-scale demonstration program to increase the commercialization of hydrogen and fuel-cell technologies.

British Columbia has established an Alternative Energy Task Force to determine how to best implement an alternative energy strategy in the region. In 2006, the Pacific Northwest Economic Region (PNWER), a nonprofit regional advocacy group, called for a regional energy strategy that combines traditional energy sources with renewables. Facilitating information sharing, transmission corridor and other infrastructure planning, and more unified permitting and standards are some of the goals of the binational PNWER effort. In the United States, the Department of Energy provides funding to states for their energy programs through Energy Efficiency and Renewable Energy grants (EERE). Renewable energy, which includes hydroelectric, is projected to have an annual average growth of 2.4

per cent in the Pacific region (California, Oregon, Washington) during the years 2004–2030 (U.S. EIA 2006b).

Although industry officials and experts work together in the international region, there is little evidence of structured regional planning for energy sustainability. A first step would be the establishment of a binational strategy with agreed-upon objectives. Included in the strategy could be an inventory of the scores of programs and initiatives currently being undertaken in the region. Efforts should be made to link the projects and develop a well-integrated educational effort focused on the economic and environmental benefits of alternative energy development and use. Another idea is to take advantage of the Vancouver 2010 Olympics, which will highlight sustainable development. The games afford a unique opportunity to meld individual provincial and state initiatives into a broader Pacific west coast strategy.

Over one thousand miles south, the Mexico–United States border has experienced comparable macroeconomic activity and accelerated use of capital and energy resources. In the San Diego/Tijuana bioregion, a large and rapidly growing population poses challenges and opportunities with respect to energy, environmental policy, and infrastructure. By 2010, the Tijuana/San Diego bioregion is projected to have a population in excess of 5 million, compared to nearly 6 million in the greater Seattle/Vancouver bioregion in the same period.

The rapid rate of economic and population growth in the Tijuana/San Diego region is creating massive opportunities for private sector involvement in infrastructure development in the energy and transportation sectors. The growing demand for energy, and new regulatory regimes developing on both sides of the border, offer a rationale for developing increased cooperation between Mexico and the United States, particularly through greater integration of Baja California's power sector into California's energy markets.

Population growth along the border in Baja, when combined with growth of manufacturing, commercial, and service sectors, exacerbates problems associated with scarcity of water and competition for energy supplies. It would seem that the states of Baja California and California have little choice but to work towards a regional energy plan, and to help each other provide enough power to fuel their growing economies. Baja California's electrical energy infrastructure consists of two large power plants (about 620 megawatts each), several smaller ones, and transmission lines, including two connecting to the San Diego power grid. Plans for expansion of the generation and transmission infrastructure of electrical energy in Baja California are critical to economic development on both sides of the border.

The majority of Mexico's liquid natural gas (LNG) facilities along the U.S.-Mexican border are in Baja California. In 2004, the California Public Utilities Commission voted to allow the import of re-gasified LNG from Mexico to California via the pipeline (U.S. EIA 2004). The most important factor driving the increase in demand for natural gas is its use for electricity generation. The opening and deregulation of the electrical sector in recent years is likely to contribute to continuing high growth in Baja California.

To satisfy the increasing demand for natural gas in Northern Mexico, a significant boost in the production of natural gas will be needed within the next few years. Otherwise, Mexico faces an energy crisis associated with competing contracted commitments of supply for industry, a low level of investment in production, and volatile price fluctuations in the international markets. Indeed, Mexico must attract investment in exploration, extraction, and commercialization of natural gas to avoid a serious shortfall in supply. The use of liquefied natural gas (LNG) as a substitute for other fuels is under consideration, since it is cheaper, environmentally cleaner, and less dangerous. Investments in the energy sector in Baja California could add significant revenues to the regional economy. Thus effective coordination between companies, energy specialists, federal entities, and the public are essential to achieve the complex planning and negotiations necessary for this task.

In California, the most important energy-related development in recent years has been the restructuring of the electric utility industry. Reorganization of the electric sector resulted in increased cross-border trade in energy services. For example, in 2001 a 50 MW natural gas-powered plant in Baja California began exporting electricity during California's energy crisis (U.S. EIA 2005b). Growth of California's electricity demand accelerated so much in the late 1990s that it substantially exceeded the state's 53,000 MW generating capacity, leaving California dependent on imports for 19 per cent of its electricity by 2004 (California Energy Commission 2005). At the same time, rapid growth in adjoining states limited the amount of surplus power available for sale, as did the capacity of interstate and north-south internal transmission lines. The basic, longer-term problem is that apart from wind power farms, very little generating capacity has been built in California since the mid-1980s, despite an average annual growth in demand of nearly two per cent.

California's recent energy crisis, which threatens to reoccur in the future, was caused by three interrelated problems: increases in wholesale electricity prices; intermittent power shortages during peak-demand periods; and deterioration of the financial stability of California's three major public utilities. For example, the price of wholesale electricity sold on the California Power Exchange escalated in mid-2000, reaching levels eleven times higher than one year earlier.

Energy projections suggest that energy trades of power and natural gas will grow substantially in coming decades in the Baja California–California region. In the open market for energy services, final price to consumers is the most important element in deciding where to purchase energy, while location of energy source becomes less relevant. As the restructuring of the California electricity sector gains momentum, it may prove cost-effective for the energy sector in Baja California to produce and sell power within the North American electricity market. Over time, the international border likely will become less of a barrier to trade in energy, a consequence of continued binational integration and regional demand (Dukert 2004).

Conclusions

The most effective approach to sustainability of the border regions is to focus on energy conservation and demand-side management. California responded to its electricity crisis with $2 billion in conservation measures, including rebates to customers who utilize energy-efficient materials and appliances. This approach depends on effective outreach to the public and the development of energy-efficiency facilities and programs that encourage using energy wisely. In addition, peak shifting programs move consumption from heavy-use to off-peak periods.

Renewable energies are less detrimental to the environment than conventional sources and have gained a degree of public support throughout the trinational region. Deregulation holds the possibility of bringing additional support for this type of technology implementation through internalization of environmental costs and marketing strategies. Evolving multiple partnerships between government entities, research institutions, and energy consumers will have the effect of reducing energy consumption and promoting efficiency.

North America is facing serious energy problems related to pricing, supply, and ecological considerations. One energy researcher stated that North America is in an "energy straitjacket," referring to shortages of coal, heating oil, gasoline, natural gas, and storage capacity (Hendricks 2005). The most obvious problem areas are in Mexico and California, but the signs are far more widespread, and certainly include the entire North American continent. The three North American countries need to focus on solving problems related to natural gas supply, oil-import vulnerability, refinery capacity, and electricity needs. The magnitude of these problems is not the same in the two Pacific west coast border regions, but each has to confront them to manage the balance between adequate energy supply and a safe and healthy environment. These problems pose risks to the economy and to society at large. Although not new, they are exacerbated by poor planning, lack of investment, and the exploitation of elements of society. In effect, economic, social, and political influences have combined to produce a uniquely North American problem. Electricity supply problems may pose the greatest threat in all three countries. Dangers include shortages and periodic failures in supply. Further, the economic impact of inefficiency is high, especially for power-intensive industries. We may see productive sectors moving out of manufacturing in North America where energy costs are highest and relocating in other lower-cost countries, resulting in higher unemployment in border regions and elsewhere.

Despite the advance of transnational cooperation and integration, energy policies are largely determined within domestic contexts. Geographic distribution of population and energy resources can provoke tension between energy-producing and energy-consuming regions. Such tension is palpable in Canada, where the interests of western producer provinces (primarily Alberta) are often in conflict with eastern population centres. On the increasingly populated border between Mexico and the United States, rising demand for energy and declining air quality are in constant conflict. Both Canada and Mexico have welcomed investment by foreign energy companies, even if they produce primarily for U.S. and off-shore markets.

Notwithstanding constitutional constraints and political realities, economic forces are slowly integrating the North American energy sector (Hufbauer and Goodrich 2003). The fact that industry players are exercising greater influence through partnerships and sectoral associations may suggest momentum in the direction of greater cooperation among energy actors and closer harmonization of regulatory frameworks. Although market forces have clearly spurred integration, further institutionalization of the relationships, perhaps through a new "energy NAFTA," may be necessary to promise adequate supply while ensuring equity in the overall system.

With emphases on continental infrastructure, deregulated markets, environmental policy, and energy security, it may be just a matter of time before the three energy systems come into greater alignment to better meet the challenges of reconciling economic demand, resource supply, and environmental health. The Pacific border regions, encountering dynamic growth, increasing environmental awareness, and more active subnational governments are experiencing an unprecedented level of interconnectedness based on proximity, common interest, and transparency. A more intensive dialogue and higher level of trust could help ensure further progress to spur a sustainable energy future for the western Mexico–United States and Canada–United States border regions.

References

BC Hydro. 2004. 2004 Integrated Electricity Plan (IEP). http://www.
bchydro.com/info/epi/epi19230.html

BC Progress Board. November 2005a. *Strategic Imperatives for British
Columbia's Energy Future.* http://www.bcprogressboard.com/
adv_work.php.

———. November 2005b. *Strategic Imperatives for British Columbia's
Energy Future Executive Summary.* http://www.bcprogressboard.
com/2005Report/EnergyReport/Energy_exec_summ_final.pdf.

Betsill, Michele M. 2005. "North American Climate Governance: NAFTA,
Electricity Generation and GHG Emissions." Paper prepared for
the 2–3 December 2005 Berlin Conference on Human Dimensions
of Global Environmental Change. Berlin, Germany. http://web.fu-
berlin.de/ffu/akumwelt/bc2005/papers/betsill_bc2005.pdf.

California Energy Commission. 2005. *California's Energy Sources.* http://
www.energy.ca.gov/html/energysources.html.

Canada. National Energy Board. 2003. *Canada's Energy Future: Scenarios
of Supply and Demand to 2025.* http://dsp-psd.pwgsc.gc.ca/
Collection/NE23-15-2003E.pdf.

———. 2004. *The British Columbia Natural Gas Market: An Overview
and Assessment.* http://www.neb-one.gc.ca/energy/EnergyReports/
index_e.htm#BritishColumbia.

Canada. Natural Resources Canada. 2002. *Energy in Canada 2000.* http://
www2.nrcan.gc.ca/es/ener2000/online/html/toc_e.cfm.

Cohen, Marjorie Griffin. 1 February 2006. "Why Canada Needs a National
Energy Plan: U.S. is now determined to control Canada's electric
power." Centre for Policy Alternatives. http://www.paymentnet.
com/ribbon/ribbon.asp?referrer=PNet.

Constantineau, Bruce. 1 June 2006. "Use of Biodiesel on the Increase."
Vancouver Sun. http://www.canada.com/vancouversun/news/story.
html?id=88ff90d8-a57c-4197-ba0a-007b.

Council for Environmental Cooperation. 2006. http://www.cec.org/home/
index.cfm?varlan=english.

De la O, Rogelio Ramirez. 2002. The Border Papers. "Mexico: NAFTA
and the Prospects for North American Integration." *C.D. Howe
Institute Commentary.* Toronto: C.D. Howe Institute.

Dobbin, Murray. 2002. "Zip Locking North America: Can Canada Survive
Continental Integration?" Ottawa: Council of Canadians.

Downing, Don, and Kevin Store. 2005. *Coal.* Natural Resources Canada.
http://www.nrcan.gc.ca.

Dukert, Joseph M. 2004. "The Quiet Reality of North American Energy Interdependence." http://cepea.cerium.ca/IMG/pdf/Dukert_Energy.pdf.

———. 2005. "North American Energy: At Long Last, One Continent." *Occasional Contributions*. Center for Strategic and International Studies (CSIS). http://www.csis.org/media/csis/pubs/oc200510.pdf.

Frankel, Stephen. 1994. "Old Theories in New Places? Environmental Determinism and Bioregionalism." *Professional Geographer* 46(3): 289–95.

Gattinger, Monica. 2005. "From Government to Governance in the Energy Sector: The States of the Canada-U.S. Energy Relationship." *American Review of Canadian Studies* 35(2): 321–52.

Gaul, David. 2004. *U.S. Natural Gas and Exports: Issues and Trends 2003*. Washington, DC: Energy Information Administration, Office of Oil and Gas.

Hendricks, Tyche. 10 December 2005. "On the Border," *San Francisco Chronicle*.

Hufbauer, Gary Clyde, and Ben Goodrich. 2003. "Toward One Continent of Energy." Edison Electric Institute. http://www.eei.org/magazine/editorial_content/nonav_stories/2003-05-01-international.htm.

Ménard, Marinka. 2005. *Canada, a Big Energy Consumer: A Regional Perspective*. Statistics Canada. http://www.statcan.ca/english/research/11-621-MIE/11-621-MIE2005023.htm.

México. Comisión Federal de Electricidad. 2004. http://www.cfe.gob.mx/es/.

North American Energy Working Group. 2005. *North American Natural Gas Vision*. http://www.pi.energy.gov/pdf/library/NAEWGGasVision2005.pdf.

Northwest Energy Coalition. 2002. *Clean Energy Options for the Pacific Northwest: An Assessment of Efficiency and Renewable Potentials through the Year 2020*. http://www.nwenergy.org//outreach/tellus_report.html.

Organisation for Economic Co-operation and Development (OECD). 2005. http://www.oecd.org/home/0,2987,en_2649_201185_1_1_1_1_1,00.html.

RAND. 2002. *Generating Electric Power in the Pacific Northwest: Implications of Alternative Technologies*. http://www.rand.org/pubs/monograph_reports/MR1604/.

Ross, John. 30 August 2003. "After the Blackout, A NAFTA For Energy?" *Counterpunch*. http://www.counterpunch.org/ross08302003.html.

Sale, Kirkpatrick. 1985. *Dwellers in the Land: The Bioregional Vision*. San Francisco: Sierra Club Books.

Selin, Henrik, and Stacy D. Vandeveer. 2005. "Canadian-U.S. Environmental Cooperation Climate Change Networks and Regional Action." *American Review of Canadian Studies* 35(2): 353–78.

United Nations. 2003. Economic and Social Affairs World Urbanization Prospects: The 2003 Revision. http://www.un.org/esa/population/publications/wup2003/WUP2003Report.pdf.

United Nations Development Programme (UNDP). 2004. *Human Development Index.*

United States. Department of Energy. Energy Information Administration (EIA). 1999. "Energy in the Americas: The Economy of the Americas." http://www/eia.doe.gov/emeu/cabs/archives/theamericas/theamericas.html#world-context.

———. 2004. *Mexico: Country Analysis Brief.* http://www.eia.doe.gov/emeu/cabs/mexico.html.

———. 2005a. *Canada: County Analysis Brief.* http://www.eia.doe.gov/emeu/cabs/canada.html.

———. 2005b. *United States: Country Analysis Brief.* http://www.eia.doe.gov/emeu/cabs/usa.html.

———. 2006a. *Annual Energy Outlook 2006 with Projections to 2030.* http://www.eia.doe.gov/oiaf/aeo/index.html.

———. 2006b. *Table 86 Renewable Energy Generation by Fuel Western Electricity Coordinating Council/Pacific Power Pool.* http://www.eia.doe.gov/oiaf/aeo/supplement/suptab_86.xls.

Washington State. Energy Facility Site Evaluation Council. 2003. http://www.efsec.wa.gov/nuclearproj.html.

World Commission on Environment and Development (WCED). 1987. *Our Common Future.* New York: Oxford University Press.

World Energy Council (WEC). 2001. *Survey of Energy Resources 2001.* http://www.worldenergy.org/wec-geis/publications/reports/ser/overview.asp.

Young, Samantha. 28 April 2006. "Energy Commission Says Keep Ban on New Nuclear Plants." http://www.signonsandiego.com/news/state/20060428_1810_ca-nuclearplants.html.

5

CONNECTIONS WITHIN THE WESTERN U.S.–CANADA BORDER REGION: TOWARD MORE SUSTAINABLE TRANSPORTATION PRACTICES

Preston L. Schiller

Abstract

The large region of Western Canada and the Northwestern United States along and across the border between the province of British Columbia and the westerly portions of Washington and Oregon states allows for the examination of several public policy discussions. These include transportation, land use patterns and policies, and the role of dominant cities in influencing the overall development of the region. Cross-border transportation of persons and freight has become especially important in the context of post–September 11, 2001, concerns. Policy discussions of these issues must be related to the environmental and social sustainability of current patterns of transportation, land use, and commerce. A considerable amount of automobile, long-distance truck traffic, and commercial aviation travel within the region could be diverted to rail in an effort to enhance the sustainability of the region's transportation system. The conclusion suggests several measures that could help lessen the current unsustainable Cascadian trajectories in the realms of transportation and land use.

Introduction

While some believe that there is an underlying regional identity to the area consisting of the lower mainland of the province of British Columbia and the westerly portions of Washington and Oregon states, there is no institutional mechanism which serves to identify it as a region for planning or political purposes. Some supporters of regionalism have dubbed the area "Cascadia" after the rugged mountain range that traverses it along a north-south axis.

British Columbia and Washington State share a busy and frequently crossed international boundary. Despite the efforts of trade liberalization in recent years, this boundary demarcates several significant political and cultural differences. Similarly, the states of Washington and Oregon share an intranational boundary that also defines several differences in policy orientation. All three entities share a major transportation corridor consisting of a motor vehicle expressway, a major passenger and freight rail route, and a heavily used commercial aviation lane.

Borders, by definition, infer boundaries, limits, separations, and transitions. For most persons the most commonly experienced border is a political boundary. Borders also may define cultural, social, economic, and linguistic differences. For purposes of this study, the border between the United States and Canada should be viewed, essentially, as a political boundary.

Before the events of September 11, 2001, the trend in U.S.-Canada border management was towards less cumbersome regulation and security measures. A special lane for precleared persons frequently driving across the border was established. There was considerable discussion about "erasing" the border to the extent that many European nations have "erased" theirs; easing the burdens placed on international travellers such as passport checks and visa requirements, as well as easing border restrictions for freight movements through preclearances and computerized and telecommunications methods of tracking freight movements. These discussions have slowed considerably or have been significantly revamped following September 11. At present there are tighter and lengthier security checks for most travellers and freight haulers.

A corridor is a passage formed either naturally or by human activity, which connects different natural or human-made features. Broadly, a corridor may also be a passageway for vegetation or animal migration. Human-made corridors may exist for the transportation of persons and freight or might be constructed for the movement of utilities such as pipelines, viaducts, and power lines. For purposes of this exploration a corridor will refer to the route or pathway by which persons and goods are transported.

Because a border defines separateness and exclusiveness, and a corridor implies connectedness and continuity between two separate places, there is a tension inherent between the two – conceptually, and in the practical realm. Inherent in the notion of a border is the tendency to limit mobility, to regulate the traversing of a boundary. Inherent in the notion of a corridor is the overcoming of barriers and boundaries and the facilitation of movement. A corridor, or the development which might occur along it, may lead to the blurring of boundaries between places previously perceived as distinct. This is what appears to be happening to several portions of the Interstate 5 corridor in Washington and Oregon, and portions of the B.C. 99 corridor to which it connects. The transportation corridor may also serve to define the points at which a border may be traversed. It is in the nature of boundary setting and border maintenance to limit and control these points, especially when the border in question divides two nations. Borders may define sovereignty or, at least, a form of privilege and entitlement. Within a nation, borders define who has the privilege of voting and receiving certain services. Corridors, on the other hand, tend to work against exclusivity.

Borders, Corridors, and Sustainability

In recent years, transportation and land use researchers, policy analysts, and environmentalists have become increasingly interested in the issue of sustainable transportation and its relation to land use. Central in this discussion is the idea that sustainable transportation and settlement patterns should reduce environmental impacts associated with increasing motor vehicle dependency and dispersed development patterns. Reducing these impacts implies a better integration of land use and transportation planning, reversal of the trajectory of highway expansion generating dispersed development ("sprawl") and damaging the fabric of cities, as well as shifting travel to less energy intensive and oil dependent modes (Replogle 1995; Benfield and Replogle 2002; Whitelegg and Haq 2003). It also implies addressing political, economic and behavioural changes to advance a sustainable transport agenda (Centre for Sustainable Transportation 1998; Organisation for Economic Cooperation and Development 1996; Wixey and Lake 1998; Newman and Kenworthy 1999; Schiller 2000). It would also imply the development of policies specifically aimed at reducing environmental damage – from air and water pollution to overconsumption of urban space by roads and parking – resulting from our current transportation arrangements (Schiller and DeLille 1997). Sustainability discussions also direct attention to the need to reduce the transportation component of goods (Böge 1995) as well as land consumption (Gersh and Congdon 1999).

Cascadia's Uneven Sustainability

The extent to which Cascadia as a region can move effectively toward sustainability is complicated by differences defined by its borders. One regional commonality is that of the growing burden of traffic. The population and job growth of the region, especially in the "high tech" sector, combined with an emphasis on automobility has been one factor in traffic growth. Another has been the exponential growth in trucks hauling international freight. Much of the freight arrives at one of the region's several large ports only to be transferred to trucks and driven through the region en route to another destination in California or the Midwest, or to be transferred to a train or ship. The growing popularity of the region as a tourist destination has also attracted large numbers of cars and recreational vehicles to the region's highways. The underdevelopment of regional and local transit systems has led to a high rate of automobile rentals among visitors arriving at the region's airports.

Increases in travel demand have been responded to in the form of highway and airport expansions. While rail transit improvements have been undertaken in Portland and Vancouver – and are in an early stage for Seattle – such improvements have not kept pace with the growth of travel demand. Hence traffic jams, and the belief in the efficacy of "traffic reports" prominent in broadcast media, are a part of everyday life in the region's major metropolitan areas (Schiller 1992).

Before discussing the issues of the corridor as a whole, it is necessary to review and compare the situations of each of the region's largest cities and their respective metropolitan areas. Understanding their situation will illuminate the broader travel issues and challenges of the Cascadia region.

Population and Density

The cities of Portland, Seattle, and Vancouver, B.C., have approximately the same population. According to 2003 statistics, Portland's is about 540,000, Seattle's is approximately 570,000, and Vancouver's is close to 550,000. The population of the Portland metropolitan area is approximately 1,500,000; that of Seattle is near 3,330,000, while that of Vancouver is close to 2,100,000. The urban and regional population densities of Portland and Seattle are considerably lower than that of Vancouver. The regional density of Vancouver also reflects the sprawl-limiting consequences of its protection of agricultural land through its Agricultural Land Reserve laws (ALR), which have had the effect of pushing population growth into already-developed municipal areas. Vancouver builds a much higher proportion of its housing as multiple-family (56 per cent), rather than single-family, in comparison to either Portland or Seattle, both of which are approximately 30 per cent multiple-family (Schiller and Kenworthy 1999; Raad and Kenworthy 1998; Schiller 1994). Multiple-family housing can be in the form of either apartments and condominiums, or shared-wall townhouses. In either case it leads to greater population densities and more efficient use of urban space.

Transportation

Both Portland and Seattle have extremely high rates of automobile ownership. Rate of owned motor vehicles per thousand persons is slightly more than a thousand, substantially higher than the U.S. average of 604 automobiles owned per thousand people (Newman and Kenworthy 1999: 80). The rate for these cities is also somewhat higher than other cities in their respective regions (whose rates of automobile ownership are still substantially higher than the national norm), possibly due to demographic factors such as smaller household size in the city in comparison to the suburbs. Vancouver, while having a slightly higher rate of automobile ownership (560 per 1,000 residents) than the average for Canada, demonstrates much less of a difference between city and suburb, and a much lower rate of automobile ownership in comparison to its counterparts across the U.S. border. The Canadian rate is 524 automobiles per thousand persons. By comparison, the rate in Europe is 392 automobiles per thousand persons.

The same significant difference is found when comparing rates of driving for the three cities. Citizens living in the city of Vancouver drive virtually half as much as do their counterparts in Seattle and Portland. Suburban Vancouverites also drive substantially less than their counterparts in the Seattle and Portland regions.

High rates of automobile ownership and driving also lead to lower rates of use for public transportation: citizens of the Vancouver region ride transit at approximately two to three times the rate of their counterparts in Portland and Seattle. The higher rates of transit use also contribute to a greater cost-efficiency for transit in Vancouver – fare boxes recover twice the proportion of transit operating expenses in comparison to the Seattle and Portland systems.

Trend data (Schiller and Kenworthy 1999) indicate that transit improvement programs, including new rail transit systems, begun in Portland and Vancouver in the 1980s, have led to incremental ridership increases in their respective regions. Conversely, Seattle's bus-only system has seen its ridership remain essentially stagnant in terms of annual per capita transit trips in recent decades. Trend data also indicate that as transit ridership increases in Portland, its rate of driving is decreasing slightly. Seattle's rate of driving, in contrast, continues to increase significantly. Vancouver appears to be achieving modest increases in transit ridership.

Some of the credit for improved public transportation in Vancouver and Portland is due to their advances in regional planning and governance. Vancouver has merged its one regional transit service and general transportation planning into one agency, the Greater Vancouver Transportation Authority (GVTA or "TransLink") directed by officials who have been elected as representatives of local jurisdictions in the region. GVTA also has taxing authority.

Portland has a directly elected regional governance structure, Metro (the Municipality of Metropolitan Portland), which has responsibility for regional transportation planning as well as a few other regional services and responsibilities. Portland also has one regional transit system, Tri-Met, serving the three counties which comprise its service area. Seattle, by comparison, has five transit agencies within its region 'as well as a heavily used state ferry system that serves, to a limited extent, as a transit service.

Seattle has a regional transportation-planning agency, the Puget Sound Regional Council (PSRC), whose principal responsibilities consist of overseeing the disbursement of federal transportation funds and monitoring the growth management and transportation plans of local jurisdictions. The government officials who comprise the directorship of the PSRC are not directly elected to it. Rather, they are elected officials nominated by the jurisdictions to which they have been elected – not dissimilar to the governance of Vancouver's GVTA.

While there are a few organizations that address some specific transportation issues on both sides of the British Columbia-Washington border, at present there is no body which is studying or planning for issues that affect the whole Cascadian region.

The heavy dependence on automobiles for local travel throughout the region, but especially in the Portland and Seattle metropolitan areas, is one major component of the transportation problems of the Cascadia region. Indeed, one could say that as the flagship cities go, so go their metropolitan regions, and as the metropolitan regions go, so goes the wider region. Within the context of our focus on borders and corridors we shall now examine some of the broader regional land use and transportation issues in Cascadia.

And the Columbia River Rolls through It ...

Most of the border between the states of Washington and Oregon, and the entire border in western Washington and western Oregon is formed by the Columbia River, whose origin is in central British Columbia. The border also defines two very differing approaches to growth management. Oregon initiated growth management legislation in the 1970s under the leadership of its then Republican governor, Tom McCall. While much of the impetus for Oregon's efforts in this area stemmed from concerns about preserving agricultural and forestry lands, and discouraging sprawl patterns of suburban development, some of the impetus addressed Oregon's desire not to grow – or at least not to grow rapidly, as was California, its neighbour to the south. McCall and the then governor of Colorado gained national publicity, if not notoriety, for discouraging the "Californication" of their states. McCall had signs placed on major highways welcoming visitors and encouraging them to enjoy their stay in Oregon – and then to go home.

Oregon's growth management legislation draws tight "urban growth boundaries" around towns and cities which define where development can occur. It has been effective in helping metropolitan regions become denser, and, in the Portland area, more interested in development around rail transit. Oregon's growth management legislation has survived court challenges, including one from the Rajneeshi cult of orange garb and salmonella salad dressing fame, (WBUR Public Radio, Boston, MA, 2002: "1984: Rajneesh Cult Attacks Local Salad Bar"; http://www.wbur.org/special/specialcoverage/feature_bio.asp) as well as developer-sponsored recall campaigns. It has not stopped Oregon from growing – indeed, in recent years Portland's rate of growth has surpassed that of either Seattle or Vancouver – but was successful in helping the city grow more gracefully. It remains to be seen what impact a recently successful statewide "property rights" initiative will have on the "Portland and Oregon" Smart Growth phenomena.

Washington State lagged almost two decades behind Oregon in initiating growth management legislation. The legislation it passed is more complicated than Oregon's and, consequently, it took several years before effective implementation could occur. One of the consequences of this "uneven development" across a border was that the area across the Columbia River immediately to the north of the Portland area, Clark County, became a haven – a "sprawl-relief valve" – for those fleeing the "horrors" of effective urban planning and seeking the comforts of sprawled exurban life.

While Oregon preserved precious farm and forestry lands, Washington's developers, fearing and anticipating growth management, subdivided wantonly and widely. In the mid-1990s, when Portland's regional transit agency offered to connect Vancouver, Washington, and Clark County to Portland with a light rail line at little cost to those on the north side of the river, Clark County voters overwhelmingly rejected this "threat" to their "rural" way of life. When Washington State requested that Oregon build another motor vehicle bridge across the Columbia to "relieve congestion," Oregon's response was that Washington can build another highway bridge so long as it doesn't cross the border in the middle of the river. But Oregon has pledged cooperation in the construction of another rail bridge across the Columbia, although plans have stalled due to lack of funding and there may be some compromise about a highway bridge if it has a transit orientation. More and more residents of Clark County, stuck in perpetual congestion in car or bus, are hopeful that a light rail, or at least a commuter rail, link to Portland where many of Clark County residents are employed, is likely in the near future. This perception is heightened as county residents see a light rail coming north from Portland, but stopping short of the river.

Children of a Congested Border

A somewhat different set of factors is at play along and astride the border between British Columbia and the state of Washington. Because it is a border between nations, there are more issues involving immigration and customs which distinguish travel between these two entities than is the case between Washington and Oregon. The most common experience shared by travellers crossing the westerly British Columbia-Washington border is that of traffic congestion at the border.

Historically, the relative position of Canadian and U.S. national currencies has had a significant influence on cross-border non-business travel, as shoppers search for bargains on either side. The decline of the relative value of the Canadian dollar in the 1990s, as well as the extensive growth of U.S.-style shopping malls in British Columbia, lessened the attractiveness of shopping south of the border. Since 2004, the steady increase in the value of the Canadian dollar has tended to increase the north-south flow, although the numbers of cross-border shoppers are not near what they were in the pre-2001 era. Another factor that has drawn Canadians south to Washington is the proliferation of casinos on Indian reservations, which was eventually met with the response of legalizing gambling in British Columbia. As Table 5.1 indicates, the trend toward decreased automobile crossings continues as more Canadian gamblers and shoppers stay closer to home. Table 5.1 also tracks the trend of truck traffic which has decreased somewhat following a dramatic rise in the 1990s as a result of trade liberalization beginning in the 1980s with the passage of the *Canada-U.S. Free Trade Agreement* and, later, with the passage of *NAFTA* in 1994. This liberalization of commerce has led to a doubling in the amount of cross-border truck traffic in the decade of the 1990s (table 5.1).

Table 5.1 Motor Vehicles Crossing Westerly B.C./WA. Border Southbound, 1991–2005.

	AUTOMOBILES	TRUCKS	TOTALS
1991	8,637,879	348,009	8,985,888
2000	4,799,746	691,579	5,491,325
2005	3,564,199	568,169	4,132,368

Note: Crossings include Peace Arch, Pacific Highway, Lynden-Aldergrove, and Sumas-Huntingdon.
Source: Whatcom Council of Governments (2001, 2006), Bellingham, WA.

During the same period there has been relatively little increase in freight rail traffic in the Burlington Northern Santa Fe (BNSF) mainline which parallel's I-5 between the border and Seattle. Numerous entities and jurisdictions are coming to resent increasing truck traffic, especially as it becomes recognized that a significant portion of the NAFTA freight traffic is simply in transit through the region; it does not originate in the Cascadia region, it is not destined for points in the Cascadia region, and it is simply moving through or being transshipped on its way to some other point in the global market (Beaulieu 1996; Gillis et al. 1995; Puget Sound Regional Council 1997). The response of transportation and political authorities to this problem has been to propose either yet another bypass around core Puget Sound communities, or yet another highway widening to increase capacity.

A more imaginative response, one proposed by the Washington Association of Rail Passengers (2002), is to examine ways in which some of the freight now carried on trucks can be transferred to freight rail. There are capacity constraints in the current BNSF line due to tunnel heights too low for double-stacking of freight containers in the Chuckanut segment. Nonphysical constraints also exist, such as the lack of effective cooperation between freight rail and port systems on each side of the border.

Improvements in an existing rail corridor that runs between Abbotsford (BC) and Burlington (WA) could divert freight both from trucks on I-5 and freight trains in the current Chuckanut line. But this would require a monetary investment on both sides of the border and greater cooperation between private sector transportation interests.

Meanwhile the public at large is left paying for the "collateral damages" of trade liberalization and deregulation through the impacts of increased air pollution, traffic noise, traffic incidents, and rapidly deteriorating roads. The situation is also influenced by the desire of B.C. truckers to save money by filling their tanks on the Washington side of the border where fuel taxes and fuel prices are lower.

Highway Modes

Traversing the province and the two states, and connecting the three flagship cities, is a land corridor. One might refer to it unglamorously as the I(nterstate)-5/BC-99 Corridor. But one could refer to it, a little more elegantly, as the "Cascadia Corridor." While most travellers think of the corridor in terms of the limited access highway which runs continuously from the city limit of Vancouver to Seattle, Portland, and points beyond, it is also a corridor for freight and passenger rail transport and, in the air, aviation. Each of these modes presents problems and challenges worthy of the attention of planners and policymakers.

It is important to note some differences between transportation policy in the U.S. and Canada, which have shaped some of the problems experienced along the Cascadia Corridor. First, the U.S. federal government has played a much more active role in the provision and expansion of highways than has the federal government of Canada. The Canadian government has never had a highway program similar in scope to that of the U.S. interstate highway program. And Canada's federal government has never funded and promoted urban and suburban highways in the same way, or to the same extent, as has the United States. This factor, itself, helps account for some of the differences in automobile dependence found when comparing cities across the border. Interstate highways, originally intended to connect distant cities in the United States, became concrete corridors which eventually pushed through and destroyed urban cores, facilitated urban sprawl, and created traffic congestion which, ironically, militated against easy intercity mobility. In a perpetual "death spiral," urban areas across the United States continue to try to build their way out of congestion by adding more lanes and creating new bypasses which only makes the traffic problem worse.

Secondly, Canadian urban planning has benefited to a certain extent from European-style town planning, where the importance of vital town centres and the provision of proper infrastructure, such as sidewalks in developed areas, are emphasized. With a few significant exceptions, most U.S. cities, especially newer western cities, have not benefited from a similar planning tradition. For example, there are few neighbourhoods in Vancouver that lack sidewalks. Fully one-third of Seattle's streets are without sidewalks and they are lacking in some Portland neighbourhoods as well. Finally, Canadian cities have not abandoned or allowed their public transportation systems to flounder and deteriorate to the extent which most American cities have.

Although the private automobile and the eighteen-wheeled truck are the mainstays of North American mobility in general, and Cascadian transport in particular, few studies are available which document their magnitude and specify their origins and destinations. Even less light is shed upon the reasons for this seemingly perpetual movement. Within traffic-dense cities and metropolitan areas there are often fairly informative studies done of vehicular volumes and flow, albeit often in preparation for a highway expansion effort. But the researcher trying to estimate the numbers of vehicles travelling daily between Vancouver and Seattle, or between Portland and Seattle, might do better consulting a reader of palms than a transportation agency's database.

Most traffic, like politics, is local. That is true for automobiles and trucks. But long-distance motoring is important to examine for two major reasons: (a) some of it might be highly susceptible to mode-shift (trucks to freight trains, automobiles to trains), and (b) long-distance trips by car or truck consume cumulatively a great deal of road space. Some help in deciphering the volumes and purposes of Cascadia Corridor highway traffic is available in bits and pieces (Whatcom Council of Governments 2001, 2006; Washington State. Department of Transportation 1992; Eriksen and Casavant 1997). It appears that approximately 11,000 automobiles and almost 2,000 trucks cross the BC/WA border southbound on weekdays. Most of the personal vehicles are travelling relatively short distances; 70 to

90 per cent of their origins and destinations are between the British Columbia Lower Mainland and north and central Puget Sound. Only a relatively low volume of automobile travel appears to be between Vancouver and Seattle, and less still between Vancouver and Portland. A larger volume appears to be travelling by automobile between the Seattle and Portland areas.

Two points in regards to these data need to be made. First, it appears that approximately two-thirds of the long-distance automobile trips in the corridor are not work or business-related. Second, while the bulk of travel is local, the long-distance trips consume a great deal of cumulative road space and add disproportionately to traffic volumes due to the length of these trips. That is, one long-distance trip may add disproportionately to congestion in more than one locale, especially if it is undertaken at peak, or "shoulder" of peak, hours. The same may be said of long-distance truck traffic. Approximately two thousand long-distance trucks originating at the border each weekday are added to another few thousand long-distance trucks in the Everett-Seattle-Tacoma area, as well as those coming into the Seattle area from the east on I-90, resulting in a very high volume of truck traffic between Seattle and Portland and points south of Portland.[1]

One of the consequences of increased global trade and travel has been a heightening of competition between the major shipping ports and airports in Cascadia, each of which is controlled by a port authority, with little scrutiny or understanding by the public. Each port vies with the others for more ships and directly connecting flights. Little or no thought is given to encouraging cooperation among the ports, or to the externalities of such competition. Such externalities include the added traffic volumes to highways connecting cities, or traffic jams surrounding airports, or the added regional pollution from ships at sea or in the air. While this trajectory may make sense to individual port entities – each trying to protect its economic interests and transportation allies – it makes little sense from the perspective of the public interest. In the case of trains and planes, as will be examined below, the marketing strategy of encouraging a large number of small "commuter" and short-haul flights from cities within one to three hundred miles of an airport in order to maintain "market share" may also be an unwise strategy, detrimental to the public interest.

Preston L. Schiller

Planes

Several thousands of feet above the car and truck-clogged BC-99/I-5 Corridor is an increasingly busy aviation corridor. Some persons tiring of the long and increasingly congested drive up and down I-5 have been turning to commercial aviation in recent years for a solution to their travel needs. They have been assisted in their efforts by smaller airlines (commuter flights or air taxis) increasingly attempting to build market share connecting smaller communities with a regional airport, as well as a willingness of regional airports to engage in costly facilities expansions to accommodate these inefficient services. In this regard, the Cascadia Region is not much different from the rest of North America. Fully 40 per cent of these airports' commercial operations are given over to short and medium-distance flights, generally undertaken in small (less than 30 passengers) aircraft. The case of commercial aviation between Vancouver (YVR), Seattle (SEA), and Portland's (PDX) regional airports, whose pertinent data are described below in table 5.2, is illustrative of a situation found across North America.

One finds that, thanks to the burgeoning spirit of trade liberalization and deregulation, exemplified in the *Open Skies Agreement*, the amount of commercial aviation activity between Vancouver and Seattle, and Vancouver and Portland, has grown considerably in recent years. Roughly 21,000 flights between Seattle and Vancouver carry approximately 700,000 passengers[2] between these two airports each year. The average flight's number of Origin/Destination (O/D) passengers is 33. The 21,000 flights represent 7 per cent of YVR's operations and 5 per cent of SEA's operations. However, the 700,000 passengers represent only 4 per cent of YVR's annual passengers and 2.5 per cent of SEA's annual passengers. When one compares the percentages of operations with the percentages of passengers served, one finds flight loadings substantially below average for the respective airports, an inefficient use of airport operational capacity.

Table 5.2 Cascadia: Trains versus Planes.

	VANCOUVER/ SEATTLE	SEATTLE/ PORTLAND	VANCOUVER/ PORTLAND
TRAINS			
Operations/yr	1,460	2,920	Included in Vancouver/
Passengers/yr	146,914	375,642	Seattle and Seattle/
Avg. Occupancy	101	129	Portland

Note: Only half of SEA-YVR trains go past Bellingham at present (2005).

	VANCOUVER/ SEATTLE	SEATTLE/ PORTLAND	VANCOUVER/ PORTLAND
PLANES			
Operations/yr	20,898	38,978	7736
Passengers/yr; O/D	700,000 (approx.)	298,000	210,000
Avg. Occupancy	33	8	27
% Total Operations	7 YVR/4.7 SEA	9 SEA/16 PDX	3 PDX/2.6 YVR
% Total Passengers	4.4 YVR/2.5 SEA	1.1 SEA/1.9 PDX	1.3 PDX/1.3 YVR

Note: Vancouver (YVR), Seattle (SEA), Portland (PDX).

	VANCOUVER/ SEATTLE	SEATTLE/ PORTLAND	VANCOUVER/ PORTLAND
AIRPORTS			
Operations/yr	295,000	446,000	251,000
Passengers/yr	16,000,000	28,400,000	16,000,000
Avg. Occupancy	54	64	64

Rail Corridor	TOTALS
Plane Operations	67,612 (18 origin/destination passengers average)
Plane Passengers	1,208,000
Train Operations	4,380 (199 passengers each average)
Train Passengers	522,556
Total Operations	71,992
Rail % of Total Operations	6
Total Air/Rail Passengers	1,730,556
Rail % of Total Passengers	30

Sources: Port of Portland (2001); Port of Seattle (2002); personal communications; Ray Allred, WSDOT Rail Division; Bob Barnet, Port of Portland.

A smaller number of travellers fly between Vancouver and Portland. There are slightly fewer than 8,000 flights per year between these airports, which represents 3 per cent of PDX's operations and 2.7 per cent of YVR's operations. These flights carry approximately 210,000 passengers,[3] which represent 1.3 per cent of PDX's annual passengers and 1.3 per cent of YVR's annual passengers. The average number of passengers per flight is 27. When one compares the percentages of operations with the percentages of passengers one finds flight loadings again substantially below average for the respective airports. In effect, this is a very inefficient use of airport operational capacity.

A large number of flights connect Seattle and Portland: almost 40,000 annually[4]; 9 per cent of SEA's total operations and 16 per cent of PDX's total operations. But this large number of flights accounts for only 298,000 O/D passengers, barely 1 per cent of SEA's annual passengers and 2 per cent of PDX's annual passengers. When the percentages of operations are compared with the percentages of passengers, one finds flight loadings[5] grossly below average for the respective airports. This represents an extremely inefficient use of airport operational capacity. Especially alarming is the rapidly increasing rate of air taxi and "commuter" flights that increased from 4 per cent of total SeaTac operations in 1970 to 46 per cent in 2000 (Port of Seattle 2002).

A look at air services to other smaller cities in the Cascadia Corridor reveals even greater inefficiencies: commercial flights between Portland and Eugene (EUG), about a hundred miles south, total almost 4,000 per year carrying a total of approximately 75,000 passengers – an average loading of 19 persons. The PDX-EUG flights represent 1.5 per cent of PDX operations while their 75,000 passengers represent less than 0.5 per cent of PDX passengers.[6] A similar inefficiency can be found for flights between Seattle and Bellingham, about a hundred miles north of SeaTac Airport. Here some 5,000 annual flights, almost 3 per cent of SeaTac's operations, account for an even smaller fraction of its total origin-destination passengers than that of the PDX/EUG market. Vancouver, Bellingham, Seattle, Portland, and Eugene are all served by an intercity train service, a cooperative venture between Oregon, Washington, British Columbia, and the United States-supported Amtrak train system. This system, the Amtrak Cascades, has been steadily improving its performance and ridership over the past decade. The many short-haul commuter and air taxi and larger flights fly over its tracks.

Trains

Running parallel and often alongside or within view of I-5 there is a not-so-little passenger train system that could and should carry a substantial number of those driving or flying between Cascadia's major cities. The environmental benefits of passenger trains compared to automobiles and commercial airplanes are well established; better energy efficiency, a much smaller footprint than either highways or airports, considerably less pollution, and much lower area noise volumes. Amtrak West runs the Amtrak Cascades passenger service, part of the United States' beleaguered national train system in partnership with Washington, Oregon, and British Columbia. The states, especially Washington, contribute generously to this service each year, both in operating subsidies, staff time, and capital improvements. Their contributions have also helped to leverage U.S. federal investments in this corridor. Unfortunately B.C. has promised, but has not yet delivered on, its rather small but expected contribution. As a result, only one train per day runs between Seattle and Vancouver. Another train runs between Seattle and Bellingham, where it stops and awaits long-promised, and relatively inexpensive, improvements to be made to the trackage between White Rock, B.C., and Vancouver.

In the corridor between Vancouver-Bellingham and Seattle some 1,460 trains, each with a capacity of approximately 240 passengers, carry 147,000 passengers each year; an average occupancy of 101 persons – which is higher most weekends, lower most weekdays (data and analysis for this section from table 5.2 above). Based upon extrapolations from current train occupancies displayed in table 5.2 one could reasonably estimate that if the trains, which now stop at Bellingham, were to continue all the way to Vancouver, ridership would likely increase at least a third immediately to approximately 200,000 per year – or an average occupancy of 137. If the additional six train runs per day envisaged by the Washington State Department of Transportation's Rail Office were added, ridership and train loadings would continue to increase. With the addition of clever marketing, ridership might soon approach capacity and the operators of the service might have to think about even more expansion.

Between Seattle and Portland there are now eight trains (four round trip) per day or 2,920 operations per year. Three of the four round trip trains travel only in the corridor and have excellent on-time records. The fourth travels from Seattle to California and back and has a rather poor on-time record, especially on its northbound segment. Total ridership is 375,642 between these two cities, or about 129 passengers per train. The ridership figures between Seattle and Portland, too, would likely increase with an increase in service to Vancouver, although probably not as dramatically as the likely increase between Vancouver and Seattle, and data are not readily available for that portion of the market which travels directly from Vancouver to Portland on the train.[7] Several more trains per day are planned in the future and ridership is projected to continue to rise, as it has on all corridor services that have been initiated or improved in just the past few years. There are also a number of operational and track improvements planned along the whole of the corridor, which should increase speeds and improve reliability, two factors which will also help increase patronage.

Turning Planes into Trains?

What happens when passenger rail and commercial aviation performance is compared in the Cascadia Corridor, as in table 5.2? One finding is that there are a total of 67,612 commercial aviation operations between the three regional airports. These carried a total of 1,208,000 passengers in the year 2000, with an average loading of 18 O/D passengers. Meanwhile the 4,380 underfunded trains running a little slower, and reliably below the short-hop planes, carried 522,556 passengers with an average loading of 119 persons, on average less than half their capacity. When plane and train operations and passengers are combined for the corridor, there is a total of 71,992 operations transporting a total of 1,730,556 passengers. The trains constitute only 6 per cent of these operations, yet transport 30 per cent of the corridor's combined plane/train travellers. If one were to include even the relatively light train ridership between Bellingham and Seattle, and Portland and Eugene, and compare these with the inefficient aviation services between these locales, one would further strengthen the case for trains in this corridor (Schiller 1995, Cooper 1995, Patterson and Perl 1999).

In the short term, aggressive marketing, some speed and reliability improvements, and more cooperation on the part of British Columbia could do much to make better use of underused capacity in the Amtrak Cascades. Modest improvements in shortening the trains' travel times would also make it competitive with airline travel times, especially from city centre to city centre in the corridor. In the longer term, adding capacity in the forms of extra tracks and train sets, and improving loadings for trains, would be easier and less expensive, and less politically contentious and environmentally damaging, than aviation expansions. In other words, a wise policy would be to "turn planes into trains."

It is also important to note that rates of air cargo shipments in and out of major airports are increasing at alarming rates. This increase is, in part, another manifestation of the "just-in-time" strategies of industrial supply logistics, as well as a manifestation of the growth of the parcel shipment industry. At SeaTac Airport, air cargo levels have grown from just under 35,000 metric tons in 1961 to 457,000 metric tons in the year 2000 (Port of Seattle 2002). While there are some fluctuations from year-to-year, the overall growth rate is increasing rapidly and air cargo is expected to reach 730,000 metric tons by the year 2010. These unsustainable levels of growth in a sector which is the least energy efficient and most polluting of freight modes should attract policy attention and intervention. It is possible that a greatly improved regional and national intercity rail system could also divert some cargo from planes to trains.

Conclusion: Unsustainable Development, Unsustainable Mobility

Cascadia, purporting to be one of the more environmentally conscious regions of North America, is challenged by some of the most rapid population growth and development in the hemisphere. Many of the issues affecting the region and its major transportation corridors are related to varying levels of governmental policymaking as well as cultural differences. For example, the aggressive role of the U.S. federal government in highway promotion stands in contrast to the comparatively limited role that Canada's federal government has played in building highways. The promotion of limited access highways through the heart of cities with closely spaced interchanges generates excessive traffic, leading to a much higher level of automobile use in U.S. urban areas compared to Canada. Evidence for this is found in significant differences in driving and transit ridership among Cascadia's main cities. Lower fuel taxes and artificially lower fuel prices along with higher rates of motor vehicle subsidization on the U.S. side of the border invite more driving and, in addition, an exponential increase in NAFTA-generated truck traffic. Increasing regional growth, suburban development, and rates of passenger air and freight, truck freight, and "automobility," illustrate a level of expansion that is inherently unsustainable.

In order for transportation to become more efficient and less unsustainable at the regional level, there needs to be more progress at the federal level. In the U.S., while some reforms were promulgated in the *Intermodal Surface Transportation Efficiency Act* of 1991 (ISTEA), their promise has only been partially realized, and highway funding has actually increased significantly in the past decade. Similarly, the Canadian federal government needs to use its powers to redirect transportation priorities at the regional level.

Additionally, current destructive transportation policies need to be addressed in both countries. "Just-in-time" delivery of goods to and from industrial concerns have led to mobile, and even airborne, warehousing of goods, representing internal efficiencies at the expense of externalizing the impacts on the public sector. For example, removing inventory from onsite warehouses to eighteen-wheelers as well as to aviation cargo, leads to greater energy consumption and traffic congestion. Much current thinking about freight movement acknowledges the necessity of moving substantial portions of freight shipment from rubber-tired (trucks) to steel-wheeled (trains) in the immediate future as highway capacity reaches freight saturation in many key U.S. corridors (American Association of State Highway and Transportation Officials 2003).

The globalization – or at least continentalization – of food supply and shipment also has serious implications for regional sustainability. The large transportation component involved in the processing and distribution of foodstuffs, where a large truck must move several metres for each little yogurt container (Böge 1995), must be addressed. A reordering of food supply and shipment should include evaluation of how much fuel is consumed to bring a product to market. Improving sustainability of food supply could also by achieved by diminishing the distance between producer and consumer, developing farmers' markets, and instituting community-supported agriculture in urban areas. This would allow "slow food" to replace fast food and just-in-time food.

At the regional level, there are several measures that could lessen the impact of currently unsustainable transportation modes and land use practices. These include:

- *Improving intermodal connections and coordination between various transportation services.* Better coordination between Greyhound coaches and Amtrak Cascades trains, and local transit connections, would result in increased use and greater efficiency for each service.
- *Exploring regional policy initiatives for improved transportation pricing and taxation.* For instance, Washington's motor fuels tax is dedicated exclusively to highway expenditures and cannot be applied to public transportation or to non-motorized modes. In effect, the more the fuel tax is raised, the more money is spent on highways, consequently generating more motorized travel. Such counter-productive taxation should be reappraised by elected officials of British Columbia, Washington, and Oregon in order to address the mobility needs of the region through improved public transportation.

- *Expanding intraregional exchange of intellectual and cultural goods.* At present much economic exchange between British Columbia and Washington – and, to a much lesser extent, Oregon – consists of consumer shopping trips, gambler tourism, and trans-shipment of goods passing though the region. This last form of exchange is costly to taxpayers and environmentally destructive.
- *Improving and expanding protected areas along the corridor.* Long stretches of I-5 and BC-99 have become an ugly and continuous strip mall, consisting of asphalt expanses, huge box stores, and food and banking drive-throughs. The remaining undeveloped stretches should be promptly protected, where they are not already sheltered under the Agricultural Land Reserve of B.C. or growth management zoning of Oregon and Washington. Interchanges along this route should be limited; some could be closed to improve traffic flow and reduce expense of maintenance, and undeveloped land around others purchased in order to maintain current road capacity and curtail additional driving (Schiller 2002).
- *Communicating "best practices" at the municipal level.* Existing informal exchanges and regional forums involving Cascadia's cities and urban areas should be institutionalized. Transit systems are steadily building ridership and improving services, as in Portland, Vancouver, and Kitsap County, Washington, should be emulated.

In the end, citizens of this environmentally conscious region must ask how their cities and the transportation networks that connect them can be redesigned to grow in ways which are not environmentally detrimental. One of the first steps in developing transportation systems that are collectively sustainable is to demand that the region's leaders and institutions shift support from a plethora of automobiles, trucks, and planes to trains and other means of public transportation.

Acknowledgments

The author would like to thank the following persons for assisting in locating data or information pertinent to this exploration: the late Ray Allred, Rail Division, Washington State Department of Transportation, Olympia – who worked throughout his career to shape transportation in environmentally sound directions; Robert Barnett, Aviation Planning, Port of Portland; Peter Beaulieu, Puget Sound Regional Council, Seattle; Hugh Conroy, Whatcom Council of Governments, Bellingham; Michael Drollinger, Aviation Planning, Port of Seattle; and Eric Jessup, Department of Agricultural Economics, Washington State University. The author alone is responsible for the interpretation of the data or information supplied.

References

American Association of State Highway and Transportation Officials (AASHTO). 2003. *Bottom Line Report, Freight Rail Mobility.* Washington, D.C.

Beaulieu, Peter D. 1996. "The 3-Cs of Freight Infrastructure Capacity: Competition + Communities + Connections." Seattle: Puget Sound Regional Council.

Benfield, F. Kaid, and Michael Replogle. 2002. "The Roads More Traveled: Sustainable Transportation in America." *Environmental Law Review* 32: 10633–10647.

Böge, Stephanie. 1995. "The Well-Traveled Yogurt Pot: Lessons for New Freight Transport Policies and Regional Production." *World Transport Policy and Practice* 1(1): 7–11.

Centre for Sustainable Transportation. 1998. *Sustainable Transportation Monitor 1.* Toronto: The Centre for Sustainable Transportation/Le Centre pour un Transport Durable.

Cooper, Hal B. H. 1995. "Prepared Testimony on the Passenger Ridership Diversion Potential for the Railroad Passenger Service Alternative to the SeaTac Airport Runway Capacity Expansion." Paper presented to Mr. Scott Lewis, Chairman, Expert Arbitration Panel of the Puget Sound Regional Council, 500 One Waterfront Place, 1011 Western

Ave., Seattle, WA 98104. Available from the author; 11715 NE
145th St., Kirkland, WA 98034.

Eriksen, Ken, and Kenneth L. Casavant. 1997. "Impact of North American
Free Trade Agreement (NAFTA) on Washington Highways." Part
I: *Commodity and Corridor Projections*. Eastern Washington
Intermodal Transportation Study (EWITS) Research Report
Number 14. Pullman, WA: Washington State University,
Department of Agricultural Economics.

Gersh, Jeff, and Chelsea Congdon. 1999. *Subdivide and Conquer: A Modern
Western*. Oley, PA: Bullfrog Films.

Gillis, William R., Eric L. Jessup, and Kenneth L. Casavant. 1995.
"Movement of Freight on Washington's Highways: A Statewide
Origin and Destination Study." Eastern Washington Intermodal
Transportation Study (EWITS) Report Number 9. Pullman, WA:
Eastern Washington Intermodal Transportation Study, Washington
State University.

Newman, Peter, and Jeffrey Kenworthy. 1999. *Sustainability and Cities*.
Chicago: Island Press.

Organisation for Economic Cooperation and Development (OECD). 1996.
Proceedings: Vancouver Conference on Sustainable Transportation.
Washington, D.C.

Patterson, Judith, and Anthony Perl. 1999. "The TGV Effect: A Potential
Opportunity for Reconciling Sustainability with Aviation." *World
Transport Policy and Practice* 5(1): 39–45.

Port of Portland. 2001. Portland International Airport (PDX), "Monthly
Traffic Report," August 2001.

Port of Seattle. 2002. Seattle-Tacoma International Airport, 2001. Airport
Activity Report, Aviational Planning Department, Seattle, WA.

Puget Sound Regional Council. 1997. "Analysis of Freight Movements
in the Puget Sound Region." Seattle, WA: Science Applications
International Corp. and Harvey Consultants, Inc.

Raad, T., and J.R. Kenworthy. 1998. "The US and Us." *Alternatives* 24
(1):14–22.

Replogle, M. 1995. "What's Sustainable?" In *Beyond the Car: Essays on the
Auto Culture*. Edited by S. Zielinski and G. Laird. Toronto: Steel
Rail Publishing/Transportation Options.

Schiller, Preston L. 1992. "Turn off the Traffic Rap." *Eastsideweek* (13 May):
2.

———. 1994. "Transportation and Trade in the Corridor." *Proceedings of the
Georgia Basin – Puget Sound – Willamette Valley Building Bridges
to Sustainable Communities International Conference*. Bellingham,
WA: Western Washington University.

———. 1995. "Fighting Airport Expansion: Turning Planes Into Trains," *The Planet,* San Francisco: Sierra Club.

———. ed. 2000. "Sustainable Transportation Issue." *Sustainable Cities* (Fall). Vancouver, BC: International Centre for Sustainable Cities (ICSC).

———. 2002. *Taking the High Road: Protecting Open Space along America's Highways.* Washington, D.C.: Trust for Public Land.

Schiller, Preston L., with Bianca DeLille. 1997. *Green Streets: The 1991 Intermodal Surface Transportation Efficiency Act and the Greening of Transportation Policy in the United States.* Washington, D.C.: Surface Transportation Policy Project.

Schiller, Preston L., and Jeff Kenworthy. 1999. "Prospects for Sustainable Transportation in the Pacific Northwest: A Comparison of Vancouver, Seattle, and Portland." *World Transport Policy and Practice* 5(1): 30–38.

United States. Department of Transportation. 1991. *Intermodal Surface Transportation Efficiency Act* (ISTEA). Washington, D.C.

Washington Association of Rail Passengers. 2002. "The Cascade Foothills Corridor: A Commerce Corridor for Western Washington," Olympia, WA.

Washington State. Department of Transportation. 1992. *High Speed Ground Transportation Study,* Final Report. Olympia, WA: Gannett Fleming, Inc.

Whatcom Council of Governments. 2001. *Cross-Border Trade and Travel Study.* Bellingham, WA: Cambridge Systematics, Inc. and TSi Consulting.

———. 2006 Cross Border Data and Reports: http://www.wcog.org/ DesktopDefault.aspx?tabid=68

Whitelegg, John, and Gary Haq. 2003. "New Directions in World Transport Policy and Practice", pp. 275–96. In *The Earthscan Reader on World Transport Policy and Practice*, eds. John Whitelegg, and Gary Haq. London and Sterling, VA: Earthscan Publications.

Wixey, S., and S. Lake. 1998. "Transport Policy in the EU: A Strategy for Sustainable Development?" *World Transport Policy & Practice* 4(2): 17–21.

NOTES

1   The author has extrapolated these 2005 estimates from Whatcom Council of Government's cross-border data (2001, 2006) and from that of the Puget Sound Regional Council (1997), which were based on 1994 data, after discussing probable increases in truck volumes with Eric Jessup of the Eastern Washington Institute for Transportation Studies, Washington State University, Pullman, WA.

2   The same supposed deregulatory "Open Skies" framework frustrates planning and research efforts by keeping secret the actual number of passengers travelling between international destinations; hence, the researcher must approximate based upon data available for specific carriers, etc. See http://www.bts.gov/programs/oai/sources.html#RESTRICT.

3   See note about "Restricted" information above.

4   See SeaTac Report for 2000, which includes scheduled and air taxi.

5   Eight passengers/flight, a low average due to air taxi loadings, even when one attempts to estimate the origin/destination passenger loadings excluding air taxis – SeaTac includes air taxis in its reporting while PDX does not, it appears that average loadings are still only in the range of 30 passengers – still less than half the average flight's loading; a very inefficient use of a major airport's operational capacity.

6   Data from personal communication, Bob Barnet, PDX planner.

7   Data are included in the breakdowns of YVR-SEA, SEA-PDX.

6

TRANSBOUNDARY ECOSYSTEM MANAGEMENT ON THE CANADA-U.S. BORDER: ORGANIZING FOR SUSTAINABILITY IN THE GEORGIA BASIN–PUGET SOUND BIOREGION

David A. Fraser

Abstract

The Georgia Basin–Puget Sound ecosystem faces enormous environmental stress from both global sources and local pressures. Coordinated institutional solutions are required to resolve these problems as these stressors are shared between neighbouring jurisdictions. This paper considers the evolution of transboundary institutional arrangements in the shared Georgia Basin–Puget Sound bioregion. Focusing specifically on the intricacies and limitations inherent in the performance of institutional and cooperative mechanisms, it concludes that close attention must be paid to complicated policy issues regarding institutional design and function.

Introduction

Border bioregions and coastal corridors – what are referred to as transboundary ecosystems in this chapter – offer an engaging yet complicated set of policy challenges for practitioners and students of transnational institutional design and function. Institutional arrangements in a transboundary context take on many forms, such as formal international treaties, legislative-based or political bilateral agreements, informal cooperative organizations, and policy or program linkages. These occur at all levels of society, from senior governments and nongovernmental organizations to community groups. A variety of design challenges are typically characteristic of initiatives to create transboundary ecosystem management institutions, including reconciliation of political with natural boundaries, accommodation of a large number of stakeholders, functional challenges to permit the free and open exchange of knowledge, and the assurance of adequate fiscal resources. Such challenges are also situated within a broader context of societal choices and trade-offs, which, especially in the face of rapid growth, affect the capacity of transboundary regimes to assist in the transition to a sustainable future.

This chapter reviews the design and function of the transboundary ecosystem-based cooperative mechanisms in the Georgia Basin–Puget Sound Region of western North America, revealing the complexities and limitations inherent in the performance of these mechanisms. This analysis focuses on institutional and cooperative arrangements within the policy field of environmental protection and conservation, and more broadly, sustainable development. The underlying premise is that effective institutional mechanisms are a crucial component of transboundary ecosystem-based management, and practitioners must therefore pay close and ongoing attention to questions of institutional design and function.

Since the late 1980s and early 1990s, when governments and other stakeholders in the Georgia Basin–Puget Sound ecosystem began looking across the border at each other in search of common solutions to their common problems, many attempts to complete a comprehensive institutional analysis in the ecosystem have been initiated. For the most part, however, these efforts have fallen short of

David A. Fraser

their stated goals due to insufficient resources and their low political priority in Canada. While a complete analysis is beyond the scope of this chapter, the following analysis does inform the evolution of transboundary arrangements in the Georgia Basin–Puget Sound ecosystem, and elsewhere.

The Georgia Basin–Puget Sound Transboundary Ecosystem

Positioned in the Pacific Northwest of the United States and the southwest corner of Canada, the Puget Sound, the Strait of Juan de Fuca, and the Strait of Georgia comprise the marine component of the Georgia Basin–Puget Sound ecosystem, while the terrestrial component of the ecosystem is loosely defined by the heights of land and watersheds (fig. 6.1). The ecosystem is ringed by the crest of the Olympic Mountains, the Vancouver Island Range, the Coast Range and the Cascades, and stretches from the City of Olympia in the south to Campbell River and Powell River in the north (British Columbia Round Table on the Environment and the Economy 1993). The boundaries of this ecosystem correspond for the most part with the ancestral home of the Coast Salish Peoples on both sides of the Canada–United States border who have traditionally referred to this ecosystem as *Sqelatses*, or "home."

Transboundary ecosystem-based management has generated widespread attention and debate within academic circles and among governmental resource managers (Fitzsimmons 1998; Callicott 2000; Kay and Schneider 1994; Slocombe 1998; Grumbine 1994; Stanley 1995). Those who champion the merits of the ecosystem approach point to the fact that previous management models have failed to help preserve environmental values in the face of society's appetite for growth. Indeed, ecosystem management represents a new and imaginative way of preparing society for more sustainable decision-making patterns. Critics of the approach argue that ecosystem management represents nothing more than a trendy recasting

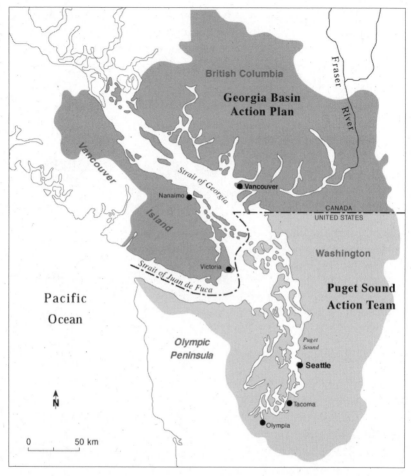

Figure 6.1   The Georgia Basin–Puget Sound Transboundary Ecosystem

of language around age-old management models, and therefore an unnecessary distraction from the serious issues at hand.

As the debate continues, characteristics of the ecosystem-based management approach are unfolding. At its most basic level the eco-system approach concentrates management attention on a particular geographically identifiable space defined by natural features such as mountain ranges, inland seas, vegetation, and animals rather than political boundaries. In other cases, specific issues requiring society's attention may also define ecosystem boundaries. The Georgia Basin–Puget Sound ecosystem, for example, is defined as a region that continues to experience rapid population growth. The 'boundaries' of the transboundary arrangements charged with offsetting the negative effects of this growth are consistent with projections of where future population growth is expected to converge. Such issue-based boundaries do not necessarily coincide with strict scientific topographical classifications and are therefore always subject to scrutiny and criticism.

Other notable characteristics of the ecosystem management approach include its promotion of interdisciplinary research and science, and its emphasis on establishing partnerships both within governments and within government agencies (horizontal integration). In addition, partnerships are required between governments at all levels (vertical integration). The meaningful inclusion of all concerned stakeholders and communities in the development and implementation of management frameworks and focus on measurable results are also important characteristics. Needless to say, credible and lasting management and institutional arrangements are an essential characteristic of effective transboundary ecosystem-based management approaches.

In the transboundary Georgia Basin–Puget Sound ecosystem, the ecosystem-based management approach is establishing itself as the *modus operandi* for region-wide partnership building, planning, and program delivery. Increasingly, individual organizations and partnership arrangements on both sides of the international border are recognizing that they can no longer fulfill their respective program responsibilities without the assistance of other stakeholders similarly engaged in the pursuit of sustainable development. Having a regional context is key to understanding the development and operation of ecosystem-based transboundary arrangements.

The Georgia Basin–Puget Sound ecosystem is a region of immense natural wealth and beauty. It offers an arguably unparalleled standard of living for residents, and is a renowned destination of choice for tourists. The region's attributes include temperate weather patterns, high biodiversity values, abundant natural resources, year-round leisure and recreational opportunities, and a unique balance between urban and rural experiences. Strategically located across the Pacific Ocean from the Asian and Pacific Rim economies, the region is a major gateway for shipping and trade and, increasingly, a lure for the high technology and entertainment industries. The multicultural make-up of the region's population provides residents with a diverse and enriching range of international experiences (Hildebrand et al. 2002).

Similar to most other regions in the world, global influences such as the integration of economic activities and the transport of contaminates including the trans-Pacific movement of air pollutants, measurably and negatively affect residents' quality of life in the Georgia Basin–Puget Sound. Other, more localized pressures on the ecosystem include the deterioration of air quality as a result of the proliferation of fossil-fuel-dependent mobile transportation pollution sources, and the effects of increased levels of this pollution on the health of residents; the degradation of marine, fresh and ground water quality and the subsequent elevated toxic burdens on aquatic fauna and flora; irreversible habitat loss which is the single most serious issue facing the ecosystem (British Columbia/Washington State Marine Science Panel 1994); the uncertain state of sentinel species most notably the resident orca whale population; and a dubious legacy of past resource extraction practices in the forestry, fishery, and mining industries.

Nevertheless, population growth is the greatest challenge facing the Georgia Basin–Puget Sound Region, and specifically the integrity of its environment and its communities. Population has tripled since 1960 and has grown by 17 per cent in the Puget Sound and 21 per cent in the Georgia Strait regions since 1992, reaching a total of almost 7 million in 2000. By 2020, the regional population is projected to increase to 9 million (Georgia Basin–Puget Sound Environmental Indicators Working Group 2002). As a result, development pressures are imposing unprecedented levels of physical, chemical, and biological stress on the ecosystem. Ironically, the increasing level of human-imposed stress places at risk the very ecosystem conditions that provide the foundation of the region's economy, the health of individuals, and the overall quality of life that attracted people to this region in the first place (Kay 1998).

David A. Fraser

The Transboundary Perspective

For several decades, regional observers and practitioners have suggested that the Georgia Basin–Puget Sound ecosystem functions as an ecologically interdependent whole, and that transboundary ecosystem-based approaches to the resolution of issues common to both sides of the border would be required in order to maintain and enhance the region's environment and residents' quality of life. As Barker (1974) noted, "The Strait of Georgia, Puget Sound, and the Juan de Fuca Strait function as a single system – a characteristic that must be recognized if planning and management programs are to be effective."

While prophetic, such reasoning proved to be far ahead of its time. Although cross-border perspectives began to materialize in 1987, it was not until 1988 when the *Nestucca* barge spilled oil in Gray's Harbor, Washington, and the oil reached the shores of Vancouver Island, British Columbia, that governments and residents on both sides of the border awoke to the fact that pollution does not recognize the international boundary (Nasser 1992). This unfortunate episode, combined with a growing emotional response in Washington State to the City of Victoria's apparent unwillingness to upgrade its sewage treatment facilities when Washington State communities had done so throughout Puget Sound, at significant cost to taxpayers, sparked an earnest commitment to cooperative transboundary management among regional authorities.

This more comprehensive, ecosystem-based, approach to transboundary management was foreshadowed by the 1987 listing of the Puget Sound as a priority estuary of concern under the United States Environmental Protection Agency's National Estuary Program (NEP). Although focused to a large extent on Puget Sound marine water quality, NEP took the first bold step of promoting an integrated management regime in the Puget Sound, thus challenging environmental managers to consider, and build partnerships around, the economic and social conditions facing Puget Sound residents. In its 1997–99 work plan for Puget Sound, NEP promoted an integrated approach by prioritizing the protection of the transboundary shared waters of the Puget Sound and Georgia Basin.

Funding commitments from NEP helped establish the Puget Sound Water Quality Authority, and its successor agencies, the Puget Sound Water Quality Action Team and Puget Sound Council as created by the Washington State legislature in 1996. The Action Team and Council are responsible for developing and tracking implementation of a comprehensive Puget Sound Water Quality Management Plan which provides the framework for managing and protecting the Puget Sound and coordinating the roles and responsibilities of federal, state, tribal, and local governments. The plan for the years 2000 and beyond highlights a Puget Sound/Georgia Basin shared waters program as a priority management area (Puget Sound Water Quality Action Team 2000).

On the Canadian side of the Georgia Basin–Puget Sound ecosystem, the now dissolved British Columbia Round Table on the Environment and the Economy was mandated in 1992 by the provincial government of the day to provide advice on how to manage the Georgia Basin in its entirety, including developing options for working with other levels of government in Canada and the United States to protect residents' quality of life. In 1993, the B.C. Roundtable developed a series of recommendations leading to the establishment of the Georgia Basin Initiative aimed at facilitating sustainable growth and development throughout the region. Managed within the former provincial Ministry of Municipal Affairs and Housing until it was integrated into the new Ministry of Community, Aboriginal and Women's Services in June 2001, the Georgia Basin Initiative launched a new wave of municipal and regional planning grounded on urban containment, compact communities, and comprehensive transportation planning goals, as well as full consideration for the health and integrity of the region's environment.

Experiences gained through the NEP and British Columbia Roundtable processes set the stage for the Premier of British Columbia and the Governor of Washington State to sign the Environmental Cooperation Agreement in May 1992. This provincial/state transboundary agreement acknowledged that "environmental concerns and impacts respect neither physical nor political boundaries" and that the province and state will "promote and coordinate mutual efforts to ensure the protection, preservation and enhancement of our shared environment for the benefit of current and future generations" (British Columbia/Washington State Marine Science Panel

David A. Fraser

1994). Upon signing this Agreement the Premier and Governor established the British Columbia/Washington State Environmental Cooperation Council (ECC), and charged this new council with the responsibility to address priority Georgia Basin/Puget Sound transboundary issues including water quality in the Abbottsford/Sumas aquifer, Nooksack River flooding, air quality, and pressures on the shared marine waters.

An independent ECC-commissioned British Columbia/Washington State Marine Science Panel subsequently identified priority issues of common concern requiring collaboration in the shared marine waters. Specified priority issues included habitat loss, marine protected areas, the protection of marine life, and the introduction of exotic species. Under ECC auspices, the Georgia Basin/Puget Sound International Task Force subsequently set in motion a formal process for mobilizing partnerships and developing work plans towards solutions to these shared concerns. Membership on this Task Force includes approximately twelve federal and state-level agencies as well as Coast Salish Tribes and First Nations. Task Force meetings are open to the general public and time is set aside at each meeting for the public to participate in the discussions. While transboundary efforts continue to address groundwater contamination, air quality and flooding problems through the ECC, U.S. Environmental Protection Agency funding, combined with the unwavering commitment on the part of the Puget Sound Water Quality Action Team, have helped to establish the Georgia Basin/Puget Sound International Task Force as one of the most active participants in, and vocal proponents for, transboundary cooperation in the shared ecosystem.

The Fraser Basin Council is acclaimed by most observers in the region as a highly credible mechanism for multi-stakeholder consensus building, and a successful institutional model for identifying and solving sustainability challenges. In 1998, the Fraser Basin Council concentrated its efforts on the promotion of sustainability in the Fraser River, the dominant freshwater influence on the Georgia Basin/Puget Sound Ecosystem, through a 'Charter for Sustainability,' which outlines a broad vision and actions for understanding sustainability, caring for ecosystems, strengthening communities, and improving decision-making (Fraser Basin Council 1997). The 'Charter for Sustainability' has proven to be an invaluable tool for rallying often-disparate interests, and focusing efforts around shared pressures in the Fraser River and Georgia Basin. It has also served as an effective precursor to a transboundary Memorandum of Understanding between the Puget Sound Action Team and Council and the Fraser Basin Council, which was signed in 1999, to enhance the water quality and biological resources of the shared ecosystem. Through the development of annual action plans under this Memorandum of Understanding, the Puget Sound Action Team and Council and the Fraser Basin Council will continue to be significant players in the broader transboundary governance regime of the Georgia Basin/Puget Sound Ecosystem.

Transboundary governance mechanisms were further supported in December 1998 with the Environment Canada and former British Columbia's Ministry of Environment, Lands and Park's (MELP) launch of the Georgia Basin Ecosystem Initiative (GBEI). The initiative was supported by a formal management structure steered by Environment Canada, Fisheries and Oceans Canada, Parks Canada, the former B.C. Ministry of Environment, Lands and Parks, and the former B.C. Ministry of Municipal Affairs. The GBEI served as an increasingly important integrator of governmental, nongovernmental, community, and individual citizens' efforts to better manage human impacts on the Canadian side of the ecosystem. Under the broad vision of *Managing Growth to Achieve Healthy, Productive and Sustainable Ecosystem and Communities*, the GBEI partnership supported an array of projects addressing the broad goals of Enhancing Environmental Health, Building Sustainable Communities, and Enhancing Human Well-being. A wide range of formal and informal partners implemented collaborative on-the-ground projects in support of these goals. Priority was placed on those policies and programs that provide local governments, communities, and citizens with the tools and information they require to make more sustainable decisions (Environment Canada 2003).

Early successes of this initiative included the formulation and sharing of capacity-building tools through information development and exchange and workshops on topics such as ecosystem-wide indicators, Smart Growth practices, leadership and innovation for urban sustainability, and storm water management. As well, the initiative supported pilot projects such as the green development project in East Clayton (City of Surrey) and the Greater Vancouver Biodiversity Conservation Pilot, as well as the development of best practices and improved stakeholder access to needed ecosystem information. In addition to specific projects, GBEI was instrumental in building a strong degree of cooperation, trust, and information exchange among scientific and policy personnel between Canadian stakeholders, and increasingly with the United States in the Puget Sound region of the Georgia Basin–Puget Sound ecosystem.

In recognition of the continuing need to support action-oriented and results-based on-the-ground projects, the GBEI was renamed the Georgia Basin Action Plan (GBAP) in April 2003 and the initiative was renewed for an additional five years. The four goals for 2003–2008 developed by the GBAP partners include: shared and informed collaborative stewardship actions to support the sustainability of the Georgia Basin; sustainable land, aquatic, and resource planning to support the conservation, protection, and restoration of the environment, enhance human well-being, and contribute to a strengthened economy; scientific and indigenous knowledge that supports improved decision-making by advancing the understanding of key ecosystem stresses; and protection and restoration of targeted ecosystems.

It is expected that the new GBAP will strengthen the collective capacity to protect and restore ecosystem health while working cooperatively to provide economic opportunities and enhance human well being (Environment Canada 2003). Strong regional and transboundary relationships will be further enhanced through GBAP and there will be increased investment in collaborative knowledge management actions such as data sharing, web accessibility, integrating science and expertise into regional and local watershed-planning approaches, First Nations relationships and capacity building, and improving networks and communities of practice for ecosystem science.

The range of ecosystem-based transboundary management arrangements in the Georgia Basin–Puget Sound region far exceeds those mentioned above. For example, the Georgia Strait Alliance and People for Puget Sound have combined forces to form the Sounds and Straits Coalition, a transboundary coalition of environmental nongovernmental organizations in British Columbia and Washington State, which serves as a credible watchdog of governments on transboundary issues. Others include the evolving Salish Sea Initiative, which is aiming to establish a representative forum of First Nation and Tribal interests, the San Juan Islands/Islands Trust partnership formed to secure a transboundary marine protected area in the region, and the Northwest Straits Marine Conservation Initiative, which is paving the way for local, tribal, state, and community representatives to work together to protect vital marine resources.

Building on these arrangements, among many others, Environment Canada and the U.S. Environmental Protection Agency agreed to help enhance the evolving transboundary work through the signing on 19 January 2000 of the *Canada-United States Joint Statement of Cooperation on the Georgia Basin and Puget Sound Ecosystem*. The vision of this *Statement of Cooperation* is one:

> ... where our common goal of sustainable communities – embracing human well-being, economic opportunities, and environmental quality – can be realised by today's generations and by those yet to come.... And ... where people of all ages can breathe clean air, drink clean water, swim on clean beaches, and enjoy unparalleled vistas of mountain, ocean and shore. (Environment Canada. United States Environmental Protection Agency 2000)

The statement outlines common goals and objectives, confirms the commitment of the two federal governments, recognizes the special interests of the Coast Salish First Nations and Tribes, and establishes a formal Canada–United States mechanism at the ecosystem level to act on the challenges of sustainability. It also commits the two federal agencies to develop annual action plans and report publicly on progress.

Goals under the 2003 annual action plan include achieving greater understanding of transboundary air quality and airshed management, providing residents and decision-makers with information on issues pertaining to sustainable growth management such as smart growth, and facilitating the participation of Coast Salish First Nations and Tribes in setting future priorities for action in the ecosystem. According to the *Statement of Cooperation*:

> We have today an opportunity for action as unique as the ecosystem itself. All the necessary factors for a successful ecosystem-wide effort are in place. Governments and the general public are aware of the many challenges to the ecosystem. We have the desire to preserve this special place. The sound science we need to make

informed policy choices is at hand. The commitment to cooperation and partnerships is stronger than ever. (Environment Canada.
United States Environmental Protection Agency 2000)

The last decade or so has witnessed significant growth in the for-
malization of partnerships around common concerns and priorities,
and around common approaches for managing the shared Georgia
Basin–Puget Sound ecosystem. These transboundary partnership arrangements take on many configurations, ranging from formal federal or provincial/state government-led institutions, charters, agreements, and consensus-based decision-making forums, to citizen-led
grassroots coalitions, not to mention the admirable achievements
undertaken by various municipalities, academia, communities, and
industry associations. For the most part, these arrangements, both
individually and collectively, are premised on the fact that in the
Georgia Basin–Puget Sound ecosystem, Canada and the United
States shared an airshed, watersheds, and migratory pathways for
birds and fish.

Most importantly, the premise behind arguably each and every
one of these transboundary mechanisms is the immediate need to
coordinate program activities with the view to mitigating the impact
of urban growth on the health of the ecosystem and therefore the
health of residents. Transboundary arrangements in the Georgia Basin–Puget Sound ecosystem share a common vision to this end – the
advancement of sustainability goals and ecosystem health protection
through the management of human population growth. This is not
necessarily to say that transboundary organizations in this region
support curtailing population growth but that they embrace the fact
that population growth management, the management of people not
the environment, requires a comprehensive ecosystem-wide response
based on governmental leadership, enhanced public awareness, the
encouragement of personal/community action, and the facilitation
of a growing regional identity among residents. Having a common
and recognizable vision within a transboundary context is a unique
and assuring condition, and affords an impressive foundation for the
furtherance of future regime building in the region. This was confirmed at the 2007 Georgia Basin–Puget Sound Research Conference
in Vancouver, where an international and multidisciplinary group
of over 800 university and government scientists, Coast Salish First

Nations and tribal representatives, regional politicians, students, and community leaders affirmed that the shared Georgia Basin–Puget Sound ecosystem is a place where common concerns and responses must transcend jurisdiction boundaries to secure regional sustainability.

Impediments to Progress

Although late in starting relative to other transboundary regions (Hildebrand et al. 2002), the recent proliferation of transboundary institution-building in the Georgia Basin–Puget Sound ecosystem is an encouraging trend. While there has been notable progress, the complexity of the task and the limitations inherent in the make-up and function of these efforts will need to be given due attention if the transboundary Georgia Basin–Puget Sound ecosystem is to retain its standing as a region perceived to be accomplishing the right balance between economic and population growth, social stability, and environmental integrity. The competence of the transboundary institutional regime to adapt and provide the necessary guidance and information to decision-makers will depend to a large extent on the recognition and amelioration of limitations in the regime's structure and function, as well as motivation of leaders to find means to overcome these limitations.

One of the most basic challenges in transboundary regime-building is the rationalization of a large and diverse set of jurisdictions, informed stakeholders, and pre-existing governance mechanisms, many of which have different interests and different capacities, along with some conflicting mandates. While by no means a unique challenge for the Georgia Basin–Puget Sound ecosystem, the international border dividing this particular ecosystem significantly complicates the multi-jurisdictional mix of interests working towards sustainability. It is no simple matter to effectively implement consensus-based transboundary programs aimed at resolving complex sustainability issues within this jurisdictional quagmire. One could argue that regime-building and decision-making in a transboundary region is equally

David A. Fraser

as complex as the interrelationships within the natural ecosystem itself. The establishment of a common vision, common goals, and a common societal will is a critical first step for reconciling interests towards a sustainable future.

Another limitation to the effective performance of transboundary institutions is the general lack of participants' information, knowledge, and understanding of each other and of their respective administrative systems. In many cases, individuals working through transboundary mechanisms have not had the luxury through their formal training to fully master the intricacies at play in neighbouring jurisdictions. This is supported by two basic facts: first, the amount of information generated and dispersed through electronic means such as internet and e-mail, has grown at such a prolific rate that participants have little capacity to absorb this information and keep pace with the affairs in a neighbouring country. Secondly, resource restrictions, among other factors such as the often immediate and seemingly never-ending need to focus attention on the resolution of domestic issues, reserves consideration of transboundary issues to the 'edge of people's desks.' It is noteworthy in this regard that few government officials on either side of the Georgia Basin–Puget Sound ecosystem have 'transboundary partnership-building' written into their job descriptions, and few, therefore, have support within their systems to undertake the continuous learning required of them.

It should come as no surprise that political factors have a significant influence on the operation of transboundary mechanisms. For instance, while it is relatively simple to galvanize political support for transboundary regimes during a time of international crisis such as an oil spill, it is less easy to maintain such support over the longer term. Additionally, politicians are bound to report to their constituents at three- to five-year election intervals thereby serving under timelines that have little applicability to those of nature and natural processes. Transboundary institutions addressing sustainability issues, on the other hand, deal with issues that are often intergenerational in scale and which require long-term planning and resource commitments. The incompatibility of these timelines results in uneven political attention to transboundary regimes and reluctance on the part of the political system generally to invest financially in those shared programs, such as data acquisition, management, and exchange, which will improve decision-making over the long term but provide little near-term benefits or results. It is worth noting that recurrent elections, leadership changes, and governmental reorganizations also affect the durability of political support for transboundary regimes as well as the congruity of players and programs.

A final note on the inherent limitations of transboundary eco-system-based institutions relates to the fact that such institutions are situated within a complex social context where interests compete and disputes are inevitable. Even though a given set of stakeholders may have the best intentions to collaborate on shared solutions to shared concerns, misunderstandings will occur, resulting in delays in program development and implementation. More often than not, however, the conflicts and delays inherent in consensus-building arrangements arise exogenous to the specific issues at hand. For example, in the Georgia Basin–Puget Sound ecosystem there is, and likely always will be, the potential for conflict between the neighbouring jurisdictions over issues such as international trade related to softwood lumber, energy generation and distribution, and natural resource management. This became painfully clear in 1997 when a serious disagreement between the United States and Canada over salmon harvest allocations resulted in the province of British Columbia suspending its involvement in all Environmental Cooperation Council activities until an agreement was reached to its satisfaction. The suspension of activities occurred regardless of the fact that 'salmon management' was not an issue under the council's mandate. Clearly, any consideration of the operation of transboundary institutions must recognize that society is comprised of many competing interests and that jurisdictions compete with each other as often as they cooperate.

Conclusions

Effective institutional mechanisms are critical to the success of transboundary ecosystem management and close attention must be paid to the complicated policy questions around institutional design and function. In the Georgia Basin–Puget Sound region, transboundary mechanisms – albeit imperfect – are currently in place to assist society in pursuing sustainable development objectives. However, the maturation of these management arrangements, and their subsequent ability to support the future health and integrity of the ecosystem's environmental, economic, and social processes will require a collective and immediate commitment on the part of the region's leaders to evaluate how best to address the current shortcomings inherent in ecosystem-based regimes, followed by collective implementation of the results of this evaluation. In a transboundary context, policy challenges such as habitat restoration, clean air and water, and the health of species, including humans, requires a reconciliation of domestic political realities with natural ecosystem-based boundaries, the cooperation of a large and diverse set of stakeholders, secure long-term funding, and unencumbered exchange of information and knowledge. This will not be a simple task. Additionally, institution-making in a transboundary context is an extremely complicated endeavour, requiring patience, personal commitment, and flexibility. Lasting arrangements, which serve the needs of as many interested stakeholders and decision-makers as possible, will not emerge without some tension and mistakes. The seemingly glacial speed at which these arrangements evolve – or adapt to changing societal values – may prove frustrating. Given the complex nature of sustainability issues, continuous learning is required. In the end, a balance must be struck between a focus of regional resources and energies on the maturation of decision-support mechanisms, a plodding exercise at the best of times, and a collective response to urgent issues currently facing the ecosystem.

References

Barker, Mary L. 1974. *Water Resources and Land Uses Strait of Georgia-Puget Sound Basin*. Ottawa: Department of the Environment, Lands Directorate.

British Columbia Round Table on the Environment and the Economy. 1993. *Georgia Basin Initiative: Creating a Sustainable Future*. Vancouver.

British Columbia/Washington State Marine Science Panel. August 1994. *The Shared Marine Waters of BC and Washington: A Scientific Assessment of Current Status and Future Trends in Resource Abundance and Environmental Quality in the Strait of Juan de Fuca, Strait of Georgia and the Puget Sound*. Report to the British Columbia/Washington State Environmental Cooperation Council. Olympia, WA, and Victoria, B.C.

Callicott, J.B. 2000. "Aldo Leopold and the foundations of ecosystem management." *Journal of Forestry* 98(5): 5–13.

Environment Canada. 2003. *Georgia Basin Action Plan: The Georgia Basin Action Plan Highlights 2003–2008*. Vancouver. http://www.pyr. ec.gc.ca/GeorgiaBasin/index_e.htm.

Environment Canada. United States Environmental Protection Agency. 2000. *Canada-United States Joint Statement of Cooperation on the Georgia Basin and Puget Sound Ecosystem*. http://www.pyr.ec.gc. ca/GeorgiaBasin/index_e.htm.

Fitzsimmons, Allan K. 1998. "Why the policy of federal management and protection of ecosystems is a bad idea." *Landscape and Urban Planning* 40(1/3): 195–202.

Fraser Basin Council. Feb. 1997. *Charter for Sustainability*. Vancouver. Document is available on the Fraser Basin Council website: http://www.fraserbasin.bc.ca/publications/charter.html.

Georgia Basin-Puget Sound Environmental Indicators Working Group. Spring 2002. *Georgia Basin-Puget Sound Ecosystem Indicators Report*. Document is available on the Puget Sound Action Plan website: http://www.psat.wa.gov/Programs/Transboundary.htm.

Grumbine. R. Edward. 1994. "What is Ecosystem Management." *Conservation Biology* 8(1): 27–38.

Hildebrand, L.P., V. Pebbles, and D. A. Fraser. 2002. "Cooperative Ecosystem Management Across the Canada-U.S. Border: Approaches and Experiences of Transboundary Programs in the Gulf of Maine, Great Lakes and Georgia Basin/Puget Sound." *Journal of Ocean and Coastal Management* 45: 421–57.

Kay, Bruce. 12 March 1998. "The Georgia Basin Ecosystem Initiative." Paper presented at the Puget Sound Research '98 Conference. Seattle.

Kay, J., and E. Schneider. 1994. "Embracing Complexity: The Challenge of the Ecosystem Approach." *Alternatives* 20(3): 32–39.

Nasser, Christine. 1 Jan. 1992. *Beyond the Border: Environmental Management in British Columbia and Washington.* Unpublished issue paper prepared for the United States Environmental Protection Agency, Region 10. Seattle, WA. USEPA.

Puget Sound Water Quality Action Team. 14 Dec. 2000. *Puget Sound Water Quality Management Plan*; http://www.psat.wa.gov/.

Slocombe, D. Scott. 1998. "Lessons from experience with ecosystem based management." *Landscape and Urban Planning* 40: 31–39.

Stanley, T. R., Jr. 1995. "Ecosystem Management and the Arrogance of Humanism." *Conservation Biology* 9: 255–62.

United States Environmental Protection Agency National Estuary Program; http://www.epa.gov/owow/estuaries/.

7

BINATIONAL GOVERNANCE OF MARINE WATERS: THE GEORGIA BASIN–PUGET SOUND EXAMPLE

J.C. Day and K.S. Calbick

Abstract

A widespread phenomenon during recent decades has been the need to confront environmental degradation by creating more effective institutional arrangements for planning and management. This task is made more difficult in shared binational environments. Following the discovery in both Washington State and British Columbia of widespread pollution in the vicinity of major urban and industrial centres in the mid-1970s, both jurisdictions adopted a variety of institutions and programs in an effort to ensure sustainable environmental quality. This paper compares initiatives adopted to manage water quality on both sides of the border and traces the evolution of binational arrangements that evolved to incorporate a variety of ecosystem components. It also assesses the effectiveness of the existing institutional arrangements for sustainable water and environmental quality management in British Columbia and Washington at the federal, provincial-state, regional, and local governmental levels. Specifically, it examines the legislation, policies, agency roles, funding, and public involvement programs that form the basic structure for water quality and environmental protection and enhancement in both jurisdictions. It also highlights mechanisms for translating this framework into planning systems for identifying water quality deterioration and other environmental problems, and remediating and preventing such problems from occurring in future.

Introduction

Canada and the United States have shared the estuary comprised of the Straits of Georgia and Juan de Fuca and Puget Sound for more than one hundred and thirty years (see fig. 6.1 in preceding chapter). Until the 1990s, each nation developed its environmental management institutions in isolation; neither the American nor the Canadian federal governments devoted much attention to binational governance issues. But the consequences of these isolationist policies, with few formal rules regarding the use of the shared waters, led to widespread recognition during the 1970s that environmental degradation was becoming common in urban and industrial areas, and estuaries, on both sides of the border. This degradation was manifest in a variety of effects, which include locally impaired water quality, as well as destruction of wetlands, marine habitats, and biota.

Many factors contributed to the water quality degradation. The present combined international population of 7 million within the binational watersheds of the estuary is projected to increase to between 9 and 11 million by 2020. As a result of the complex development of urban, industrial, agricultural, and transportation land uses in the binational bioregion, the rich ecological diversity that includes 220 species of fish, 26 mammals, and 100 birds in Puget Sound is stressed. Three fish are listed under the *Endangered Species Act* in the United States and many other populations are declining. Seventy per cent of tidal wetlands have been lost, 33 per cent of shorelines altered, and shellfish beds have decreased by 25 per cent, while sediments in urban areas are contaminated (PSWQAT 2000, 2004). Although comparable figures could not be located for the shared British Columbia waters, the destruction is believed to be at least as severe in Canada.

Over the past quarter century, the response to environmental degradation has been to progressively strengthen environmental management systems at all levels of governance in each country. During the 1990s, institutions for international cooperation were gradually introduced in an effort to harmonize policies and actions. While the development of this binational management system is still in its infancy, initial progress in moving toward sustainable management of the shared marine waters in both countries has occurred.

This paper traces efforts in each country as well as the development of binational arrangements to confront the challenges posed by degradation of the waters in the binational Georgia-Puget Sound basin. It evaluates the strengths and weaknesses of new institutions on both sides of the border developed to resolve environmental problems in the basin. Using a standard set of criteria, the paper begins by summarizing the characteristics of four new institutional systems created to deal with emerging, large-scale ecosystem problems on the west coast of North America, as well as one national agency in the United States. These new binational agencies are then compared with other modern management systems. Finally, conclusions are drawn about whether a sustainable, high-quality shared environment can be recreated based on the existing binational institutions. Recommendations are made on measures that will be needed to move toward environmental sustainability in the shared Georgia Basin–Puget Sound, although the major focus is on a comparative assessment of water quality management systems in the shared binational waters.

Evaluative Criteria

Recent research evaluated the institutional arrangements adopted by a variety of agencies created to manage large, complex, ecosystems or political jurisdictions (Calbick 2003). In each case, the goal is to create long-term ecological, social, and economic sustainability. These agencies include: the Fraser Basin Council in British Columbia, the Land Conservation and Development Commission in Oregon, the Bay Conservation and Development Commission in California, and the U.S.D.A. Forest Service. Based on this work, seven factors are used to evaluate ecosystem protection institutions in the Puget Sound–Georgia Basin.

- Legislation in terms of comprehensiveness and integration with existing acts, agencies, and policies, whether it is prioritized with respect to other environmental responsibilities, enforceable, and founded on civics-based decisions that rely on strong and continuing public involvement.
- Adaptive planning, implementation, and monitoring in terms of clear goals, priorities, and targets; based on a wide range of potential initiatives, public evaluation of outcomes, and ecosystem analysis.
- Representation that involves all stakeholders at the decision table working with politicians who observe and contribute to the debate.
- Alternative dispute resolution to reduce costs and speed up decision-making. Traditional court proceedings and line agencies are always available in the event that stakeholders are unable to resolve complex issues themselves.
- Financing for existing and new environmental agencies and their activities is sustainable and adequate.
- Innovative leadership supported by all relevant levels of government.
- Outcomes promoting social, economic, and environmental sustainability.

Georgia Basin–Puget Sound

The Setting. By the mid-1970s it had become apparent that the approach in both British Columbia and Washington State to managing marine water quality was ineffective. Elevated levels of metals, PCBs, and other organic substances were found in Seattle's harbour and river, while similar deterioration was noted in the vicinity of Vancouver. In response, each country adopted dramatically different systems of planning and institutional arrangements in an effort to correct the deficiencies and protect the aquatic environment in future.

Institutions and Planning Focus

This section traces the individual national approaches implemented to deal with environmental deterioration in each country, as well as binational efforts.

Water Pollution and the Coastal Zone. The United States and Washington State recognized the pollution problem and created new coastal management legislation in the early 1970s (table 7.1). Water quality standards had been under development at the federal and state level since the early 1970s as well. In contrast, neither Canada nor British Columbia established water quality and coastal legislation to control water quality and land and water uses in the Georgia Basin ecosystem. Studies undertaken between 1977 and 1984 culminated in a federal-provincial agreement in 1985 and the Fraser River Estuary Management Program or FREMP (table 7.1). Federal and provincial agencies created a new institution for the Fraser Estuary, which, with the exception of influence of the Greater Vancouver Regional District (GVRD) and federal harbour commissions, has remained tightly under their control for water quality management. Their limited effort focused on the Fraser River estuary and, indeed, only the wetted area between the flood-control dikes, for water-quality concerns until the late 1990s (fig. 7.1). In contrast, little attention

Table 7.1 Major Georgia Basin–Puget Sound Binational, National, and Provincial-State Environmental Management Agencies and Agreements.

GOVERNMENT LEVEL	DATE CREATED	AGENCY/ AGREEMENT	JURISDICTION
Federal-Provincial	2003	Georgia Basin Action Plan (GBAP)	Canada–British Columbia
Federal	2000	Joint Statement of Cooperation: GB-PS Ecosystem Initiative	Environment Canada (EC) and U.S. Environmental Protection Agency (EPA)
Federal	1998	Dept. of Fisheries Oceans Act: coastal management	Canada
Federal-Provincial	1998 (renamed in 2003)	Georgia Basin Ecosystem Initiative (GBEI)	Canada–British Columbia
State-Provincial	1992	B.C.-Washington Environmental Cooperation Council	British Columbia–Washington State
Federal-Provincial	1991 (BIEAP)	Burrard Inlet Environmental Action Plan	Canada–British Columbia
Federal-Provincial	1985 (FREMP)	Fraser River Estuary Mgmt. Program	Canada–British Columbia
Federal-State	1985	Puget Sound Water Quality Program (renamed Action Team)	United States–Washington
Federal-State	1972–71	*Coastal Management Act* and agencies	United States–Washington

was paid to the Straits of Georgia and Juan de Fuca until the late 1990s, and the level of interest in the shared waters remains limited to the present time.

The Fraser River Estuary Management Program (FREMP) is comprised of Environment Canada (EC), Fisheries and Oceans Canada (DFO), Transport Canada, the B.C. Ministry of Environment, North Fraser and Fraser Port Authorities, and GVRD (FREMP 2006: 1–2) (table 7.1). FREMP's goal (Canada and British Columbia 1986a,b) is to provide the means for accommodating a growing population and economy, while maintaining the quality and productivity of the Fraser estuary's natural environment.

These objectives and goals are to be achieved through a linked management system, a public participation process, coordinated referrals and assessment process, and the Fraser Estuary Information System. FREMP has been coordinating decision-making among more than thirty agencies representing federal, provincial, and local governments, port authorities, and First Nations on conservation and development in the estuary. In 1994, partnering agencies adopted a coordinated plan with a vision, goals, and actions for managing the estuarine environment, as well as sectors of the economy that depend on the river for their success. Management issues include: water quality; remediation of contaminated lands; fish and wildlife habitat, water birds, and resident fish; navigation, dredging, and log management; marine cargo and employment; land available for, and employment in, water-dependent industry; recreational visits to regional parks, shoreline corridors, boating, and registered archaeological and heritage sites (FREMP 2001), although only water quality is considered here. Over the next twenty years it is expected that intense pressure for space and resources will develop as the population of the area increases from 2 to 3 million. Public advisory bodies and stakeholders have a restricted ability to influence water quality issues under this administrative system.

A companion organization was created in 1991, the Burrard Inlet Environmental Action Program (BIEAP), composed of five of FREMP's partners (table 7.1; fig. 7.1). The only difference is that the Vancouver Port Authority replaces the Fraser harbour commissions. BIEAP coordinates a joint action program to improve and protect environmental quality in Burrard Inlet. Administration of FREMP and BIEAP was amalgamated in 1995.

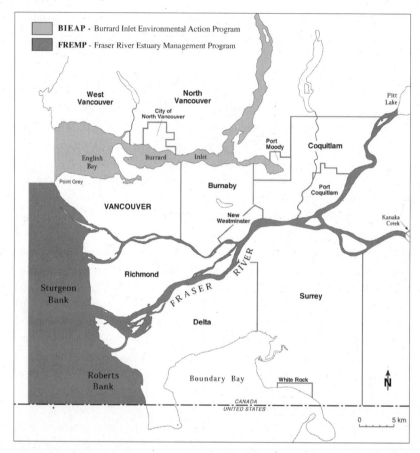

Figure 7.1 BIEAP and FREMP.

Geographically, BIEAP encompasses the marine foreshore and tidal waters east of a line between Point Atkinson and Point Grey, including False Creek, Port Moody Arm, and Indian Arm. The majority of the Vancouver Port Authority is located within Burrard Inlet. With 72 million tons of cargo handled annually, the port is one of the world's largest in terms of the volume of goods moved (Vancouver Port Authority 2003a,b). Port activities and industrial operations within the harbour contribute significantly to regional, provincial, and national economies. Burrard Inlet is an equally important ecological area, providing important habitat for fish and a variety of other aquatic life. Productive tidal areas are also an integral part of the Pacific flyway. Traditionally, Burrard Inlet supported First Nations through an abundance of fish and wildlife. While it still provides an environment for a large number and diversity of biota, a century of industrial, port, and urban activity has substantially changed the original character of the inlet and adversely impacted its local ecology (Daykin 1999).

Management of Burrard Inlet is complex, involving a multitude of federal, provincial, regional, and local governments. Seven municipalities are involved in the management of the land base that surrounds the inlet. Under the traditional institutional system, the separate line agencies created to manage diverse aspects of the environment and the economy have largely operated independently, without legislative coordination or the necessity to involve related agencies or the publics in the planning and implementation processes.

The formally linked management structure established through BIEAP represents a significant improvement over the previous sectoral management system. However, a recent study found that the institutional restructuring to establish BIEAP had been insufficient for adequately meeting the necessary preconditions for effectively implementing ecosystem management (Daykin 1999). Reforms must extend beyond mere coordination if institutions are to overcome conventional barriers and effectively adopt the holistic perspective required by ecosystem management. Specific recommendations for increasing institutional effectiveness of BIEAP pertaining to implementing ecosystem management include: clarifying and strengthening the program vision and goals; strengthening program management; strengthening the skills and knowledge associated with ecosystem management; expanding the program perspective and its zone of influence; increasing emphasis on ecosystem-level planning and management; broadening public involvement; providing adequate, committed resources; adopting an adaptive management approach; and intensifying emphasis on addressing root causes, as opposed to symptoms, of environmental degradation. The discharge of combined sewers into the inlet continues to cause water quality degradation, although this problem is slowly being resolved, for example, with recent sewer improvements in Burnaby (BCFacts. Org May 2003b), as well as Vancouver's continuing sewer separation program that will eliminate combined sewer overflows by 2050 (City of Vancouver 1999).

Water Quality and the Coastal Zone. Canada and British Columbia were comparatively slow to respond to the water-quality degradation by failing to adopt an integrated system to manage the coastal zone. Further, the federal and provincial governments have been unable to agree on minimum water quality standards for either fresh or marine waters, opting instead for objectives and criteria which citizens can only challenge with great difficulty (Sierra Legal Defence Fund 1999a). Only in exceptional instances of severe water quality degradation, such as pollution associated with mines and pulp mills, have standards been adopted in Canada. Nor did the federal government assign the responsibility for coastal management to the Department of Fisheries and Oceans until 1998. British Columbia has not yet created special legislation that outlines a vision, goals, or objectives, nor has it designated a lead agency, to coordinate provincial agencies in an effort to protect its coastal environment. Currently this protection, such as it is, is being handled in a piecemeal approach based on individual regional coastal land and resource management plans in the absence of a provincially created vision and related goals, objectives, and targets. Unfortunately the central and northern coastal tables to whom this task fell were both unable to consider the coastal environment in their deliberations. As a consequence, the establishment of a coastal policy for the province was assigned in 2006 to a new federal-provincial task force under the direction of Department of Fisheries and Oceans Canada. Establishment of a coastal policy for British Columbia remains an elusive goal.

Washington State. Elevated levels of metals, PCBs, and other organic substances were found in Seattle's harbour and associated river following a large spill of PCBs in the mid-1970s. Research, conducted in 1975, revealed that bottom fish had a variety of liver diseases (Washington, PSWQA 1987). Rising bacterial levels in the early 1980s led to advisories limiting recreational fish consumption in urban areas and to closing commercial shellfish beds in rural areas. The ensuing public concern over these events led to the creation of a citizen's coalition in 1983 that resulted in the creation of the Puget Sound Water Quality Authority (PSWQA) in 1985 (Washington, chpt. 90.70), subsequently renamed the PSWQ Action Team a decade later (table 7.1). Its area of concern is the entire Puget Sound drainage basin. The authority prepared a plan in December 1986, which was revised on six occasions through 2004. Its duties were later extended to oversee plan implementation and to influence enforcement activities. In addition, selected federal programs were used to increase the capacity for sensitive resource management in the area. A National Estuary Program (NEP) was created in Puget Sound and jointly administered by the U.S. Environmental Protection Agency (U.S. EPA), the state Department of Ecology, and PSWQ Program and subsequently the Action Team. The authority was invited to join this program because it was developing a comprehensive management plan for the sound. Thereafter, the sound was designated an estuary of national significance under section 320 of the *Clean Water Act* (U.S. EPA 1987) and the National Estuary Program in 1988 (Day et al. 1993).

In pursuing these objectives, the original Action Plan embraced fourteen components in an effort to arrest and remediate water quality. An unfinished agenda of other issues was presented that required study when the first fourteen were under control. For each issue discussed, the agencies responsible for the work were identified, timetables and deadlines for completion were specified, and budgets and funders were listed. Over the ensuing fifteen years, the topics investigated have increased until the list is now comprehensive and impressive (table 7.2). Although this agency did not identify its work as ecosystem based, because the initial mandate preceded the popularization of this term, its mandate has evolved to the point where it may be characterized as such an approach. In comparison, a comprehensive water pollution plan has not been prepared for either the Georgia Basin nor the Strait of Juan de Fuca in British Columbia, and progress on comprehensive water quality control for the GVRD and Capital Regional District in Victoria lag (Venton and Werring 2003; SLDF 1999b) in comparison to settlements on the American side of the border. For example, even the small settlement of Port Townsend in Washington State, forty kilometres south of Victoria on the shore of the Strait of Juan de Fuca, has installed secondary sewage treatment. Sierra Legal Defence asserts that Victoria is dumping PCBs into the sea at 160 times the provincial guideline for protecting aquatic life (BCFacts.Org April 2003a). On behalf of the T. Buck Suzuki Environmental Foundation and the Georgia

Table 7.2. The Evolving PSWQAT Estuary Management Plan Interests.*

Growth management strategy
Local watershed management strategy
Aquatic nuisance species
Wetlands, fish, and wildlife protection
Spill prevention
Monitoring, research, laboratories
Public education and involvement
On-site sewage systems
Household hazardous materials
Pest management
Forestry practices
Agriculture practices
Marinas and boaters
Shellfish protection
Contaminated sediments and harbor dredging
Municipal and industrial discharges
Storm water management and combined sewers

*Source: Washington (2000).

Strait Alliance, Sierra Legal Defence requested that the province designate underwater areas surrounding Victoria's sewage outfalls as contaminated sites as these outfalls contain toxic chemicals higher than the levels prescribed under provincial legislation and national guidelines (Sierra Legal Defence Fund 15 Nov. 2005). In response, the B.C. Ministry of Environment stated that the provincial rules on contamination do not apply to an active source of pollution and implies their application would only be considered if the use of the outfalls were to cease. These conservation agencies continue to urge the province to instruct the Capital Regional District to move quickly to install secondary sewage treatment to remedy this problem (Sierra Legal Defence Fund 8 Feb. 2006).

The goal of the action team is to prevent pollution, and to restore and protect the biological health and diversity of Puget Sound (Washington 2000). This restoration goal is much more ambitious than FREMP's maintenance goal. To do so, the team has characterized the condition of the water, sediments, plants, animals, and habitats in Puget Sound and its watersheds. To achieve these goals, the plan aims to protect and enhance three resources: water and sediment quality, fish and shellfish, and wetlands.

· PSWQAT deals with a complex institutional environment in all waters and lands draining into Puget Sound, the Strait of Georgia south of the Canadian border, and the Strait of Juan de Fuca. More than 480 governmental bodies – federal, state, local, and tribal – play a role in regulating water quality. These include 6 federal agencies, 5 state agencies, 12 counties, 10 cities, 14 tribes, 40 ports, 13 sewer districts, 15 flood control districts, 121 soil and water districts, 14 park and recreation districts, and 9 public utility districts (Washington 1987). About 400 industries and sewage treatment plants have permits to discharge effluent in the sound while urban development, agriculture, forestry, and roads also contribute to surface water degradation.

The action team coordinates, and oversees the work of federal, state, and all other levels of government in meeting commitments established in the Puget Sound Water Quality Management Plan. A major weakness in this institutional system, however, is that the action team can only use moral suasion in its efforts to achieve compliance in the event that an agency with the legislative power to do so fails to meet its commitments under the plan.

Summary Assessment

By the mid-1980s, the Americans recognized that their existing institutions were incapable of improving water quality within a reasonable period in their portion of the shared international water body. In response, they created a new agency to create a plan and then oversee its implementation. In contrast, the responsible federal and provincial bodies in British Columbia created a forum composed of existing managers to control FREMP and to integrate federal and provincial actions in the lower Fraser River (table 7.3).

Table 7.3 FREMP and BIEAP Scorecard.[a]

Legislation	Must rely on members' legislation; few enforceable water quality standards.
Adaptive	Limited data on which to base decisions but 2006 synthesis coming; little long-term monitoring available to publics; GVRD has assumed this task.
Civics representation	Agencies secretive with water quality data; only recently beginning to release; no politicians or citizens on either body; difficult to obtain information. GVRD will report conditions to the publics on an ongoing basis for the first time.
Alternative dispute resolution	No; leads to problems when differences of opinion among agencies emerge.
Financing	2001 $783,079[a] 2005 $390,881.
Leadership	Report to funding agencies, secretive with stakeholders; one-way communication on water quality.
Sustainability: economic, social, environmental	Needs more financial support and firmer political direction to monitor environment; inadequate municipal sewage treatment.

[a]BIEAP and FREMP (2002): 17; (2005): 18.

The study area adopted for Puget Sound water quality management in the mid-1980s was the entire Puget Sound basin; in British Columbia, the Fraser River channels and banks within GVRD were investigated to the extent possible, while the rest of the estuary, the Fraser River basin, and the Strait of Georgia received comparatively little attention until the 1990s, and then only on a modest scale compared to the Puget Sound initiative.

There were other notable binational differences in the approaches adopted. The Washington State water quality management initiative was a civics-based process with widespread involvement of public stakeholder groups in the solution of pollution problems, as well as thorough public access to water quality data. In contrast, the program in British Columbia was professional, elitist, and secretive. This system continues to exist to the present day. Only highly generalized information is released to the public on water quality conditions in the Georgia Basin, the Greater Vancouver Regional District, and the Fraser River estuary and Burrard Inlet as all levels of government have failed to fund environmental agencies to the level required to undertake a transparent system of water quality governance (BIEAP and FREMP 2003). GVRD recently assumed the responsibility for water quality monitoring and coordination within its boundaries.

The *Puget Sound Water Quality Action Team* has emerged as a continental, if not global, model of the way forward in water quality and ecosystem management. From the beginning, this experience has been based on an ambitious program combining public participation and involvement of all relevant stakeholders, education, and research.

The action team has had the solid support of successive federal and state governments for twenty years. Over time it defined a promising program of actions in all aspects of biophysical, social, and economic systems that need to be changed if a sustainable aquatic environment is to be achieved. This joint initiative is supported by federal water quality standards, U.S. EPA research, receptiveness to public interests, and public involvement and education, as well as ongoing oversight by politicians from both the state house and senate. Moreover, the state has funded the initiative generously on a continuing basis until the early years of the twenty-first century when there was a decrease in annual revenues. Washington Governor Chris Gregoire revitalized the Puget Sound initiative on 19 December 2005 when she announced a $52 million supplemental budget proposal to create a new road map to achieve sustainability in Puget Sound by 2020. Although the environment had been taken for granted for more than a hundred years, the action team has charted a course in an effort to stabilize and remediate the widespread damage from this long period of neglect (table 7.4).

Table 7.4 Puget Sound Water Quality Action Team Scorecard.

Legislation	Focused, clear, comprehensive, effective; federal Clean Water Act + Washington State equivalent and National Estuary Program support
Adaptive	Fully + sustainability indicators + abundant data available to stakeholders
Civics representation	Stakeholders advise and oversee, agencies implement; comprehensive information; thorough representation; house and senate representatives on council
Alternative dispute resolution	Yes; consensus of stakeholders-agencies
Financing	2001–2003 U.S.$15.4 MM; 27.9 MM nonproviso
Leadership	Innovative, adaptive; nontechnical director; reports to governor. Action team has no power to force compliance if member agencies with legislative power do not implement plan
Sustainability: economic, social, environmental	Problem areas identified; need long-term initiatives to achieve

In contrast to the development of effective institutions to confront the threat of water pollution in Puget Sound, FREMP and BIEAP have struggled against enormous odds to protect the GVRD ecosystem. Compared to the action team, the approach to water quality has been based on agency secrecy and confidentiality. Federal guidance in terms of environmental standards and dependable financial support to assist with the construction of infrastructure to treat emissions to water bodies adequately has not been available consistently. Nor have provincial and local governments set a funding priority to have the required studies and monitoring completed on an ongoing basis. As a consequence, only three of five treatment plants have been upgraded to secondary treatment, and 20 per cent of GVRD sewers remain as combined sanitary and storm water systems (Sierra Legal Defence Fund 1999b), although this problem is slowly being resolved. Recently, the provincial government moved to replace the *Waste Management Act* with the *Environmental Management Act*, which would exempt all but "high risk" industries from the need to obtain a permit to discharge waste into the environment. Medium and low risk activities will experience a lower level of surveillance. At the same time, the North American Commission for Environmental Cooperation reported that pollution is growing in North America with small- and medium-sized polluters responsible for the growth (BCFacts.Org May 2003a). This action was taken at a time when Vancouver and Victoria were collectively dumping about 460 billion litres of sewage and toxic chemicals into marine waters annually, including some 69 billion litres of untreated raw sewage (Sierra Legal Defence Fund 1999b). The province recently approved liquid waste management plans for both cities that permit Vancouver to modernize its facilities within thirty years (Greater Vancouver Regional District 2003; BCFacts.Org April 2002) but Victoria does not need to do so during the twenty-five-year life of its plan (BCFacts.Org April 2003a; Venton and Werring 2003; Capital Regional District July 2000). Clearly, BIEAP, FREMP, and the Georgia Basin Ecosystem Initiative, discussed below, face enormous challenges in moving toward the creation of a plan for the sustainable management of the shared binational waters.

Given the current structure of the Canadian institutional system, it is becoming more difficult to achieve sustainable development and protect the environment in the shared marine waters. Furthermore, the provincial government eliminated the independent office of the Commissioner for Environment and Sustainability before the post could be filled and repealed the *Protection of Public Participation Act*, which provided safeguards against frivolous lawsuits usually filed by companies against citizens who question company activities (BCFacts.Org August 2001). Indeed, in 1999, Canada was heralded as the "promised land" for polluters in the *Globe and Mail*. Citing a 78 per cent drop in prosecution rates since 1992, the article documented the lenient approach to environmental crimes (Wristen 1999). In a related initiative, the Sierra Legal Defence Fund laid charges before the B.C. courts against the Capital Regional District in Victoria for dumping raw sewage into the Strait of Juan de Fuca, as well as five other private prosecutions. All of these cases have been taken over by the province and stayed (Sierra Legal Defence Fund

1999a). Clearly, neither the federal nor provincial governments have been decisive in protecting the aquatic environment shared with our neighbours in Washington State.

There are a number of serious weaknesses in the current approach to protecting the British Columbia area of the shared binational waters. A comprehensive council of stakeholder groups has never been created to advise BIEAP–FREMP on a continuing basis about questions regarding water quality policy and priority, or to resolve disputes. Nor do politicians sit as members on these boards. Although sporadic water quality reports were released by FREMP in 1994 and 1996, data are sparse and seldom updated on its website (BIEAP–FREMP 2003: 16–17). In 2006, BIEAP posted the first summary and interpretation of all the available water quality data in GVRD in five years (FREMP 2006). However, virtually no data have been available to the public on Burrard Inlet. BIEAP–FREMP normally has inadequate resources to take on this task and GVRD has only recently assumed the responsibility to do this work. The water quality data reported are based on GVRD monitoring, rather than federal or provincial stations. As a consequence of the rigidly enforced policy of secrecy over water quality in the Fraser Estuary, Burrard Inlet, and the Strait of Georgia generally, the populace remains ignorant about regional water quality. Therefore, few in society, with the exception of specialized nongovernmental organizations such as Sierra Legal Defence, have been in a position to comment on shortcomings of this approach to governance and the slow progress in improving and protecting the local environment. Annual reports on water quality have not been made public, nor are they published on the Internet. The scientists, engineers, and other agency members of these two bodies have had a very low level of financial, legislative, and institutional support as they have attempted to stabilize the regional environment at a time of rapid population growth. Given this lack of support for their efforts by the federal and provincial governments, it is amazing that regulators at all levels achieved as much as they have over the past quarter century. Clearly, until widespread public debate occurs regarding the current shortcomings in the environmental management system, steady progress towards sustainable development cannot be expected. More than a quarter century after serious pollution was recognized in the Vancouver area, it is the regional government that has begun to assume the responsibility to establish an integrated monitoring system and protect water quality in the region. This is a very positive development given GVRDs record of openness in dealing with interested publics on environmental issues since the early 1990s.

Georgia Basin Ecosystem Initiative (GBEI). It was not until December 1998 that Canada and British Columbia created an institution comparable in interest and geographic scope to the PSWQ Action Team. In January of 2000, Environment Canada and the B.C. Ministry of Sustainable Resource Management were joined by the Department of Fisheries and Oceans Canada and the B.C. Ministry of Communities to begin planning for the Canadian portion of the shared waters. The initiative's vision is to manage growth to achieve healthy, sustainable ecosystems and communities based on three priorities. These priorities include the enhancement of: air, water, habitats, and species' health; sustainable communities through scientific and knowledge transfers; and human well being through programs to be developed. Water quality, however, has received comparatively little attention to date. Currently, Canadian federal agencies continue their historic approach of seldom engaging a broad range of stakeholders for setting policies and priorities, as well as resolving conflicts in an ongoing attempt to further such an ambitious task as managing the Georgia Basin. Conversely, the province has an impressive record of involving all interested parties in the solution of complex problems beginning in 1992 and continuing to the present time (Frame et al. 2004). In comparison, GBEI is no different than past federal initiatives in both BIEAP and FREMP. The stated intention of permitting public participation at "one meeting per year ... to enable interested pubic, stakeholders, and other levels of government to provide input to the planning process, as well as receive information on progress to date" (Canada and British Columbia 2000: 9) is simply inadequate to achieve the necessary widespread public consensus and support for such an ambitious initiative. This policy needs to be expanded and modernized to include a substantial civic component if the environment is to receive the priority required for rehabilitation and sustainability.

The Georgian Basin Ecosystem Initiative (GBEI) was renamed the Gerogian Basin Action Plan (GBAP) in 2003 and five Coast Salish First Nations were added to the Joint Management Committee as well as to planning and implementation teams. However, no other levels of government, stakeholder groups, or politicians were included in the governance structure and an oversight committee of stakeholders has not been created. A plan to protect and remediate water quality on the British Columbia side of the shared waters with goals, objectives, and priorities to guide future management actions remains an elusive objective (GBAP 2007).

Summary Assessment

While GBEI has only had time to begin initial planning, it faces enormous problems. Perhaps most importantly, like its sister program – BIEAP–FREMP – it has neither a legislated mandate nor a comprehensive council of stakeholders to provide policy advice and thus keep its actions consistent with public goals and objectives. Currently, the program could not be considered adaptive as few long-term data have been collected in the Georgia Basin over the past quarter century. Hopefully, such data collection will become a long-term objective. Its annual funding for the first five years was $5 million. Even when added to the 2001 annual FREMP–BIEAP budget ($783,079) (BIEAP–FREMP 2002: 21), this level of funding is totally inadequate. (Over the past two years, the BIEAP–FREMP budget has been reduced from $783,079 to $280,000). In comparison, the PSWQ action team annual education and public involvement expenditures are more than half of the total budget in British Columbia in equivalent terms during the 2001–2003 biennium budget (WA, PSWQAT 2001: table 3) and its budget was reduced dramatically during this biennium in comparison to earlier years. Indeed, funding in Canada represents only 18 per cent of the Action Team's total annual budget to plan for a larger area, and the Action Team has had this comparatively generous level of funding since 1985. Given the magnitude of problems the initiative faces, the structure and funding for GBEI are inadequate for the task at hand.

Binational Agencies

The Canada–United States *International Joint Commission* (IJC) mandate was restricted to freshwaters under the Boundary Waters Treaty (Canada, United States 1909). Thus, an institution dealing specifically with marine issues at the interface between Canadian and the United States has not evolved. During the 1990s, steps were taken to correct this deficiency.

B.C.-Washington Environmental Cooperation Council (BC-WA ECC). International issues are traditionally considered a responsibility of the federal governments in Canada and the United States. However, given the reluctance of Canadian federal agencies to become involved with binational environmental issues, as recently as the early 1990s, Mike Harcourt, then premier of British Columbia, undertook with the Washington governor, Booth Gardner, to begin cooperating on the solution of shared environmental problems. A binational body was created to address environmental concerns between the state and the province. This body has the potential to deal with transboundary water pollution on rivers as well as other environmental issues, including marine waters, and has taken initial steps to do so. On 7 May 1992, British Columbia and Washington State signed the *Environmental Cooperation Agreement* establishing a framework to foster regional cooperation in environmental protection (British Columbia and Washington State 1992). The agreement created the British Columbia-Washington Environmental Initiative and Council, whose mandate is to promote and coordinate mutual efforts to ensure the protection, preservation, and enhancement of the shared environment for the benefit of current and future generations. Such efforts involve action and information sharing focused on matters of mutual concern, identified by British Columbia and Washington in their preliminary action plan (British Columbia-Washington Environmental Initiative n.d.a). Council members include representatives from the B.C. Ministry of Sustainable Resource Management and the Washington Department of Ecology. In addition, federal representatives from Environment Canada and U.S. EPA have informal observer status.

The council meets semiannually and reports annually to provincial and state officials (British Columbia-Washington Environmental

Initiative n.d.b). Given the limited human resources of the council, it can establish subcommittees to deal with specific matters, or, by formal agreement, establish international task forces to address issues of special, or major, significance. For example, its Georgia Basin–Puget Sound Task force was effective in mobilizing an international effort to investigate the status and trends in habitat, fish, shellfish, marine protected areas, exotic species, toxics, and spills. Within the broader shared basin, additional studies are completed, or underway, on water quality, water availability, groundwater, flooding, wetlands, and regional air quality in the mid-1990s. Many examples of this excellent research may be found in the literature, such as Wilson et al. (1994).

While this initiative is in its infancy in comparison to the IJC, it shows promise. The agreement is enabling, rather than regulatory, and encourages participants to seek solutions to binational problems at the regional level before resorting to federal agencies, the IJC, or higher levels of dispute resolution. The Environmental Cooperation Council filled a major void created by the lack of interest exhibited by Canadian federal agencies and should be maintained to work with federal agencies now that the Canadian federal government has decided to become engaged in binational aspects of the west coast marine environment.

Joint Statement of Cooperation: Georgia Basin–Puget Sound. In June of 2000, Environment Canada entered into an agreement with the U.S. EPA, in effect replicating the agreement between British Columbia and Washington State eight years earlier. It formally recognized existing efforts underway and declared its mandate to confront not only transboundary but also transpacific and global environmental challenges as well. Its immediate tasks in 2001 were identified as air quality, sustainability, and the development of mechanisms of cooperation to deal more effectively with Tribes and First Nations. It has promised to produce an annual action plan and report to the public.

As reported above for GBEI and GBAP, Canadian stakeholder groups and local politicians have little prospect of playing a major, continuing role in creating policy and providing an oversight function under the Joint Statement on Cooperation. Clearly, it is important to ensure continuing federal cooperation on coordinated international management of shared drainages and the marine environment under

GBAP on the west coast. However, before this new institution can become effective, a need exists to open the decision-making system on the Canadian side of the border to a much broader range of stakeholders than are currently involved.

Conclusions and Recommendations

Canada and British Columbia lagged in adopting modern institutions in an effort to stabilize and remediate water quality in the binational Puget Sound-Georgia Basin. There has been a failure to create effective legislation, in which minimum acceptable standards for fresh and marine waters are established as well as goals and objectives for the Canadian waters based on widespread civic participation and continuing public involvement. The development of a system of planning for the shared waters is in its infancy in British Columbia. To date, it has been based on agency preferences, rather than direction from a broad council of stakeholders; no politicians have been assigned to keep abreast of management initiatives. Monitoring reports on ecosystem conditions, including water quality, are not systematically made available to stakeholder groups. Alternative dispute resolution cannot be attempted in such an institutional setting in which a forum has not been created where alternative policy options, management plans, and data are made available to all interested parties as a basis for discussion. Secrecy continues to shroud the management process to the present time. Clearly the Salish Sea, as the shared estuary is known by First Nations, is a low federal priority in Ottawa and provincially in Victoria. And this situation cannot be expected to change until widespread stakeholder involvement is created to garner public support for such a major management initiative as the Georgia Basin Action Plan.

Thus, there is a marked contrast to the four modern institutional systems developed for the Fraser Basin Council in British Columbia, the Land Conservation and Development Commission in Oregon, the Bay Conservation and Development Commission in California, and the U.S.D.A. Forest Service, as well as the legislated and

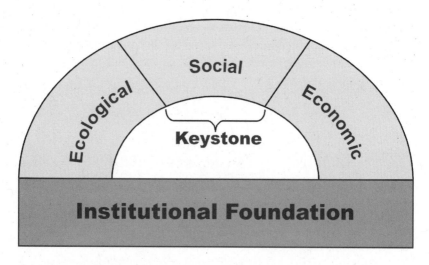

Figure 7.2 The Sustainability Arch: A new paradigm for considering sustainability issues (Source: Calbick 2003).

innovative federal and state arrangements in Puget Sound (Calbick 2003). Collectively, these agencies were used to choose the evaluative criteria by which to judge governance actions in the shared waters. Comparatively, the institutional arrangements adopted on the Canadian side of the Georgia Basin–Puget Sound shared estuary during the 1990s require redesign to be effective. Immediate steps that would assist movement toward environmental remediation and sustainability at all governance levels include the creation of a sustainability framework to guide the development of new institutions. Such an approach explicitly depicts the necessary foundation provided by an institutional framework, as well as the importance of its social aspects. If institutional aspects of a sustainability framework, rather than being expressly identified and defined, are buried in the social dimension, as has traditionally been the case, specific efforts focusing on closing so-called 'institutional gaps' may not be considered, or such efforts may prove inadequate because a problem has not been clearly defined. One such model, the arch of sustainability (fig. 7.2), captures these subtleties, since it clearly emphasizes the social dimension of sustainability, as well as the requisite institutional foundation.

When new, or existing, agencies are being designed or designated for implementing ecosystem-based management regimes, the statute should ensuring policy directions remain clear and concise to avoid confusion and conflict. Furthermore, such a statute should provide jurisdiction over sufficient factors so that the potential of attaining specified objectives is enhanced. Consideration should also be given to the likely effects of proposed legislation on a target population as well as unforeseen consequences for other stakeholders. This type of implementation structure maximizes the probability of compliance from implementing officials and target groups.

The following policies are recommended for consideration in the redesign of relevant institutions on the Canadian side of the shared waters:

- Federal, provincial, and local harmonization agreements, or legislation, are needed for all actions in shared coastal, estuarine, and river basins. These arrangements should include management priorities and shared responsibilities. Consistency should be adopted as a principle to ensure that two levels of government will not compete for the same task and that all monitored data will be published and shared. Given the limited budgets that confront all environmental agencies, inefficiency is no longer an option.
- A council of stakeholders should be created to assist in setting priorities and policies at all stages of Georgia Basin planning and management. This body should operate in an open, civics-based collaborative planning and management manner as exemplified by the five institutions reviewed by Calbick (2003).
- Environmental agencies must be provided with the necessary funds to achieve their mandates. When crafting funding scenarios, consideration should be given to alternate funding sources such as increased permit fees, or retention of financial enforcement penalties, in addition to the traditional source of federal or provincial general revenues. Since budgetary cutbacks are a reality, agencies should cultivate and maintain close associations with decision-makers and special interest groups. Through such linkages, agencies will be better positioned to influence funding decisions. Furthermore, decision-makers must be

informed of all benefits that accrue due to the existence of a program in relation to what may be a comparatively small cost.

- Minimum legislated, legally enforceable water quality standards are needed. Interested publics should play a role in defining both end-of-pipe effluent concentrations, as well as ambient conditions.

- All monitoring data should be made available in an easily understandable form just as FREMP achieved for water quality in 2006. This format should include bad news, as well as good news, on a wide range of environmental parameters. For example, in light of the fact that a variety of government agencies have been responsible for these environments for so many decades, the current situation whereby few water quality data are accessible to interested publics on the Strait of Georgia and within FREMP and BIEAP is unacceptable.

- A new kind of senior manager who is sympathetic to a wide range of environmental values, public involvement, collaborative planning, and openness should be chosen to direct our environmental agencies. To the present time, these qualities have not characterized the federal and provincial agencies in charge of governance of the Georgia Basin. Traditional scientific and technical educational programs are not necessarily the most fertile areas for the new kinds of managerial expertise that will be needed in coming decades when collaborative planning, principle-based negotiation, compromise, and an eclectic perspective will be essential in all planning initiatives.

The adoption of these measures would help in promoting sustainable social, economic, and environmental outcomes in the binational waters of the shared Georgia Basin–Puget Sound. In the meantime, an important experiment has been underway for more than a quarter century in Canada and the United States. Both nations adopted radically different policies for managing their shared waters. Time will reveal which management systems and components are most effective in moving society toward sustainability of the shared waters.

J.C. Day and K.S. Calbick

References

BCFacts.Org. Aug. 2001. *Government Eliminates Anti-Slapp Protections.*
———. April 2002. *Government Allows Vancouver Water Pollution for Another 30 years.*
———. April 2003. *Government to Weaken BC's Main Pollution Act.*
———. May 2003a. *Government Approves Ongoing Raw Sewage Dumping from Victoria.*
———. May 2003b. *Government Invests in Sewage Upgrades.* http://www.bcfacts.org/index.cfm?Group_ID=1014#a1032; accessed: 25 July 2003.
British Columbia and Washington State. 1992. *Environmental Cooperation Agreement Between the Province of British Columbia and the State of Washington.* Victoria, B.C. and Olympia, WA: B.C. Ministry of Environment, Lands and Parks and Washington, Department of Ecology.
British Columbia-Washington Environmental Initiative. n.d.a. *Terms of Reference.* Victoria, BC and Olympia, WA: B.C. Ministry of Environment, Lands and Parks and Washington, Department of Ecology.
———. n.d.b. *Preliminary Action Plan/Work Priorities.* Victoria, BC, and Olympia, WA: B.C. Ministry of Environment, Lands and Parks and Washington, Department of Ecology.
Burrard Inlet Environmental Action Plan (BIEAP) and Fraser Estuary Management Program (FREMP). 2002. *Annual Report: Burrard Inlet Environmental Action Plan, Fraser Estuary Management Program: 2001–2002.* Burnaby, B.C. http://www.bieapfremp.org; accessed: 14 August 2003.
———. 2003. *A Living Working River: The Estuary Management Plan for the Fraser River.* Burnaby, B.C. http://www.bieapfremp.org/fremp/management plan.html; accessed: 14 August 2003.
———. 2005. *Annual Report: Burrard Inlet Environmental Action Plan, Fraser Estuary Management Program: 2004–2005.* Burnaby, B.C. http://www.bieapfremp.org; accessed: 19 April 2006.
Calbick, K.S. 2003. *The Use of Program Theory for Identifying and Evaluating 'Best Practices' for Implementing Land-Use Policies.* Research report 325. Burnaby, B.C.: School of Resource and Environmental Management, Simon Fraser University. http://www. rem.sfu.ca/sustainableplanning.

Canada and British Columbia. 1986a. "Management Committee Formed."
    FREMP Newsletter, no. 1–1. Vancouver.
———. 1986b. "What is FREMP?" *FREMP Newsletter*, no. 1–3. Vancouver.
———. 2000. *Working Together for the Georgia Basin: A Framework for
    Action.* Environment Canada. Fisheries and Oceans Canada. British
    Columbia. Ministry of Environment, Lands and Parks. Ministry of
    Municipal Affairs. NP, 21 November.
Capital Regional District. July 2000. *Core Area Liquid Waste Management
    Plan: Colwood, Langford, Esquimalt, Oak Bay, Victoria, Saanish
    and View Royal.* http://www.crd.bc.ca/es/lwmp/pdf/; accessed:: 29
    August 2003. [This plan was approved by the Province of British
    Columbia in April 2003.]
City of Vancouver. 1999. *Policy Report: Environment.* To Vancouver City
    Council, from General Manager of Engineering Services. CC.
    File No. 3753. 5 October 1999. http://www.city.vancouver.bc.ca/
    ctyclerk/cclerk/991005/p1.htm; accessed: 12 August 2003.
Daykin, Margo M. 1999. *Ecosystem Management – The Institutional
    Challenge: An Analysis of the Burrard Inlet Environmental Action
    Program (BIEAP).* Research report 238. Burnaby, B.C.: School of
    Resource and Environmental Management, Simon Fraser University.
Day, J.C., J. Paul Georgison, and Sandra P. Tippett. 1993. "Coastal
    Management on the West Coast of Canada and the United States:
    Lessons for the Great Lakes," pp. 31–60. In: *Managing the Great
    Lakes Shoreline: Experiences and Opportunities,* ed. P.L. Lawrence
    and J.G. Nelson. Occasional Paper 21. Waterloo, ON: Heritage
    Resources Centre, University of Waterloo.
Frame, Tanis M., Thomas I. Gunton, and J.C. Day. 2004. "The Role
    of Collaborative Planning in Environmental Management: An
    Evaluation of Land and Resource Management Planning in British
    Columbia." *Journal of Environmental Planning and Management*
    47(1): 59–82.
Fraser River Estuary Management Program (FREMP). 2001. *Monitoring
    the Estuary Management Plan.* Burnaby, B.C. (See also www.
    bieapfremp.org.)
———. 2006. *2006 Fraser River Estuary Management Program Monitoring
    Report Update.* Burnaby, B.C. http://www.bieapfremp.org/main_
    fremp.html; accessed: 30 November 2006.
Georgia Basin Action Plan (GBAP). 2007. www.pyr.ec.gc.ca/georgiabasin/
    CoastSalish_e.htm

Greater Vancouver Regional District (GVRD). 2003. *Long-Range Plans: Sewerage*. Burnaby, B.C. http://www.gvrd.bc.ca/sewerage/plans. htm; accessed: 15 August 2003.

Sierra Legal Defence Fund (SLDF). 1999a. *Sewage Charges Raise Capital Stink*. Newsletter no. 22. Vancouver. http://www.sierralegal.org/ newsletter.html; accessed: 30 July 2003.

——. 1999b. *The National Sewage Report Card (Number 2): Rating the Treatment Methods and Discharges of 21 Canadian Cities*. Vancouver. August. http://www.sierralegal.org/.

——. 15 Nov. 2005. "Contaminated Sites Created by Victoria's Sewage."

——. 8 Feb. 2006. "Groups Urging B.C. to Clarify its Stand on CRD Sewage."

U.S. Environmental Protection Agency. Office of Regulations and Standards. 1987. *Clean Water Act of 1977*. Title 33 U.S. Code Service. Sections 1251 et seq. Rochester, NY: Lawyers Cooperative Publishing, and San Francisco: Bancroft-Whitney.

Vancouver Port Authority. 2003a. *Port Vancouver: Media*. (Site accessed: 6 July 2003; www.portvancouver.com/media/port_facts.html)

——. 2003b. *Port Vancouver: Statistics*. http://www.portvancouver.com/ statistics/2002_statistical.html; accessed: 6 July 2003.

Venton, Margot, and John Werring. 11 July 2003. *Tests Reveal High Levels of PCBs in Victoria's Sewage: Group Calls for Immediate Investment in Secondary Treatment*. Sierra Legal Media Releases. Vancouver, BC: Sierra Legal Defence Fund. http://www.sierralegal. org/m_archive/pr03_07__11.html; accessed: 30 July 2003.

Washington. 1985. *Washington Water Quality Authority Act*. Chpt. 90.70 RCW. Olympia, WA.

Washington. Puget Sound Action Team. 2001. *Final Budget for the 2001– 2003 Puget Sound Water Quality Work Plan*. *Puget Sound Online*. http://www.psat.wa.gov/Publications/workplan_01/wp01_index. htm; accessed: 16 October 2003.

Washington. Puget Sound Water Quality Action Team. 2000. *Puget Sound Water Quality Management Plan*. Olympia, WA. http://www.psat. wa.gov/Publications/manplan00/mp_index.htm; accessed: 6 July 2003.

——. 2004. *State of the Sound 2004*. Olympia, WA. http://www.psat. wa.gov/; accessed: 29 November 2006.

Washington. Puget Sound Water Quality Program (PSWQA). 1987. *Puget Sound Water Quality Action Plan*. Olympia, WA.

Wilson, R.C.H., R.J. Beamish, Fran Aitkens, and J. Bell, eds. 1994. *Review of the Marine Environment and Biota of Strait of Georgia, Puget Sound, and Juan de Fuca Strait*. Proceedings of the BC/Washington Symposium on the Marine Environment, 13 and 14 Jan. 1994. Canadian Technical Report of Fisheries and Aquatic Sciences no. 1948. Sponsored by Washington State, Province of British Columbia, and Fisheries and Oceans Canada. Ottawa: Minister of Supply and Services Canada. 398pp.

Wristen, Karen. May 1999. "Canada 'Promised Land' for Polluters?" *Newsletter* no. 22. Vancouver: Sierra Legal Defence Fund. http://www.sierralegal.org/newsletter.html; accessed: 30 July 2003.

8

WATER MANAGEMENT IN THE SAN DIEGO–TIJUANA REGION: WHAT LESSONS CAN BE LEARNED?

José Luis Castro-Ruíz and Vicente Sánchez-Munguía

Abstract

Urban centres located along the U.S.-Mexico border share a set of conditions and problems related to the available water. Despite the proximity of the binational pairs of cities, profound regional dispari-ties exist in the ways that water is managed across the border, which are indicative of a fundamental asymmetry between the systems of governance in each country. These differences present an obstacle for cooperative planning and management at the local and regional level. As water supply becomes the most pressing and complex issue in this region in coming decades, it is important to learn from the accumulating binational experience, so as to define strategies that promote a sustainable water supply for sister cities in both countries. The San Diego–Tijuana region is the most dynamic urban complex along the border and one that faces critical water supply problems.

The aim of this paper is to examine the design and operation of management systems adopted on both sides of the border, as well as institutional constraints within border cities, states, and federal agencies in Mexico and the United States that make it difficult to plan for sustainable water supplies. Such analyses are necessary in order to identify a range of potential options to support a binational policy framework for shared water management.

Introduction

The cities along the U.S.-Mexico border not only share the same physical and climatic characteristics, but also the problems stemming from limited water availability and a growing demand to meet the needs of conflicting urban uses. Concurrently, profound regional disparities exist in the ways that water is managed across the border, which are indicative of a fundamental asymmetry in the systems of governance in each country. Despite the close proximity of most of the thirteen binational city pairs, their historic economic, social, and political differences present difficult obstacles that must be overcome if cooperative local and regional binational water supply initiatives are to be adopted.

Water supply will undoubtedly be one of the most pressing and complex problems faced by the Mexican-U.S. border region in the twenty-first century. However, this challenge offers an opportunity to learn from our mutual experience in an effort to develop sustainable systems of water supply and use. This study examines urban water management in the San Diego–Tijuana region, the most dynamic urban conglomerate along the border, where water supply problems are critical. We compare the current urban water management arrangements in each city, from both institutional and operational perspectives, in search of lessons and efficiencies that may support the establishment of a binational water management system in the future. To do so, we address the following questions: What are the major similarities and differences between the systems on each side of the border at present? What is the current status of binational collaboration in water supply in the region? Can potential efficiencies

José Luis Castro-Ruíz and Vicente Sánchez-Munguía

be identified associated with future collaborative development? If so, what steps need to be taken to develop an integrated, binational, urban water supply system?

The paper is organized into three sections. It begins with a description of the growth that characterizes the U.S. and Mexican border region, with emphasis on the area of study. The natural occurrence of fresh water in Mexico and the current variability of supply as well as the components of the present demand are examined first. Then, we examine the ways water is managed on each side of the border, emphasizing the particularities of service in both countries. The study ends with conclusions and recommendations related to basic policy changes that are necessary to contribute to the development of sustainable binational water management both in the case-study area as well as the shared border environment.

Growth and Water Availability

The historical growth of the urban centres along the border region has brought the water availability issue to the attention of policymakers in each country (fig. 8.1). For the past sixty years, development of the border region was a major objective of the Mexican federal government, based on implementation of programs to promote new industrial activities in the main cities to generate employment. Such programs included fiscal policies designed to stimulate investment in maquiladora industries. Then, during the 1980s, the Mexican border became an economic policy priority in the country.

Over the past twenty years, population growth in Mexican urban areas was considerably higher than in their U.S. counterparts along the U.S.-Mexico border. These growth rates were 1.9 per cent in the United States and 3.6 per cent in Mexico (table 8.1). At the state level, the border populations were concentrated in California and Texas in the United States (78.3% in 2000), and in Baja California, Chihuahua, and Tamaulipas in Mexico (86% in 2000). The proportion of the population on the Mexican side increased from 42.5 to 46.7 per cent of the total border population between 1980 and 2000 (based on data in table 8.1). The San Diego–Tijuana conurbation

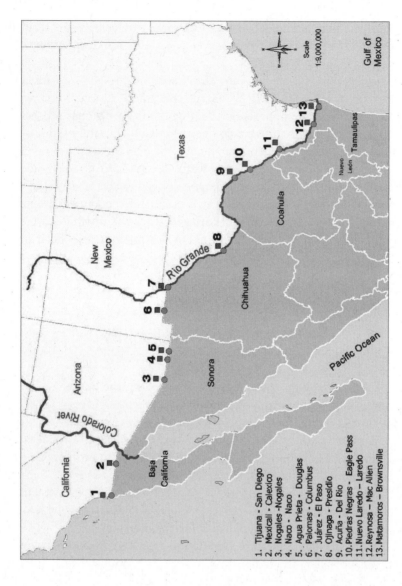

1. Tijuana - San Diego
2. Mexicali - Calexico
3. Nogales -Nogales
4. Naco - Naco
5. Agua Prieta - Douglas
6. Palomas - Columbus
7. Juárez - El Paso
8. Ojinaga - Presidio
9. Acuña - Del Rio
10. Piedras Negras - Eagle Pass
11. Nuevo Laredo – Laredo
12. Reynosa – Mac Allen
13. Matamoros – Brownsville

Figure 8.1 Main city pairs along the U.S.–Mexico border

Table 8.1 Population along the U.S.-Mexico Border, 1980–2000.

AREA	1980	1990	2000	ANNUAL GROWTH RATES 1990–2000 (%)
Border Total	6,976,694	9,103,319	11,797,954	2.63
U.S. Subtotal	4,009,151	5,213,774	6,286,194	1.89
California	1,953,956	2,607,319	2,956,194	1.26
Arizona	728,142	914,919	1,159,828	2.40
New Mexico	117,974	159,978	205,630	2.54
Texas	1,209,079	1,531,958	1,964,517	2.52
Mexico Subtotal	2,967,543	3,889,545	5,511,785	3.55
Baja California	1,002,459	1,400,873	2,053,217	3.90
Sonora	312,079	394,712	515,979	2.72
Chihuahua	635,490	869,951	1,294,214	4.05
Coahuila	151,623	191,135	263,885	3.28
Nuevo León	16,475	17,312	18,524	0.68
Tamaulipas	849,417	1,015,562	1,365,966	3.01

Sources: Peach and Williams (2000): 40; México (2000); U.S. Bureau of the Census (2000).

experienced even faster growth than the rest of the border and the Tijuana municipal population increased at more than four times the rate of San Diego County (table 8.2).

Population forecasts made by some specialists for the U.S.-Mexican border region suggest a total population of 24 million for the year 2020, at the growth rates during the 1990–95 period. The corresponding shares are 10,671,054 for the U.S. side and 13,427,748 for the Mexican side (Peach and Williams 2000: 50). A second scenario, based on more moderate growth rates, estimates a population of 19,460,216 on both sides of the border with 8,957,026 on the U.S. side, and 10,503,187 in Mexico (ibid.: 53). In both cases, the population on the Mexican side is predicted to be larger than its U.S counterpart, representing an addition of 13,500,000 and 8,875,000 inhabitants respectively to the whole border region.

Table 8.2 Border Population California-Baja California, 1980–2000.

Area	1980	1990	2000	Annual Growth Rates 1990–2000 (%)
COUNTIES:				
San Diego	1,861,846	2,498,061	2,813,833	1.20
Imperial	92,110	109,303	142,361	2.68
Subtotal California	1,953,956	2,607,319	2,956,194	1.26
MUNICIPALITIES:				
Tijuana	461,256	747,379	1,210,820	4.94
Tecate	30,540	51,556	77,795	4.20
Mexicali	510,663	601,938	764,602	2.42
Subtotal Baja California	1,002,459	1,400,873	2,053,217	3.90

Sources: Peach and Williams (2000): 59–60; México (2000); U.S. Bureau of the Census (2000).

Such an increase would double the demand for water in the domestic sector, with a corresponding requirement for investment in infrastructure and service levels.

Under the previous growth scenarios, urban systems such as Tijuana-Rosarito-Tecate in Baja California, and Reynosa–Rio Bravo–Matamoros in Tamaulipas would tend to coalesce into metropolitan conglomerates. Also, the mutual interaction between the binational pairs of cities along the border is expected to be reinforced. These conditions would create specific challenges for the governments, in turn, to organize and manage efficiently land uses, public services, and environmental preservation.

The San Diego–Tijuana region has an extreme desert climate and scarce rainfall (fig. 8.2). These conditions define an initial panorama of limited water resources to meet the urban and rural demand on both sides of the border. The historical trends of population growth have made the entire region highly dependent on imported water to assure the needed volumes. In this context, the Colorado River represents today the only reliable source to meet the demand from the different sectors in the long run. However, this resource is also under pressure not only by the other U.S. states that claim rights over it, but other cities in California that are also serviced by the Metropolitan Water District (MWD). Recently, California lost a long-standing right to water from the Colorado River and a complex series of adjustments are currently underway in urban water supply for the Coachella Valley and the Los Angeles–San Diego corridor.

Water Management in a Binational Region

Differing legal frameworks on each side of the border have created important differences in the way that urban water systems operate in the San Diego–Tijuana area. In the U.S., the law recognizes property rights to the resource, under certain limits and modes of use. At the federal level, water legislation in the United States evolved under two premises. The first, which guided the corresponding policies during the second part of the nineteenth century and the early years of the twentieth, considers the water as a resource which may be exploited, either as a means for navigation (*Rivers and Harbors Act*, 1899), for irrigation (*Reclamation Act*, 1902), or for power generation (*Federal Water Power Act*, 1920). This period was characterized by the development of the country's water resources. The second principle has to do with the laws expressly developed to regulate water quality and environmental protection. Though the first legal efforts to control water quality occurred in 1948 (*Water Quality Act*), it was not until the 1960s and 1970s that the first environmental protection laws began to appear. The instruments approved to meet these objectives were grouped into two categories: those focused on water quality, such as the *Clean Water Act* of 1977, and those dealing indirectly with different water problems, such as the *Comprehensive Environmental Response, Compensation, and Liability Act* of 1980. Such characteristics are established by every state in the country. Most American states have agencies that operate as counterparts to federal programs. Water quality control agencies, which work closely with the Environmental Protection Agency (EPA), are examples. A *public authority* is created to be responsible for urban water management in Anglo-Saxon countries; this concept refers to a form of government organization widely used in the United States and other Anglo-Saxon countries throughout the twentieth century to administer a variety of services (Mitchel 1992: 1–13).

In contrast to the American case, Mexican law bestows property rights to water on the federal government. Article 27 of the Mexican Constitution establishes the principles of property and control by the nation over its natural resources, including water. Access by individuals and other sectors to those resources is established through permits. In the case of water, the *Law of National Waters* (1992), and its subsequent 2003 and 2004 modifications, represent the legal instrument that provides the guidelines for the use and management of water resources in Mexico. This law confers on the National Water Commission (CNA) the sole capacity to implement its precepts, which include – among others – the formulation of the National Water Program, the development of both potable water and sewage systems at the local level, water reuse, issuing of water permits, administration of the public registry of water rights, and the promotion of efficient water uses (Téllez 1993: 107). When it comes to water management for urban uses, local and state governments invoke the constitutional principles (article 115) that bestow on them the responsibility for such services at the local levels.

In the case of Baja California, the agencies that operate water services have evolved toward more dynamic, managerial-type bodies that resemble their American counterparts more than traditional Mexican agencies. This concept is particularly appealing in the present Latin American context, where neoliberal political and academic actors are attempting to improve the efficiency of the water systems in an effort to meet the rapidly growing urban demand for water.

The City of San Diego

San Diego County depends on water imports from Northern California and the Colorado River for 90 per cent of its urban needs (fig. 8.2; table 8.3). This water is purchased by the San Diego County Water Authority (SDCWA), and then conveyed to its twenty-three member agencies responsible for water services at the urban level. The City of San Diego, by far the largest consumer of water from the SDCWA, provides water and sewage services through two agencies: the Water Department (SDWD), which is responsible for meeting the demand of all urban users, and the Metropolitan Wastewater Department (SDMWD), which is in charge of wastewater collection and treatment. During 2001, SDWD serviced a population of 1,277,168 in urban and contiguous rural areas. In addition to the residential sector, which accounts for 57 per cent of the total water demand, other uses include industry and commerce (13%), agriculture and irrigation (19%), public and other uses (10%), as well as users of treated wastewater such as golf courses and public parks and gardens (1%).

In recent years, the search for long-term solutions to meet water demand has been one of the main priorities of the county's water authority and its member agencies. In 1998, the SDCWA began talks with the Imperial Irrigation District (IID) for an annual transfer of 200,000 acre-feet during a forty-five-year period, with the possibility of an extension for another thirty years. The agreement to secure that water was finally accomplished on October 2003 (www.iid.com/water/transfer.html).

A second agreement with the MWD will deliver another 77,000 acre-feet to the authority's jurisdiction once the lining of the All American Canal in Imperial Valley is completed. These agreements created an important degree of certainty for the different agencies and actors depending on the support of the SDCWA.

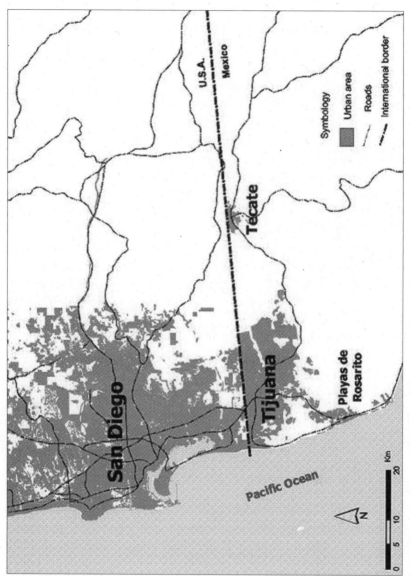

Figure 8.2 The Tijuana-San Diego Border Region.

José Luis Castro-Ruíz and Vicente Sánchez-Munguía

Table 8.3 San Diego County Water Sources, 2001–2002.

IMPORTED WATER (MWD)	VOLUME IMPORTED	%	% OF MWD SUPPLY
Colorado River	504,207 AF	73	
State Water Project	146,488 AF	27	
Total	650,695 AF	100	90
LOCAL SOURCES			
Surface water	39,380 AF	55	
Reclamation/Brackish Groundwater	13,693 AF	19	
Wells	12,435 AF	18	
Desalination	5,449 AF	8	
TOTAL	70,957 AF	100	10

Source: San Diego County Water Authority (2002). Annual Report 2001–2002.

Other options considered by the SDCWA to complement the transfers of water in the future include the recycling of wastewater, desalination, and groundwater recharge. In the later case, it is estimated that, between 2002 and 2020, recycling of tertiary treated sewage in the county will increase from 8.6 to 121.3 MGD, thus securing the reliance of member agencies on this type of alternative source (Brown et al. 2003).

Tijuana and Rosarito

The region comprising the cities of Tijuana and Playas de Rosarito is highly dependent on imported water to serve its needs. Unlike San Diego, however, the Colorado River represents the only reliable source for these cities, providing 90 per cent of their supply through the Colorado River–Tijuana Aqueduct (ARCT). Most surface streams in Baja California are short and seasonal and remain dry most of the year. This situation leaves the Colorado River as the basis of future plans of the agencies that manage water at the local level. The state receives an annual quota of 1.5 million ÁF by virtue of the 1944 International Treaty between Mexico and the United States. Approximately 81,070 AF are assigned by CNA and the state's water agency through ARCT to the cities of Tecate and Tijuana in the west.

The total supply available also includes local groundwater sources (table 8.4). The municipal agency in charge of water and sewage services is the State Commission of Public Services for Tijuana (CESPT), a state-owned entity whose functions are sanctioned by an administrative board headed by the Governor of Baja California and includes representatives of the public and private sectors in the city. The State Commissions of Public Services (CESP's) are the agencies responsible for the services at the municipal level. Their origins go back to 1954, when Baja California acquired statehood. That same year an *Urban Planning Law* was enacted to meet urban infrastructure needs. In the case of potable water and sewage services, the implementation of this law required the creation of the *Juntas Federales de Agua Potable y Alcantarillado* for each urban district. Tijuana's junta evolved into the current CESPT in 1961 (Castro and Sánchez 2000). As part of its operation, CESPT maintains a close relationship with the State Commission of Water Services (COSAE) that intervenes at the state level in the purchase of water from the National Water Commission (CNA). Another agency, the State Water Commission (CEA), provides planning support from the state government.

Table 8.4 Water Sources for Tijuana and Playas de Rosarito, 2001.

IMPORTED WATER	VOLUME IMPORTED	%	% OF CESPT SUPPLY
ARCT	80,097 AF		94
LOCAL SOURCES			
Surface Water (Abelardo L. Rodríguez Dam)	973 AF	21	
Tijuana River wells	1,865 AF	40	
La Misión wells	1,297 AF	28	
Rosarito wells	567 AF	11	
TOTAL	4,702 AF	100	6

Source: Comisión Estatal de Servicios Públicos de Tijuana (2003).

Despite the previous trends, the current challenges faced by CESPT are substantial when compared with its counterpart in San Diego. Most local and state agencies in Mexico are powerless to meet the growing demand for water and sewage services. In Tijuana, service levels are continuously pressed by high in-migration rates. During 2001, CESPT reported service levels of 94.6 per cent for potable water and 79 per cent for sewage. The treatment level of wastewaters was close to 50 per cent during the same year. On November 30, 1995, the municipality of Playas de Rosarito was created from Tijuana's territory, but no agency was created to service the water infrastructure demands of the newly formed entity, leaving CESPT with the responsibility.

The case of CESPT has become quite unique within the national context. During the second half of the 1980s, Baja California became the first state with an opposition government in Mexican history. Subsequent administrations have worked to strengthen a rather unique management model based on entrepreneurial principles. These included improvement of the internal flows of information and decision-making processes, an accountability relationship with the users, better response in contingency situations, and an incipient long-range planning project. Over time, these conditions enabled the agency to become one of the most efficient in the country.

One major difference that exemplifies the asymmetric framework of operation of water systems in the San Diego–Tijuana region is reflected by economic and political factors that restrict planning activities of the later. In this context, the perspectives to meet the demand for the next fifteen or twenty years continue to be based mainly on higher volumes of water conveyed from the Colorado River. Other alternatives such as wastewater reuse, water desalination, or the implementation of programs to educate the public about efficient methods of water use have not as yet advanced beyond the conceptual level in planning documents. Their reality has yet to involve a long process of operational changes, with heavy capital investment to improve the current infrastructure. Education, pricing, and new technologies are also urgently needed to increase the efficiency of water use.

Binational Cooperation

Despite the obvious asymmetry that characterizes water management on both sides of the border in the study region, the process of binational integration was slow to develop and is a recent development. These endeavours originated primarily from concerned groups outside government, and they evolved into more inclusive organizations including representatives and actors from both sides of the border. In the early 1990s, the Extension Division at the University of California, San Diego, promoted an initiative to address different problems in the San Diego region. Eventually, key actors and groups from Tijuana were also included in the discussions. In 1996 the San Diego Association of Governments (SANDAG) supported an innovative project to address the region's problems from a binational perspective: the creation of the Committee on Binational Regional Opportunities (COBRO), a consulting body that exchanges regional information based on a binational agenda of mutual interests. The participation of the Consuls General of the United States and Mexico in COBRO has provided a supportive framework to promote the legitimacy of this body's activities. COBRO has sponsored an annual conference on issues of major binational concerns, beginning with water in 1997. COBRO's operations rely, in turn, on two instruments: the Border Liaison Mechanism (BLM), a formal vehicle for binational cooperation, and the Border Water Council (BWC). This institution originated in 1997 from the need for transborder cooperation and regional water concerns (Brown et al. 2003). The BLM convenes local actors from all levels of government on both sides of the border to address shared concerns (Ganster and Sánchez 1999: 48). The BWC functions with the binational water authorities in the region – the San Diego County Water Authority and CESPT – as cochairs, and it has been active in searching for new options to convey water from the Mexicali and Imperial valleys to Tijuana and San Diego, in line with the principles of Minute No. 301 of the International Boundary and Water Commission to make more information available on the water supply options for the region.

The Tijuana River watershed (TRW) has been a key component of binational cooperation in the San Diego–Tijuana region. This 1,758 square mile watershed, two-thirds of which is in Mexico (fig. 8.2), embraces a wide range of topography, climates, biological resources, land uses, and social-political institutions. More than 1 million people live within the limits of the TRW, in political jurisdictions that include the County of San Diego, the City of San Diego, the City of Imperial Beach, several Native American reservations, and the municipalities of Tijuana, Tecate, and Ensenada in Mexico.

In recent years it has been the locus of a variety of binational efforts conducted by actors and organizations on both sides of the border. Since 1994, over a dozen projects have been carried out by different institutions, including El Colegio de la Frontera Norte (COLEF), which developed a GIS for the watershed and its use in community outreach, education, and scientific research (Brown et al. 2003). North of the border, San Diego State University (SDSU) sponsored the Binational Vision Project for TRW to address different environmental and social problems in the watershed. This project has promoted the organization of a Binational Watershed Advisory Council (BWAC) to identify stakeholders from various sectors to provide views on the ideal state of the watershed in the near and distant future (http://trw.sdsu.edu).

What Lessons Can Be Learned?

We have examined the forms of water management that coexist in the San Diego–Tijuana region. Although this case may be unique at the transborder level, given the characteristics and size of the urban areas on each side of the border, our preliminary analysis allows us to advance some reflections in the context of viable binational cooperation scenarios for the shared management of the water resources between Mexico and the United States. In this sense, there are two elements that cannot be ignored in our discussion: the regional, associated with our case study, and the border region as a whole.

Regional Policy Implications. Profound regional disparities exist in the ways that water is managed across the border, which are indicative of a fundamental asymmetry between the systems of governance in each country. These differences complicate collaboration in water planning and management within the binational region. Despite the relative progress made by the responsible agency in Tijuana and Playas de Rosarito, its slow evolution in developing and implementing comprehensive plans for sustainable water management on the Mexican side of the border makes full cooperation with its counterpart agencies in San Diego improbable at best, and perhaps impossible. This agency exemplifies the persistence of traditional institutional structures in Mexico that affect the operational efficiency of most systems (table 8.5). These conditions impede, rather than promote, innovation and favour personnel with no professional training in comprehending and developing the range of social and economic measures that will be required to move toward more sustainable, long-term solutions. They also inhibit the ability to constrain and direct growth within the region so as to recognize physical and economic limits. Indeed, these same constraints affect water management throughout the country as a whole.

Table 8.5 Major Differences in the Urban Water and Sewage Systems along the U.S.-Mexico Border.

CHARACTERISTICS OF RESPONSIBLE AGENCY	U.S.	MEXICO
Legal/structural characteristics	Public; entrepreneurial management; public authority	Public; bureaucratic, politicized management
Organization	Professional	Traditional[a]
Managing staff appointment criteria	Professional capabilities/ experience	Political: affiliation to a political party/personal relationships
Political head of the organization	City mayor	State governor
Management autonomy	Comprehensive	None
Recruitment method	Civil service	Union/personal relationships
Internal environment in the organization	Stable	Unstable[b]
Financial capacity	Adequate	Limited
Planning capacity	Comprehensive; long-term	Limited; medium-term
Social participation	Representative, comprehensive	Corporate type; limited
Current water service coverage	100%	85–95%
Service quality	Excellent/very good	Unsatisfactory
Current priorities	Long-range project consolidation and integration	Project development to meet current service coverage; working on long-term plans

Source: Castro and Sanchez (2003).
a. This refers to the long-established post-revolutionary model still present in many public organizations in Mexico.
b. This relates to the absence of clear rules on the permanence of professional staff in the organization.

Water management under guidelines that explicitly establish the efficiency and financial autonomy as an objective of the responsible agency is an incipient process in Mexican cities. Even the largest metropolises, whose growth and related problems monopolized the attention of the central government half a century ago, were characterized as rather elementary management models, which basically emphasized the immediate needs created by rapidly growing water demand. It was not until the 1970s that new federal legislation explicitly recognized the importance that urban water uses had for the country's future development. Subsequently, institutional changes were made in response to the development models currently in use, as well as the growing global concern for the sustainable use of the natural resources and preservation of ecosystems. Despite these tendencies, operational changes have been introduced slowly by most agencies at the local level in the country, due mainly to the persistence of obsolete and inefficient management methods. Indeed, the border Mexican cities are not isolated from these constraints (table 8.5). Against this backdrop, the innovation process adopted by Tijuana emerges as a unique model that can be considered as a beginning step forward by other governments and agencies throughout Mexico as they consider reforms to modernize Mexican water and sewage systems. And along the border with our U.S. neighbours, it is of utmost importance that this knowledge be transmitted to cities with antiquated, inefficient systems of governance if Mexico is to contemplate binational cooperation based on the joint management of our shared water resources.

Another aspect that needs to be emphasized about the San Diego–Tijuana case refers to its history of binational collaboration projects to address the region's issues, particularly water availability. This experience should be a clear indication of the necessity to involve nongovernmental sectors in the solution of regional problems. Unfortunately, it has mainly been organizations and groups in San Diego that have undertaken these initiatives. The participation of representatives from Tijuana has been rather uneven and based more on the existence of social networks than on social recognition of the importance of civic participation. Federal and state governments have not formally recognized and supported participation in such efforts yet, given the rigid, narrow, institutional framework that continues to exist in Mexico. Still, the Tijuana–San Diego process has

José Luis Castro-Ruíz and Vicente Sánchez-Munguía

led to the existence of a group of actors on both sides of the border that share a basic degree of information from which to maintain a continuous search for shared solutions to the region's water needs.

Clearly, binational cooperation to develop a sustainable water future for the region must be promoted by Mexicans as well as their counterparts in California, even in the absence of an explicit need on the part of San Diego to take part in such a project. While for Mexico the benefits of this option are clear, a solid argument is still needed to persuade American counterparts of the benefits that such collaboration would bring to the region as a whole. Indeed, Southern California is not entirely immune from unexpected water shortages in the long run, given recent drought conditions in the region and the potential for growing intrastate conflict over the water from the Colorado River. Situations like those raise fundamental questions related to long-term policy options associated with the choice of agricultural or metropolitan water districts as the preferred alternative to meet the future demand of the cities.

There are advantageous conditions already in place that should be nurtured and extended which will require an integrated approach by all levels of government working cooperatively with nongovernmental bodies to make them workable. In cases of other city pairs along the border, such conditions may exhibit a wide range of scenarios, so that the potential to generate binational cooperation initiatives will probably be based, at least in part, on the knowledge and support of existing arrangements in the largest cities. One potential asset in a context of future options for the region might be San Diego's role in providing technological support to promote water reuse on both sides of the border. This strategy is already being considered by the SDCWA member agencies in their long-run plans, and its development could eventually benefit their Mexican counterparts. Another relevant problem relates to water contamination on the Mexican side, which represents a significant threat to water availability everywhere in this region. In this respect the participation of San Diego could be instrumental in advancing technological solutions that would benefit the entire binational community. An ideal plan of cooperation will also require a more flexible, integrated Mexican governmental framework to promote sustained participation of Mexican NGOs and related decision-making processes.

To date, Mexican government institutions have maintained a rigid format when it comes to dealing with binational affairs at the local level, based on the legal documents that sustain them. This structure leaves the responsibility for any matter related to binational relationships, whether national or local in nature, in the hands of agencies such as the Comisión Internacional de Limites y Aguas (CILA), the Mexican counterpart of the IBWC in the United States. In effect, CILA deals only with the federal mandate in each country, leaving local governments little potential to intervene. Conversely, other agencies that were created to remedy the need for binational cooperation, such as the Border Environmental Cooperation Commission (BECC) and the North American Development Bank (NAD-Bank), do consider local input as part of their operational guidelines, but their capacity to promote binational interlocal communication is limited. However, it is imperative that, in future, both governmental and nongovernmental actors combine their interests without compromising the normative rules of the former. A successful illustration of this kind of scenario exists in the search for solutions to air quality problems of the Juarez–El Paso region by the *Paso del Norte Air Quality Task Force* (PDNAQTF) (Castro and Sanchez 2003). One desirable quality of the PDNAQ Task Force relates to its capacity to combine both governmental and nongovernmental concerns with the aim of developing a transboundary air-quality district that attempts to reduce contamination levels throughout the binational region. The project included the creation of a *Joint Advisory Committee on Air Quality Improvement* for the region under the guidelines of the La Paz Agreement, thus assuring federal recognition for the objectives of the plan. The successful aspects of PDNAQTF led to the adoption of a similar initiative to consider problematic water management issues in the Juarez–El Paso region. In this case, the Paso del Norte Water Task Force (PNWTF) has faced quite a different set of circumstances due to the complexity of factors involved in both the supply and demand for water. Despite this, PDNAQTF creates interesting elements that are relevant in the context of this discussion of border water sustainability issues.

Border Region Policy Implications. In examining why binational cooperation has generally achieved limited success in resolving Mexican-U.S. border environmental problems, Sánchez (2003: 53) attributed this outcome to the fact that most binational actions have not responded to the needs of Mexican border communities. This is because binational actions tend to respond to political pressure from groups in the United States and media attention to environmental problems at the border, rather than adhering to a comprehensive long-term strategy. Further, the managerial approach used in the design of binational programs creates a fragmented perspective of environmental issues that isolates problems from their structural causes and their social and economic consequences. Generally, the inability of Mexican border cities to keep pace with the need for urban infrastructure at a time of rapid population growth is strongly related to the absence of adequate financing. Resources provided to municipalities by the central government are only 4 per cent of the federal budget and barely enough to pay employees' salaries, with little left for construction of new facilities. The needs of border municipalities have not been high on the federal agenda. Sánchez (2003: 66) advocated a new approach to binational cooperation involving alternative development strategies based explicitly on border community needs. In a related argument, Levesque and Ingram (2003: 178) suggested that governments in both countries must increase the capacity of grassroots actors involved in environmental management to both mobilize and act effectively in the political arena, as well as fostering binational linkages among all stakeholders in both countries to work together.

Water, as with other environmental issues along the U.S.-Mexico border, does not recognize international boundaries. Any problem arising from its use, such as the overexploitation of aquifers or the contamination produced by wastewaters on one side, frequently ends up affecting communities in the other country. Therefore the search for solutions requires an integrated approach, where the concurrence of many agencies and other affected stakeholders becomes essential. A number of scholars have observed the multitude of interactions that currently take place along the U.S.-Mexico border in spite of the structural asymmetries that separate both societies (Bustamante 1981; Herzog 1990; Alegría 1992). Thus, border communities are conceptually different in the sense that they have rich and up-to-date knowledge of their counterparts in the other country. This heightened level of understanding represents a base from which to construct the kinds of innovative transboundary relationships for water supply and sewage management discussed in this paper.

References

Alegría, Tito. 1992. *Desarrollo urbano en la frontera México-Estados Unidos*. Mexico City: Consejo Nacional para la Cultura y las Artes.

Binational Watershed Advisory Council. http://www.trw.sdsu.edu.

Brown, Christopher, Jose Luis Castro-Ruiz, Nancy Lowery, and Richard Wright. 2003. "Comparative Analysis of Transborder Water Management Strategies: Case Studies on the U.S.-Mexican Border," pp. 279–362. In *The U.S.-Mexican Border Environment: Binational Water Management Planning*, ed. Suzanne Michele. SCERP Monograph Series no. 8. San Diego: San Diego State University Press.

Bustamante, Jorge A. 1981. "La interacción social en la frontera México-Estados Unidos: un marco conceptual para la investigación," pp. 26–46. In *La Frontera del Norte. Integración y Desarrollo*, Roque González (comp.). Ciudad de México: El Colegio de México.

Castro, José Luis, and Vicente Sanchez. 2000. "Descentralización y eficiencia operativa: los servicios de agua potable y alcantarillado en Baja California." *Estudios Sociales* 10(19): 119–38. [Hermosillo, Sonora, México: Universidad Autónoma de Sonora].

———. 2003. "Binational Relationship and Water Supply in Mexican Border Cities: Challenges and Opportunities." Paper presented at the 27–29 March 2003 meeting of the Latin American Studies Association (LASA). Dallas, TX.

Comisión Estatal de Servicios Públicos de Tijuana. 2003. *Plan Maestro de Agua Potable y Saneamiento en los Municipios de Tijuana y Playas de Rosarito*. Tijuana, B.C. (CD-ROM).

Ganster, Paul, and Roberto A. Sanchez. 1999. *Sustainable Development in the San Diego-Tijuana Region*. Discussion papers prepared for a binational community forum. San Diego: Center for U.S.-Mexican Studies, University of California.

Herzog, Lawrence A. 1990. *Where North Meets South: Cities, Space, and Politics on the U.S.-Mexico Border*. Austin: Center for Mexican American Studies, University of Texas.

Imperial Irrigation District. http://www.iid.com/water/transfer.html.

Levesque, Suzanne, and Helen Ingram. 2003. "Lessons in Transboundary Resource: Management from Ambos Nogales," pp. 161–82. In *Transboundary Environmental management Issues Facing Mexico and the United States*, ed. Linda Fernandez and Richard T. Carson. Boston: Kluwer.

México, 2000. *Population Census 2000.* Instituto Nacional de Estadística, Geografía e Informatica.

Mitchel, Jerry. 1992. "Policy Functions and Issues for Public Authorities," pp. 1–13. In *Public Authorities and Public Policy: The Business of Government,* ed. Jerry Mitchel. New York: Praeger.

Paso del Norte Water Task Force. http://www.sharedwater.org.

Peach, James, and James Williams. 2000. "Population and Economic Dynamics of the U.S.-Mexican Border: Past, Present, and Future," pp. 37–72. In *The U.S.-Mexican Border Environment: A Road Map to Sustainable 2020,* ed. Paul Ganster. SCERP Monograph Series, no. 1. San Diego: Southwest Center for Environmental Research and Policy (SCERP), San Diego State University.

Sánchez, Roberto A. 2003. "Binational Cooperation and the Environment at the U.S.-Mexico Border: A Mexican Perspective," pp. 53–71. In *Transboundary Environmental Management Issues Facing Mexico and the United States,* ed. Linda Fernandez and Richard T. Carson. Boston: Kluwer.

San Diego County Water Authority. 2002. *Annual Report 2001–2002.* San Diego, Ca.

Téllez, L. 1993. *Nueva legislación de tierras, bosques y aguas.* Ciudad de México: Fondo de Cultura Económica.

U.S. Bureau of the Census. 2000. *Population Census 2000.*

U.S. Congress. *Rivers and Harbors Act,* 1899.

———. *Reclamation Act,* 1902.

———. *Federal Water Powers Act,* 1920.

———. *Water Quality Act,* 1948.

———. *Clean Water Act,* 1970.

———. *Comprehensive Environmental Response, Compensation, and Liability Act,* 1980.

9

HIDDEN WATERS: THE ROLE OF LOCAL COMMUNITIES IN TRANSBOUNDARY ENVIRONMENTAL MANAGEMENT ACROSS THE FORTY-NINTH PARALLEL

Emma Spenner Norman and Jean O. Melious

Abstract

This study investigates the ability of organizations, at different geo-political scales, to reduce pollution inputs across a political border. Based on a study of the Abbotsford-Sumas aquifer, the nature of shared resource management problems within two divergent cultural regions are investigated in western Washington and southern British Columbia, bisected by the Canada-U.S. border. Coordinated management of a number of organizations is quantified through the development of an index system that ranks the groups according to their "institutional capacity." Groups with the least geographic representation such as the Abbotsford Sumas Stakeholder Group and the Industry Stewardship Group had the greatest ability to reduce pollution. The groups' success relied on their ability to receive political support, but not directives, while maintaining a strong community focus. Community-based success was largely contingent on supporting scientific research on specific questions by senior government agencies in both countries. This new knowledge allowed local stakeholders to reach consensus on what problems needed to be resolved so that mutually acceptable binational solutions to environmental problems were attainable.

Introduction

A discussion of border bioregions and coastal corridors of North America would be incomplete without analysis of one of the least visible environmental issues: groundwater pollution. Groundwater pollution follows the familiar "out of sight, out of mind" adage, where, even in the best of circumstances, it is difficult to raise awareness of issues that are invisible to the human eye. This study evaluates an issue that is complex not only because of transboundary complications, but also because of the literally invisible nature of the resource in question.

The spatial scale of this study area is confined to the limits of the Abbotsford-Sumas aquifer, which underlies a portion of the Canada-U.S. border in western Washington State and British Columbia (fig. 9.1). It investigates the ability of organizations at a variety of geopolitical scales to reduce groundwater pollutants from moving across an international boundary. This aquifer has been the focus of local, provincial/state, and federal attention over the past decade and significant steps have been made towards reducing pollution inputs into the aquifer. This progress, which has been slow and incremental, has involved industry organizations, nonprofit groups, and agencies on many levels of government, including the transboundary level.

This study is based on a system designed to measure the institutional capacity of these actors. The index system quantifies the level of cooperation among groups working to solve shared transboundary pollution issues, incorporating qualitative information based on interviews, written correspondence, archival research, meeting and conference participation, and a review of relevant literature. The index serves as an indicator of two underlying factors: the effectiveness of different groups' participation in transboundary pollution reduction efforts, and the overall effectiveness of efforts to reduce pollution entering the aquifer. A review of the historical events that led to the cross-border cooperation of the aquifer augments the discussion of the index.

The Study Area

The 100-square-mile (260-square-kilometre) Abbotsford-Sumas aquifer provides drinking water for more than 60,000 people (Washington State. Department of Ecology 2005) on both sides of the border. The aquifer is used by rural and urban dwellers in the towns of Lynden, Everson, Nooksack, and Sumas in Whatcom County, Washington, and in Abbotsford, British Columbia, during the summer months when surface water is limited.

The bioregion of the study area is characterized by a low-lying floodplain surrounded by the Northern Cascades mountains. It is an agricultural area that is rapidly urbanizing, especially in British Columbia. Recent studies (Almasri and Jagath 2004; Almasri and Kaluarachchi 2004; Zebarth et al. 1998; Wasenaar 1995; USGS 1999) have shown that agricultural sources are the primary cause of elevated nitrate concentrations in the aquifer. In particular, the leaching of manure from dairy farms in Washington and poultry farms in British Columbia is a main source of nitrate pollution in the aquifer. The application of manure to fertilize raspberry fields is another source of nitrate leaching (Zebarth et al. 1998).

The aquifer is particularly susceptible to such contamination because it is close to the surface and lacks a barrier to nutrients. The aquifer is "unconfined," or located in loose, unconfined soil, with the water table no more than fifteen feet (0–5 metres) below the surface at the edges of the aquifer. In the central portion, the water table descends to a maximum of a hundred feet (30 metres) below the surface. The pollution problem associated with high nitrate concentrations

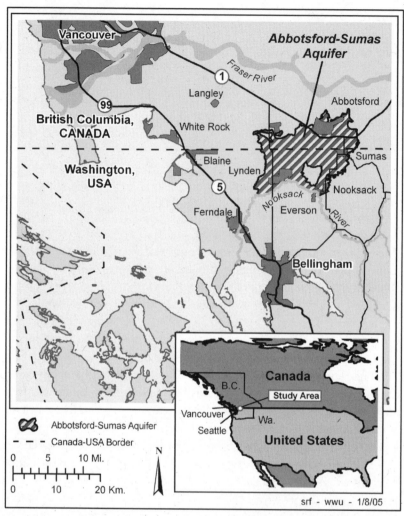

Figure 9.1 The Canada-U.S. Border bisecting the Abbotsford-Sumas Aquifer.

Emma Spenner Norman and Jean O. Melious

is compounded by high annual rainfall, which leads to rapid infiltration of nitrates through the soil. Profligate irrigation practices and increasing intensification of dairy farms further exacerbate the pollution problem (USGS 1999).

Due to high nitrate concentrations, the water quality of the Abbotsford-Sumas aquifer does not meet acceptable levels for drinking water. Both Canadian and American drinking water standards limit nitrates to ten parts per million, expressed as ten milligrams per litre in Canada (Washington State. Department of Health 1999: 29; Hii et al. 1999). Studies (Almasri and Jagath 2004, Almasri and Kaluarachchi 2004; British Columbia. Ministry of Environment 1999; USGS 1999) indicate that better control of the application of agricultural wastes to farmland will help to improve water quality and that a decrease in nitrate leaching is crucial to maintaining the quality of the aquifer. Efforts to reduce pollution entering the aquifer, however, face the added bureaucratic complexity of coordinated action across the border.

Management Agencies for the Abbotsford-Sumas Aquifer

Although the border between the United States and Canada divides the aquifer in two parts for political management purposes, water within the aquifer flows freely across the border from British Columbia south into Washington. The political border is significant, however, because it delineates somewhat different economics; the greater emphasis on poultry operations in British Columbia, for example, affects the identity of the industry groups involved in addressing pollution inputs.

The border also more than doubles the number of government agencies that are responsible for the management and protection of the shared resource. In addition to the domestic agencies involved in pollution regulation and water quality in both countries, transboundary agencies have emerged to bridge the divergent political systems associated with the political border. Listed in descending order of the geographic scope of their authority, these agencies include the North American Free Trade Agreement, Commission for Environmental Cooperation (CEC), International Joint Commission (IJC), British Columbia/Washington Environmental Cooperation Council (ECC), Abbotsford-Sumas Aquifer International Task Force (task force), Abbotsford-Sumas Aquifer Stakeholders Group (stakeholders group), environmental nongovernmental organizations (ENGOs), and industry stewardship groups (ISGs). Some of these agencies only have the potential to be involved in the clean-up of the Abbotsford-Sumas aquifer, while others were created expressly for that purpose. To clarify the role of each management agency of the Abbotsford-Sumas aquifer, each group is described below.

North American Free Trade Agreement: The Commission for Environmental Cooperation (CEC)

CEC is an international organization created by Canada, Mexico, and the United States under the North American Agreement on Environmental Cooperation (NAAEC). The agreement was designed to complement the 1994 North American Free Trade Agreement (NAFTA) by incorporating provisions relating to the resolution of environmental concerns arising from free trade. CEC was specifically established to "address regional environmental concerns, help prevent potential trade and environmental conflicts, and to promote the effective enforcement of environmental law" (CEC 2004). The formal obligations of the countries include "periodic publication of reports, education, scientific research, assessments of environmental effects and promotion of environmental goals" (Marchak 1998: 144).

CEC has catalogued approximately 350 transboundary environmental issues along the Mexico-U.S. and Canada-U.S. borders, including the Abbotsford-Sumas aquifer. Although the aquifer is not currently under review, the council could take a role in aquifer-related issues at the request of either national government, or if a party filed a petition with CEC alleging that either country has failed to follow the requirements of its own national environmental laws with respect to the aquifer. While no party has expressed interest in CEC involvement in aquifer protection, CEC is included in this study because of its theoretical and potential role in transboundary deliberations relating to the Abbotsford-Sumas aquifer.

International Joint Commission (IJC)

The IJC was created in 1909 to review applications for transboundary water use, to investigate water pollution issues involving Canada and the United States, and to deflect and mitigate potential transboundary water conflicts (Hildebrand et al. 1997: 2). The six-member group acts as an advisory board to the two federal governments with respect to transboundary water issues anywhere along the border (Jolly 1998). Upon request of the governments, the IJC "investigates environmental questions or matters of difference along the shared frontier; monitors and coordinates the implementation of recommendations for dams or canals in the shared waters; and approves or disapproves projects such as dams or water divisions" (Hildebrand et al. 1997: 2).

Historically, the IJC has focused largely on the Great Lakes region and has had a minimal presence along the British Columbia/Washington State border. However, Puget Sound/Georgia Basin issues such as oil transportation and the raising of Ross Dam on the Skagit River both involved the IJC (Alper and Monahan 1986: 164). Like the CEC, the IJC has the potential for involvement in the Abbotsford-Sumas aquifer. This particular transboundary water issue has never been referred to the IJC for its consideration. Given that local, state, and provincial politicians normally prefer more local problem-solving approaches and often view the IJC as relating to far-off national capitals than to local on the ground efforts, the IJC is not likely to become involved in this issue in the near future (Alper 1997).

British Columbia/Washington State Environmental Cooperation Council (ECC) and the Abbotsford-Sumas Aquifer International Task Force (Task Force)

British Columbia and Washington are parties to a unique nonfederal transboundary agreement. The signing of the Environmental Cooperation Agreement (ECA) in May 1992 by then-premier of British Columbia, Michael Harcourt, and then-governor of Washington State, Booth Gardner, is a significant symbol of the two governments' commitment to environmental cooperation (Alper 1996: 10). The ECA committed the state and the province to "promote and coordinate mutual efforts to ensure the protection, preservation, and enhancement of our shared environment" (British Columbia and Washington State. *Environmental Cooperation Agreement* 1992).

As a result of the ECA, the British Columbia/Washington ECC was established to oversee these coordinated environmental activities (Alper 1996: 10). The ECC, in turn, established five task forces to address ECC's highest priorities, including the Abbotsford-Sumas aquifer. The Abbotsford-Sumas International Task Force has been meeting since 1991, although its cochairs reported in 2003 that "[d]eclining attendance by U.S. and Canadian agencies ... due to funding cuts, other priorities and retirements are affecting the task force's ability to conduct subcommittee activities" (Grout and Zubel 2003).

The Abbotsford-Sumas Aquifer Stakeholders Group

The stakeholders group was formed under a mandate from the City of Abbotsford in January 1997. The group meets monthly to discuss its goal of "develop[ing] practical and reasonable solutions" that "lie with the voluntary actions of the stakeholders, not with the establishment of new laws and regulations and more bureaucracy"

(Andzans 1998: 1). Based in the City of Abbotsford, the group is composed of local community members representing agriculture (including raspberry farmers and the poultry industry, two locally important agricultural sectors), small business owners, urban and rural dwellers, and representatives of the City of Abbotsford, the B.C. Ministries of Environment, and Agriculture Canada. Agency representation is aimed at coordinating information exchange, rather than implementing regulatory approaches (Andzans 2000). Unlike most groups dealing with international environmental problems, the stakeholders group is comprised primarily of local citizens who both use and pollute the aquifer (Pelley 2000).

Industry Stewardship Groups (ISGs)

A number of ISGs in the Abbotsford District of British Columbia have united under the umbrella of the Abbotsford-Sumas Aquifer stakeholders group. Monthly meetings bring representatives of the ISGs together to discuss methods of reducing pollution inputs into the aquifer. The representatives act as a correspondent between the stakeholders group committee and its particular groups' stakeholders. The representatives relay information back to their members as well as explaining their industries' objectives to the stakeholders group (Andzans 2000). The goal of the ISG is to design solutions that reduce pollution inputs while maintaining their respective business objectives. The most active ISGs include the B.C. Raspberry Growers' Association, the B.C. Auto Recyclers' Association, and the Sustainable Poultry Farming Group (Andzans 1998).

Environmental Nongovernmental Organizations (ENGOs)

Historically, ENGOs have played an important role in fostering unique grass-roots solutions because of their ability to bypass the limitations posed by the red tape of governmental regulation and political bureaucracy (Alper 1997: 372–74). Funded by private sources and grants, ENGOs usually have more flexibility than government agencies in finding solutions to environmental problems. It is not surprising, then, that ENGOs have "emerged as central players in domestic and international environmental advocacy" (Alper 1997: 372).

The role of ENGOs in transboundary environmental issues often focuses on building community relationships across the border (Andzans 2000; Gray 1999; Hinkle 1999). These relationships foster a community-oriented approach to managing resources and therefore are an essential component of managing transboundary environmental issues (Ellis 1995; Meyers and Papademetriou 1999; Towers 2000; Waak 1995). Although as many as sixty ENGOs are involved in transborder issues along the British Columbia and Washington border (Alper 1997: 372), the Abbotsford-Sumas aquifer has received limited attention. Transboundary ENGOs such as the People for Puget Sound and the Georgia Strait Alliance are active participants in transboundary environmental issues; their priority lists, however, do not include the Abbotsford-Sumas aquifer.

Emma Spenner Norman and Jean O. Melious

Development of an Index to Measure Cross-Border Cooperation

An index was designed to measure the "institutional capacity" of cross-border cooperation across the Abbotsford-Sumas aquifer. Variables and performance indicators were chosen after twelve months of direct and indirect observation of issues surrounding the aquifer. The authors observed meetings, interviewed government and nongovernment employees, and spoke with concerned citizens and local governmental officials. This methodology was based on Scheirer (1994) and Wholey's (1994) work on designing program evaluation. After extensive field research and a thorough literature review, the authors identified five variables that embody an ideal cross-border program.

These variables are: (1) adequate decision-making power, (2) an institutional structure that contributes to transboundary management, (3) the ability to modify behaviour to reduce the amount of pollutants entering the aquifer, (4) a strong ability to read and modify public opinion, and (5) the ability to modify British Columbia and Washington policies.

Performance indicators then described the five variables. The performance indicators were assigned a nominal value of 1, 0 for yes or no questions or an ordinal scale of 0–3 for relative-scale questions. Zero indicates "No presence of performance indicator," 1 indicates "Low presence," 2 indicates "medium presence," and 3 indicates a "high presence of performance indicator." The variables were assigned between 2 and 5 performance indicators, for a total of seventeen indicators (table 9.1).

The variables and performance indicators were adjusted to take into account the comments of knowledgeable observers, including three community members familiar with the Abbotsford-Sumas aquifer and four Western Washington University faculty members. A score was then assigned to each of the organizations. The faculty reviewers were also asked independently to score each of the organizations. The final score was based on the authors' scores, amended slightly in several categories to reflect consistent themes in the other reviewers' analyses (fig. 9.2).

Table 9.1 Numerical Scale for the Variable and Performance Indicator.

VARIABLE	PERFORMANCE INDICATORS	ASSIGNED NUMERICAL VALUE
Decision Making Power	Adequate funding	Yes = 1 No = 0
(D)	Ability to implement programs	Scale 0–3
	Ability to enforce programs	Scale 0–3
	Prioritization of the aquifer	Scale 0–3
Institutional Lay-Out	Committed committee members	Scale 0–3
(I)	Geographic proximity to issue	Close = 1 Not Close = 0
	Presence of strong leadership	Scale 0–3
	Longevity of program	> 5 yrs = 1 < 5 yrs = 0
	Frequency of meetings	Scale 0–3
Change Pollution Input	Decrease in manure (cattle/poultry)	Yes = 1 No = 0
(MN)	Decrease N input on berry farms	Yes = 1 No = 0
	Change in business behavior	Yes = 1 No = 0
Public Opinion	Ability to influence public opinion	Scale 0–3
(PO)	Ability to read public opinion	Scale 0–3
Procedural change	Change in inspection ratio	Yes = 1 No = 0
(PC)	Increase of staff/ volunteers	Yes = 1 No = 0
	Procedural change	Yes = 1 No = 0

Findings

The results clearly indicate a converse relationship between geographic representation and institutional capacity to alleviate cross-border pollution (with the exception of the ENGOs) (table 9.2; fig. 9.2). For example, the CEC and IJC (the groups covering the largest geographic area) scored the two lowest scores of 1.52 and 1.65 out of 5. The highest scores went to the organizations that have the least geographic representation. For example, the stakeholders group earned the highest percentage points, with 72 per cent, or 3.58 out of a possible 5, and the Industry Stewardship Group earned the second highest percentage, with 68 per cent out of 3.40 points. The international task force came in third earning, 51 per cent of the possible points. The environmental NGO's low score is a regional phenomenon based on lack of funding for cross-border cooperation.

Table 9.2 Index Results: Highest Ranking Groups and Geographic Representation.

ORGANIZATIONS	POINTS (OUT OF 5)	PER-CENTAGE	GEOGRAPHIC REPRESENT-ATION
ASA Stakeholders Group (ASASG)	3.58	72%	5
Industrial Stewardship Groups (ISGs)	3.40	68%	6
ASA International Task Force (ASAITF)	2.54	51%	4
Environmental Cooperation Council (ECC)	2.47	49%	3
Environmental NGOs (ENGOs)	2.00	40%	7
International Joint Commission (IJC)	1.65	30%	2
Commission for Environmental Coop. (CEC)	1.52	24%	1

Figure 9.2 Institutional capacity per organization.

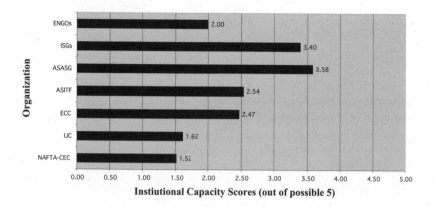

The index measures the institutional capacity of the organizations within a defined cross-section of time. During that period (1999–2000), the ASASG and the ISG revealed themselves as the most capable of reducing pollution. However, as the timeline below indicates (table 9.3), a series of prior events and relationships occurred that provided the foundation for the aforementioned groups to succeed. These efforts provided the framework in which the groups formed and functioned and also may have affected their willingness and ability to participate effectively in pollution reduction efforts.

Table 9.3 Timeline: Canada–U.S. Transboundary Water Issues and the
Abbotsford-Sumas Aquifer.

YEAR	EVENT
1907	Trail Smelter Arbitration (Canada-U.S.)
1909	Boundary Waters Treaty enacted
	The International Joint Commission (IJC) created
1928–1941	Trail Smelter Arbitration (Canada-U.S.)
1988	Oil spill on Gray's Harbor, WA
	Washington–B.C. Joint Oil Spill Task Force created
	Exxon Valdez oil spill in Prince William Sound, Alaska
	Other west coast states joined the Oil Spill Task Force
1989	States/B.C. Oil Spill Task Force issued a comprehensive report
1992	Washington and B.C. expanded coordinated transboundary efforts
	The Environmental Cooperation Agreement (ECA) signed by Premier Harcourt and Governor Gardner
	The BC/WA Environmental Cooperation Council (ECC) established to oversee the coordinated activities as discussed in the ECA
	The Abbotsford-Sumas aquifer was prioritized under the ECC and the Abbotsford-Sumas International Task Force (ASITF) created
1994	NAFTA implemented
	The Commission for Environmental Cooperation (CEC) established
1996	Memorandum of Agreement (MOA) on Water Rights Applications signed by state and provincial environmental agencies
	City of Abbotsford, B.C., mandates nonregulatory solutions for reduction of aquifer's pollutant inputs
1997	Abbotsford-Sumas aquifer inaugural stakeholders meeting
1999	United States Geologic Survey Abbotsford-Sumas aquifer report published
2000	Environment Canada Abbotsford-Sumas aquifer report published the Memorandum of Understanding (MOU) for the Abbotsford-Sumas aquifer signed by the governor of Washington and the premier of British Columbia

This time line clearly depicts the long-term interest in solving transboundary issues. The Trail Smelter Arbitration of 1928–1941, for example, significantly affected international law and cross-border cooperation by establishing the obligation of states to use their own property in such a manner as to not injure the property of other states (*Trail Smelter Arbitration* 1938, 1941). With the enactment of the Boundary Waters Treaty two years later, in 1909, Canada and the United States officially recognized the importance of coordinating decisions on shared waters. This treaty was designed to resolve water disputes on the U.S./Canada border. It also institutionalized the IJC, which was created to review applications for transboundary water use and to investigate water pollution issues involving the two countries when requested to do so by both countries (Jolly 1998). The IJC is the longest-standing committee between the United States and Canada with the primary purpose of addressing transboundary environmental issues.

While transboundary water quality issues along the western Canada-U.S. border did not receive a great deal of attention until the last quarter of the twentieth century, the pace of cooperation has accelerated over the past twenty years. Significant oil spills in 1988, including the Exxon Valdez oil spill in Alaska, and an oil spill in Gray's Harbor, Washington, prompted a series of actions to solidify the transboundary coordination of regional water issues between Washington and British Columbia. The Gray's Harbor oil spill prompted Governor Gardner of Washington and Premier Van der Zalm of B.C. to create a Joint Oil Spill Task Force. The transboundary task force was charged with investigating prevention of future oils spills, coordinating emergency responses, and assessing methods for expediting compensation (Jolly 1998). This task force laid the foundation for future regional, cross-border collaboration.

These events indicate that the analysis of the aquifer in isolation may tend to downplay the significance of the foundation laid for transboundary cooperation over the past hundred years. The timeline acts as a reminder that a quantitative metric such as the index only represents a diminutive period of time. The index is a useful, but limited, tool that is intended to relay a large amount of information in a condensed version. This information, in turn, then must be considered within the broader historical and political contexts of transboundary cooperation in the region.

Emma Spenner Norman and Jean O. Melious

Promoting Scientific Knowledge and Understanding: A Governmental Role

The role of the government in funding scientific research is another important component of transboundary environmental management. Although the index results did not directly divulge this outcome, individual and organizational interviews clearly recognized the role of higher political organizations. Discussions with both high-level bureaucratic officials and grass-roots community workers revealed that the government's support of scientific inquiry was an essential component to ensuring the eventual local support of an environmental issue (Andzans 2000; Cole 1999; Hinkle 1999; Pelley 1999; Robinson 1999).

Once a concern is validated through scientific research, a community is able to develop initiatives that are in line with the community's characteristics and goals (Palumbo and Calista 1990; Wondolleck 1997; Uitto 2000). The institutional support can fund scientific research and provide the communities with the information needed to implement and designs site-specific solutions to remedy the issue (Andzans 1999).

The acquired, and proven, knowledge then acts as an impetus for communities to gain popular support for local efforts (Palumbo and Calista 1990). Without the funding for research to prove that an environmental issue exists, local groups often experience resistance, making it difficult to gain momentum. Thus, in order for local action to operate effectively, it is imperative that organizations with larger geographic scope focus time, energy, and resources into exploring the problem.

In the case of the Abbotsford-Sumas aquifer, the problem of a polluted water source was identified by scientific research on both sides of the border. The United States Geological Service (USGS) conducted an in-depth research study that clearly identified the need for nitrate reduction in the aquifer (USGS 1999). Environment Canada also conducted a study of the aquifer, which identified the area as highly polluted with nitrates resulting from agricultural practices such as chicken manure and fertilizer pollution from raspberry productions (Hii et al. 1999). Both scientific studies provided tools to empower communities to take action towards changing behaviour to reduce groundwater pollution.

Local communities and citizens' groups often do not have the resources to fund extensive studies. Although it is unlikely that community members will read each scientific study, or perhaps even see the completed documents, it is vital that the science was conducted and that it is available for public review. The scientific verification provides the local community with the empowered knowledge to move forward and to act to reduce the pollution.

Conclusions and Recommendations

The primary research goal of this study was to assess the "institutional capacity" of organizations to reduce pollution inputs in the Abbotsford-Sumas aquifer. Seven organizations were ranked using the index, which measured the groups' ability for: (1) adequate decision-making, (2) institutional contributions to transboundary management, (3) modification of behaviour to reduce the pollutants entering the aquifer, (4) modifying public opinion, and (5) modifying British Columbia and Washington policies.

The study found that groups with the least geographic representation had the most ability to reduce pollution inputs in a transboundary setting. The groups' success primarily relied on their ability to receive political support, but not directives, while maintaining a strong community focus. The groups that could enjoy the benefits of structure through political involvement, and the benefits of local support through community-involvement, ranked the highest. For example, the stakeholders group and the industry stewardship group scored the highest largely because the local government supported their efforts to design and implement initiatives with limited bureaucratic regulation.

The community-based success was largely contingent on supporting scientific research on specific questions by senior government agencies in both countries. This new knowledge allowed local stakeholders to reach consensus on what problems needed to be resolved so that mutually acceptable binational solutions to environmental problems were attainable. The role of the higher level governments to provide financial support for expensive scientific studies helped provide the necessary impetus for action at the local level. This was indicated by the use of the U.S.G.S. and Environment Canada studies to provide the general public with information on the elevated levels of nitrates in the Abbotsford-Sumas aquifer. This information was used by regional groups to educate the public through health and environmental campaigns which brought the aquifer's water pollution issue to the fore.

The federal support of scientific studies provided an impetus for local effort. However, in general, we found a converse relationship between geographic representation and institutional capacity to deal with transboundary water issues at the local level. The ENGO sector was the only significant variant to this trend. Despite the very active participation in environmental stewardship activities within each respective border community, the nonprofit and local grassroots organizations did not score well with the index. The ENGO's lack of institutional capacity to work on transboundary issues was primarily a regional phenomenon, limited by the lack of funding for cross-border environmental projects and the lack of constituent support.

Although the respective communities were interested in ensuring clean water in their neighbourhoods, on their side of the border, constituents surrounding the Abbotsford-Sumas aquifer were not willing to allocate funds towards local transboundary environmental issues. However, transboundary issues with a larger scale, such as water pollution in Georgia Strait/Puget Sound received more generalized constituent support because of the larger scope of the issue. Although localized issues such as the Abbotsford-Sumas aquifer receive support from the community, the support does not transcend the political border, despite its international setting.

On the other side of the geographic spectrum, the Commission for Environmental Cooperation, with a mandate that encompasses all of North America, and the International Joint Commission, which can be involved in issues along the entire Canada-U.S. border, also received low scores. Consistent with the converse relationship between geographic representation and institutional capacity, CEC and IJC did not score well because of their overly broad commitment to transboundary problem-solving, their lack of attention to localized cross-border issues, and the fact that neither agency had a mandate to address this specific transboundary pollution problem. In order for these supranational groups to become involved in transboundary issues at a local level, they need an invitation to participate or reference. Had this occurred, their score would undoubtedly have increased as they became active participants. However, as the groups were working well at a local level – with no conflict – there was no need to call in these supranational organizations to help bring about solutions.

In order for the analysis to be more comprehensive, however, it is important to look at the long-term involvement of each group. For example, although the British Columbia-Washington Environmental Cooperation Council (ECC) did not score as well as predicted, it has historically played a crucial role in laying the foundation for cross-border cooperation. It could be argued that, without the presence of groups such as the ECC and IJC, local groups would not have had as much long-term success.

It is crucial to situate the results of the index within a larger historical context. This historical narrative is particularly important in the case of transboundary issues, where two countries dealing with a singular issue could react with significant variance. Transboundary management of the Abbotsford-Sumas aquifer is a success because of the presence of strong leadership to coordinate efforts, the foresight of governments to set up task forces, and the unyielding dedication of local communities.

The questions posed, therefore, should not only have been "which organization possesses the most institutional capacity to alleviate groundwater pollution," but also, "in what capacity did institutions work together?" The relationships between the organizations are an essential component in transboundary management analysis. Efforts, ideas, and programs trickle up and down between organizations. This movement, albeit somewhat invisible, is a crucial communication mechanism that ultimately leads to instigating change.

Despite these shortcomings, the exercise of assessing and ranking groups within an index does have some advantages. One of the main assets of a quantitative assessment is its ability to effectively and efficiently quantify a large amount of qualitative data. Condensing a large amount of information into a standard format makes the assessment of transboundary groups straightforward; it becomes simple to compare groups' strengths and weaknesses and quickly surmise which group has a higher capacity for transboundary management. This index is particularly useful for audiences with limited time to read through extensive narratives. The index provides the reader with a condensed version of each groups' strengths and weaknesses and a glimpse of their potential.

What the index does not provide is a historical context for the scores. Thus, by situating the results within a historical framework, the quantitative analysis gains greater applicability. With the supplemental information, the reader decides whether he or she wants a quick synopsis or a more comprehensive, temporal analysis. Although this mechanism is just one attempt to gain insights into a complex, multivariate, and dynamic process, the authors hope that it will prove useful for other groups or individuals working on transboundary environmental management issues. Those interested in employing this application, however, will undoubtedly need to negotiate a balance between capturing a large amount of information in a limited amount of space and situating the relationships within a wider historical context.

Acknowledgments

The authors would like to thank the editors, Don Alper, Chad Day, and James Loucky for their encouragement throughout this project. Special thanks also to Stefan Freelan, Huxley College of the Environment, Western Washington University for producing the location map. We also gratefully acknowledge Environment Canada and the American Association of University of Women whose financial support helped make this project possible. This research is based on Norman's master's research project at Western Washington University, which was supervised by Melious.

References

Almasri, M. N., and J. K. Jagath. 2004. "Assessment and management of long-term nitrate pollution of ground water in agriculture-dominated watersheds." *Journal of Hydrology* 295(1–4): 225–45.

Almasri, M. N., and J. J. Kaluarachchi. 2004. "Implications of on-ground nitrogen loading and soil transformations on ground water quality management." *Journal of the American Water Resources Association* 40(1): 165–86.

Alper, Donald K. 1996. "The Idea of Cascadia: Emergent Transborder Regionalisms in the Pacific Northwest-Western Canada." *Journal of Borderlands Studies* 10(2): 1–22.

———. 1997. "Transboundary Environmental Relations in British Columbia and Pacific Northwest." *American Review of Canadian Studies* 27(3): 359–83.

Alper, Donald K., and R.L. Monahan. 1986. "Regional Transboundary Negotiations Leading to the Skagit River Treaty: Analysis and Future Application." *Canadian Public Policy* 12(1): 163–74.

Andzans, Peter. 1998. "Report of the Abbotsford-Sumas Aquifer Stakeholders Group, Abbotsford, British Columbia." Unpublished.

———. 5 Dec. 2000. City of Abbotsford Community Planner. Telephone Interview by author. Abbotsford, British Columbia.

British Columbia. Ministry of Environment, Lands and Parks and Environment Canada. 1999. *Trends in Water Quality in British Columbia*. Victoria, B.C. Ministry of Lands, Environment and Parks.

Cole, Wendy. 12 Oct. 1999. Whatcom County Dairy Education Extension Officer. Interview by author. Bellingham, WA.

Council for Environmental Cooperation (CEC) website [cited, 2004]. http://www.cec.org/who_we_are/index.cfm?varlan=english.

Ellis, E.A. 1995. "Bordering on Disaster: A New Attempt to Control the Transboundary Effects of Maquiladora Pollution." *Valparaiso University Law Review* 30: 621–99.

Province of British Columbia and Washington State. 1992. *Environmental Cooperation Agreement between the Province of British Columbia and the State of Washington.* http://wlapwww.gov.bc.ca/cppl/ecc/documents/mouair.pdf.

Gray, Darrell. 12 Oct. 1999. Nooksack Salmon Enhancement Association. Telephone interview by author. Bellingham, WA.

Grout, Richard, and Marc Zubel. 2 April 2003. "Abbotsford-Sumas Aquifer International Task Force." Presentation to the Environmental Cooperation Council Victoria, B.C. http://wlapwww.gov.bc.ca/cppl/ecc/documents/April2003/ASAITF%20ECC%202003%20(3).pdf.

Hildebrand, Larry, Victoria Pebbles, and Holly S. Ross. 1997. *Cooperative Ecosystem Management Canada and U.S.: Approaches and Experiences of Programs in the Gulf of Maine, Great Lakes and Puget Sound/Georgia Basin*. A Report, Coastal Zone 97 meeting, Boston, MA.

Hii, Basil, Hugh Liebscher, Mike Mazalek, and Taina Tuominen. 1999. *Ground Water Quality In the Abbotsford Aquifer British Columbia*. Vancouver, B.C.: Environment Canada, Pacific and Yukon Region.

Hinkle, Irene. 7 Oct. 1999. Resources for Sustainable Development Education Coordinator. Interview by author. Bellingham, WA.

Jolly, Carol. 29 Jan. 1998. Lecture to International Environmental Law class at University of Washington.

Marchak, P. 1998. "Environment and Resource Protection: Does NAFTA Make a Difference?" *Organization and Environment* 11(2): 133–57.

Meyers, D., and Demetrio G. Papademetriou. 1999. "Walking a Fine Line: Issues in Canada-United States Border Management." *International Migration Policy Program*. Washington, D.C.: Carnegie Endowment for International Peace. Unpublished.

Palumbo, Dennis J., and Donald J. Calista. 1990. *Implementation and the Policy Process: Opening up the Black Box*. Westport, CT: Greenwood.

Pelley, Joan. 7 Nov. 2000. Department of Ecology, Communications Manager. Written correspondence with author, Bellingham, WA.

Robinson, Marion. 10 Dec. 1999. Written correspondence. Fraser Basin Council: Fraser Valley Regional Coordinator. Abbotsford, B.C.

Scheirer, Mary Ann. 1994. "Designing and Using Process Evaluation," pp. 40–68. In *Handbook of Practical Program Evaluation*, ed. J. Wholley. San Francisco: Jossey-Bass.

Towers, George. 2000. "Applying the Political Geography of Scale: Grassroots Strategies and Environmental Justice." *The Professional Geographer* 52(1): 23–36.

Trail Smelter Arbitration (United States v. Canada). 1938, 1941. *United Nations Reports of International Arbitral Awards*. Vol. 3.

United States Geological Survey (USGS). Department of the Interior. 1999. *Hydrogeology, Ground-Water Quality, and Sources of Nitrate in Lowland Glacial Aquifers of Whatcom County, Washington and British Columbia, Canada*. Report 98-4195. Tacoma, WA.

Waak, Patricia. 1995. "Shaping a Sustainable Planet: The Role of Nongovernmental Organizations." *Colorado Journal of International Environmental Law and Policy* 6(2): 345–62.

Washington State. Department of Ecology. 15 March 2005. "Environmental Cooperation Council Letter to WA Governor Locke and B.C. Premier Campbell 2003" [cited, 2005]. http://wlapwww.gov.bc.ca/cppl/ecc/documents/ecc_03.pdf.

Washington State. Department of Health. Oct. 1999. *Public Health Assessment: Whatcom County Groundwater.* Draft for Public Comment.

Wassenaar, L. 1995. "Evaluation of the origin and fate of nitrate in the Abbotsford Aquifer using the isotopes of 15N and 18O in NO^3." *Applied Geochemistry* 10: 391–405.

Wholey, Joseph, ed. 1994. *Handbook of Practical Program Evaluation.* San Francisco: Jossey-Bass.

Zebarth, B.J., B. Hii, H. Liebscher, K. Chipperfield, J.W. Paul, G. Grove, and S.Y. Szeto. 1998. "Agricultural Land Use Practices and Nitrate Contamination in the Abbotsford Aquifer, British Columbia, Canada." *Agriculture, Ecosystems and Environment* 69: 99–112.

10

COMMUNITY-BASED MANAGEMENT OF GRAY WHALE ECOTOURISM IN BAJA CALIFORNIA SUR, MEXICO

Duncan Knowler, Peter Williams, and Salvador Garcia-Martinez

Abstract

Gray whale-watching is generally viewed as a useful means of achieving wildlife conservation objectives along the entire Pacific coastline of the United States, Canada, and Mexico, including the Bahia Magdalena region in the Mexican State of Baja California Sur. However, some researchers argue that there is a need to limit this industry's growth to avoid adverse impacts on whale populations. It is also suggested that community-based management of whale-watching be promoted to ensure local communities benefit. To determine sustainable levels of community-based ecotourism development requires a greater understanding of the dynamic links between tourism, whale ecology, and economic benefits. This chapter outlines resource management problems in Baja California Sur related to gray whale breeding habitat and the associated whale-watching industry. An appropriate management approach requires an interdisciplinary planning perspective that transcends international borders. Trinational research and management collaboration are recognized as prerequisites to achieving sustainability of this species and the associated industry.

Introduction

The recovery of the Eastern Pacific gray whale (*Eschrichtius robustus*) population is one of the great conservation success stories of modern times. As a highly migratory resident of North America, the gray whale relies on habitat in all three countries of North America as it swims annually from Baja California Sur to Alaska during the spring each year and returns again during the autumn (fig. 1.1 in an earlier chapter of this volume). Gray whales rely upon food resources in northern waters during the summer to meet energy needs through the winter breeding period spent in the vicinity of Baja California, Mexico. Of critical importance during the winter breeding period are the lagoons and bays of the West Coast of Baja California Sur, where much of the mating, bearing, and nursing of calves takes place (fig. 10.1). The spectacle created by the whales' presence in the breeding areas is the focal point for a rapidly expanding whale-watching industry (Hoyt 2000). While whale-watching and other forms of ecotourism have been viewed as a feasible alternative for achieving wildlife conservation, some researchers have suggested there is a need to limit capacity in the industry to avoid adverse impacts on the associated whale populations (Heckel 2001).

Achieving a sustainable ecotourism whale-watching industry has important implications for the continental-scale management of gray whales. For example, the greatest numbers of foreign whale-watchers visiting the bays of Baja come from Canada and the United States. Indeed, resource "users" are not restricted to the local whale-watching industry, but also include recreational and commercial whale-watching operations along the Pacific coast of North America as far as Alaska. Various studies have recognized the economic values associated with these activities involving Mexico's North American

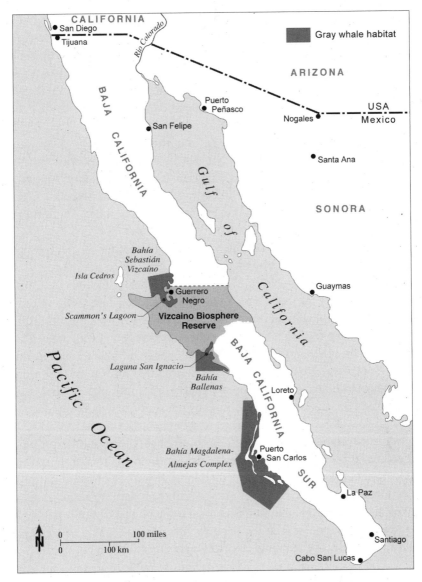

Figure 10.1 Gray whale habitat, Baja California.

neighbours (Hoyt 2000; Chien 1994; Loomis and Larson 1994). Thus, to be successful in the long term, the management of this species requires a coordinated international program of habitat protection and viewing protocols. This concern is reflected in various initiatives intended to integrate management of gray whales across the borders of the three North American countries involved, such as the Baja to Bering Sea (B2B) program, partially funded by the North American Commission for Environmental Cooperation (Bowman 2006; Jessen and Lerch 1999). Numerous nongovernmental organizations are also active in promoting conservation of habitat for gray whales in all three countries, including Pronatura in Mexico, Wild Coast in the United States, and the Canadian Parks and Wilderness Society (CPAWS) in Canada.

A substantial portion of the breeding and nursing habitat in Baja California Sur is now protected, having been designated as the Vizcaino Biosphere Reserve in November of 1988 (CONANP 2000). The creation of the largest reserve in the country, and a recent federal government decision to withdraw a salt works proposal within Vizcaino, suggest that the Mexican government recognizes the importance of the lagoons for the gray whale. However, significant threats remain. For example, one breeding area does not fall within the reserve. Located four hundred kilometres south of Vizcaino, Bahia Magdalena is used by a significant share of the whale population during its winter stay in the waters of Baja California Sur. As this is not a protected area – and there is no prospect at present that it will become one – there is a need to consider the pace and direction of regional economic growth and its potential impact on local natural resources, including the migratory whale population. Management strategies to ensure sustainable resource use policies are needed, and a key component will be the need to ensure that local communities will benefit from the presence of the whale population.

The conservation of the gray whale population using the Baja Region, and the need to develop new community economic opportunities, could create conflicts between the main resource use stakeholders in Bahia Magdalena and with stakeholders in the other two countries hosting gray whale populations for part of the year. Inevitably, such a situation makes it difficult to set an appropriate level for human activities in the bay that could detrimentally impact the whales. For example, local whale-watching companies using

Bahia Magdalena have expressed a desire for more whale-watching permits (Garcia-Martinez 2004), yet an appropriate limit on the total number of such permits from a conservation perspective is uncertain. The problem is made more challenging since there is presumably some level of disturbance that could cause the whales to abandon the bay as a wintering area. Ultimately, the unprotected status of the bay calls for the careful design of appropriate incentives that serve to reconcile conservation and economic development objectives.

In this chapter, we set out a number of considerations that will be important for the sustainable management of Bahia Magdalena and its resources, especially its itinerant gray whale population. The next section reviews the research problem in more detail. Subsequently, we address two sets of key issues in separate sections: the first considers community-tourism linkages from a social science point of view; and the second discusses the further linkage with whale ecology and population dynamics, outlining this in terms of an appropriate ecological-economic systems model. The final section extracts the important elements from the preceding discussion in order to identify gaps for further study.

An Overview of the Resource Management Problem

In this section we provide an outline of some of the resource management problems affecting gray whales in the bays of Baja California Sur. For example, continued growth of ecotourism based on gray whales may be problematic if this activity is seen as a panacea for economic problems in the Baja California region, especially in the fisheries, without regard for its impacts on the whales themselves. Therefore, an important objective is to analyze whale-watching activities to determine what level of whale-watching is sustainable from both a biological and a tourism marketing perspective. This level should ensure minimum impacts on the gray whale population to avoid negative effects on reproductive success as well as to recognize the particular attributes of the experience valued by tourists. However, whale-watching cannot be viewed in isolation, since there are numerous other potential threats facing the whale population's use of unprotected breeding areas like Bahia Magdalena. These threats include fishing, industrial pollution, tanker traffic, aquaculture, large-scale tourism development, and urban development. Such concerns must be factored into management planning, along with consideration of the opportunities available from ecotourism.

In addition, as the gray whale constitutes a charismatic species from a global conservation perspective, the values associated with this species are of wider interest. As demonstrated with other species and habitat conservation issues, compelling support from decision-makers and the funding necessary to conserve biodiversity is easier when valuation estimates are available to support the necessary management actions. Thus, it is imperative that the few extant studies of gray whale economics be consolidated (Loomis and Larson 1994; Chien 1994) and that gaps be filled to provide a better picture of the benefits derived from whale-watching. This work also needs to be linked to whale ecology and biology. Such an effort may help to convince individuals and nations that they must provide more support for the protection of whale habitat, if whale-watching is to be managed as a sustainable industry.

An important aspect of the valuation exercise is an assessment of local and global economic benefits of whale-watching. In the former case, the benefits accruing to local communities are an important determinant of local people's willingness to contribute to whale conservation. Thus, determining what constitutes these benefits and how they vary according to different management regimes is a useful exercise and one that should be undertaken in close association with the communities themselves. At the larger regional or global level, the influence of Bahia Magdalena on the health of the whale population and on the economic benefits generated by whale-watching activities is uncertain. Clearly, the loss of the bay as breeding habitat aligns conservation and local community interests, since both groups would lose in such a scenario. Current bioeconomic modelling and valuation techniques can shed light on the size of the benefit from retaining Bahia Magdalena as viable breeding habitat.

No program for the sustainable management of natural resources in the Bahia Magdalena Region can be successful without the involvement of local communities, recognizing that coordination as well as support from the other North American nations involved – the United States and Canada – will be needed as well. Special attention must be paid to the likelihood of community action, as demonstrated by the level of social capital in the communities, as one indicator. Financial incentives and the community interest and attitudes towards ecotourism management are important dimensions to such an analysis as well. In the end, there is a need to analyze ecotourism as a potential source of diversified economic activity at the community level and to consider its integration with existing activities, such as the shrimp fishery.

Key Issue I: The Community-Tourism Connection

An emerging view among conservationists is that the successful management of coastal marine resources must include the cooperation and support of local people (Gjerdalen and Williams 2000; Agardy 2000; Cocklin et al. 1998; Luttinger 1997). Excluding people who live adjacent to protected areas from use of such resources without providing them with alternatives is increasingly viewed as politically infeasible and ethically unjustifiable (Brandon and Wells 1992).

Many subsistence coastal communities are increasingly looking to expand their economy and standards of living through ecotourism. However, *ex post* assessments of tourism developments in a variety of cultural and biophysical settings have demonstrated that ecotourism is not an easy option or a panacea for the development of coastal areas (Williams 1994). Ecotourism can have adverse economic, social, and environmental implications, such as:

- detrimental impacts on wildlife and fragile ecosystems (Young 1999a, Butler 1991);
- the breakdown of local cultural traditions (Dearden 1991; Brower 1990);
- few economic benefits for local people (Bookbinder et al. 1998; Dedina and Young 1995) and for protected areas (Brandon and Wells 1992); and,
- aggravated conflicts over access to resources (Barkin 1996).

Despite these potential shortcomings, ecotourism continues to be widely promoted as a means of linking development with conservation in coastal ecosystems, especially through the establishment of marine protected areas (MPAs) (UNESCO 1999; Agardy 1993). The general position is that often the tourism linkages between coastal resources and local communities are a necessary condition for securing initial support for the development and sustainable management of such areas in the developing world.

Nonetheless, few comprehensive studies have been conducted to critically examine the linkages between community participation, ecotourism, and successful management of coastal resources. This absence highlights the need for more research that addresses key questions concerning linkages between community involvement, ecotourism, and the conservation of the gray whale. The principles developed by Becker and Ostrom (1995) concerning the management of common pool marine resources are a useful guide in analyzing the linkages between community-based ecotourism and coastal resource conservation. In particular, these principles can be used to investigate the extent to which:

- The boundaries and the community's rights to use the resources for ecotourism purposes have been clearly defined.
- Ecotourism initiatives receive a fair distribution of costs and benefits within the local community.
- The management rules governing coastal resources such as gray whales can be modified by a community's ecotourism users to meet their needs as long as sustainability of the resource is protected.
- The management and monitoring of ecotourism operations is fair and accountable.
- Sanctions and enforcement of ecotourism guidelines are well understood, fairly implemented, and appropriate.
- The resource management regime has workable mechanisms for conflict resolution between ecotourism operators, conservationists, and other resource users.
- The rights of local ecotourism operators to devise their own sustainable management regimes are not challenged by external governmental authorities, and ecotourism

Duncan Knowler, Peter Williams, and Salvador Garcia-Martinez operators have long-term tenure rights to the area's marine resources.

- The organizations set up to deal with ecotourism regulations are flexible and adaptive.

The focus must be on gaining an understanding of how local inhabitants' use of gray whales for ecotourism has been shaped by community-based management practices, regional economic and political structures, and government policies. More specifically, answers must be sought to questions such as whether the community is aware of, and in favour of, the resource management regime; whether the community is supportive of ecotourism; whether the management regime's linkage with ecotourism can reduce resource conflict, regulate extractive pressures, and promote stewardship of marine resources among local people; and, finally, what the northern nations with a clear stake in gray whale management can contribute to the process. Previous research in the Baja California region can assist in this pursuit (Dedina 2000, Young 1999b). In the end, the objective is to learn how to enhance community-based ecotourism so that it can become an effective tool for achieving conservation objectives.

Key Issue II: Linking Tourism Management with Gray Whale Ecology

The previous section detailed concerns that must be factored into the management of ecotourism operations to ensure that communities benefit and that the resources at stake are managed sustainably. The linkage between ecotourism activity levels and resource dynamics will be an important consideration if these aims are to be achieved in addition to the community-based dimensions of management that were the focus of earlier studies. Since the analysis of resource dynamics involves elements of economics and ecology, it is best attempted using tools that allow for integrated modelling of ecological-economic systems. In our case, this perspective argues for the use of bioeconomic modelling. As a result, this section details a possible approach that could characterize the interrelationships between eco-tourism activity and gray whale population dynamics and considers some potential implications for management. As this study design is a preliminary formulation, only a rough sketch of the approach is provided.

A typical bioeconomic model employs a 'stock transition' relationship describing changes in the adult population or breeding stock from one period to the next (Munro and Scott 1985). Stock growth for species such as the gray whale may depend on factors other than stock size, such as the availability of suitable breeding habitat, which we introduce later. Following Clark (1990), we can express the stock-transition relationship as comprising adult gray whales that survive natural mortality from one year to the next plus the addition of younger whales to the adult population, or 'recruitment.' In the latter case, a delay of several years between birth and recruitment to the breeding population is explicitly recognized by using a delayed-recruitment model (Clark 1976). Given the present moratorium on commercial whaling, we can ignore the relatively insignificant indigenous catch of gray whales as an influence on population numbers.

Since we assume that the whale-watching industry is essentially unregulated, we must specify a process whereby whale-watching operators enter into, or exit from, the industry. Typically, this is expressed as a function of lagged financial profits in the industry. That is, new whale-watching operators might be expected to enter the industry when profits are high and exit when they are negative (Conrad 1995). This specification yields an 'adjustment' expression for the number of whale-watching operators or vessels in a given year. Together, the equations formulated along the lines suggested above capture the open access dynamics of a small-scale, community-based, whale-watching industry.

As depicted here, the industry represents an undesirable management situation for the reasons cited in many critiques of open-access resource regimes (Hardin 1968). By introducing some sort of management or regulation of local operators, the community-based industry could increase profits and provide more substantial benefits to the community. This 'system' can be modelled empirically, adding in additional sophistication when needed, to provide a tool for

Duncan Knowler, Peter Williams, and Salvador Garcia-Martinez testing management alternatives. Various alternatives exist, such as licensing, quotas and tradable permits. Even if retained locally, industry profits might not be the only objective of management (Charles 1988), so that striking the right trade-off among objectives will need to be factored into any regulatory action. Modelling this preferred situation is possible using the representation presented above as a starting point.

What is missing in the formulation so far has already been hinted at above; it does not include a possible feedback effect from increasing levels of whale-watching activity on whale population dynamics. Yet there is mounting evidence that gray whale behaviour is affected by human activity (Heckel 2001). While not fully understood, this impact may normally be relatively trivial, although under certain circumstances it may be more profound. For example, could heightened levels of human disturbance alter breeding activity or other aspects of the biology of gray whales? There is some evidence for supporting the latter interpretation occurring in the key breeding lagoons of Baja, Mexico: industrial salt production caused the abandonment of one lagoon for breeding purposes for several years (Ortega-Rubio et al., 1998). Could a similar problem develop if whale-watching activity were to surpass unknown thresholds of tolerance on the part of gray whales? If so, how could this be included in management modelling and planning? We turn to this question now.

Modelling this added risk from whale-watching requires a probabilistic, or 'stochastic' analysis, since we do not know where any tolerance thresholds may lie, or whether these would even be fixed in any way. Yet such an analysis can be incorporated into the model presented above. To formulate a representative stochastic analysis, we might assume that:

- At some unknown level of whale-watching activity at a given breeding site, gray whales would abandon the site and that this can be modelled as a temporary structural change in their reproductive success.
- The period of abandonment is determined by the persistence of the disturbance above the tolerance threshold.

- The regulator of the industry is risk neutral and knows the relevant probability distributions and magnitudes of the two possible states of the world, that is, use or abandonment of the breeding site in question.

Under these assumptions, a stochastic transition equation equivalent can be easily formulated that depicts the two states of the world referred to above. Either the whale population is making use of its full breeding range and its reproductive behaviour has not been affected by tourism activity and the initial recruitment relationship prevails; alternatively, the gray whale's breeding activity has been disturbed, leading to abandonment of a breeding site and the alternative recruitment relationship. As the system shifts from use of a breeding site to its abandonment, the recruitment relationship governing the whale population 'jumps' from one variant to the other.

The stochastic variable in the analysis is the unknown threshold in any year that may trigger abandonment. This random variable is measured in terms of the number of whale-watching operators or trips that would trigger abandonment under a given set of circumstances. Setting up and then solving the stochastic problem can now follow the approach described in the previous section with only minor modification.

It should be emphasized that this is just one way of formulating a model to capture the linkages between the community-based tourism aspect of the management problem and its biological or ecological component. Nonetheless, there are several implications from such an analysis and these should be explored in further research. For example, an expansion of whale-watching activity leads to an increased risk of abandonment and this must be weighed against the benefits of more whale-watching revenues in the short term. Ultimately, recommended regulatory limits would be different from those if no risk of abandonment were present. Thus, there may be a strong argument for some sort of precautionary approach until more is known about such linkages, especially in light of recent concerns about gray whale mortality and ecological changes in the Bering Sea summer range (Le Boeuf et al. 2001).

Implications for Managing a Cross-Border Natural Resource

Several key questions need to be addressed concerning the conservation of gray whales and the prospects for community-based wildlife management in Baja California Sur, as part of a broader international (cross-border) management regime. These questions are:

1. What are the potential local and international benefits to the United States and Canada from ecotourism involving gray whale watching in Baja, Mexico and elsewhere, and do current and projected levels of economic activity threaten these benefits, especially ecotourism itself?

2. How should ecotourism be managed, both locally and in the neighbouring countries through which the gray whales traverse in their annual migrations, to ensure that the goals of biodiversity conservation and community development are compatible and jointly realized?

3. What are the prospects for institutional development at the community level to ensure that sustainable whale-watching utilization occurs, and what support is needed across borders in the United States and Canada, which also have a stake in gray whale management?

To answer these questions, it is necessary to consolidate existing data from whale watchers in all three interested countries, local communities and industry surveys, and undertake new primary data collection to fill the gaps. We believe that new research should concentrate on surveys of local households to assess various social capital and related characteristics, as well as surveys of whale watchers to determine the relationships needed to derive economic values and devise management strategies.

Conclusions

This chapter has outlined a resource management problem in the Baja California peninsula of Mexico involving gray whale breeding habitat and the associated whale-watching industry. It recognizes that this problem has an important cross-border dimension involving both the United States and Mexico. We discussed aspects of the resource management problem, focusing on key issues such as the linkage between community development and ecotourism and further linkages to whale ecology and biology and to activities in bordering nations. All such links must be an integral part of research addressing the issue. Clearly, understanding these connections is a prerequisite for sustainable management. An appropriately designed management approach requires an interdisciplinary planning perspective, but also one that transcends borders. As the gray whale is a highly migratory species, its life cycle links habitat in three North American countries. Therefore, collaboration across borders will be an additional prerequisite to success. Initial steps in this direction look promising.

Acknowledgments

The authors would like to recognize a number of individuals who contributed to the development of this work. The research assistance of Jenny Dalton, Center for Coastal Studies, School for Field Studies, Puerto San Carlos, Baja California Sur, was invaluable. The section on communities and tourism is based on research prepared by Peter Rossing, a graduate student at the University of British Columbia, under Peter Williams' supervision; his research focus is the Vizcaino

Biosphere Reserve, north of Bahia Magdalena. Consultations were also carried by D. Knowler under a U.S. Department of Education trilateral grant between Western Washington University, El Colegio de la Frontera Norte, and Simon Fraser University, Canada. We would especially like to thank: James Loucky (WWU); Chad Day (SFU); Jose Luis Castro (COLEF); Ana Maria Escofet, Gisela Heckel and Lucila Lares (CICESE, Ensenada); Francisco Aranda, Ana Luz Quintanilla, Manual Gardia and David Fisher (Marine Sciences, UABC, Ensenada); Carlos De Alba Perez and Jennifer Dalton (School for Field Studies, San Carlos); Luis Fleischer and Hector Perez-Cortes (Regional Center for Fisheries Research [CRIP], La Paz); Jorge Urban Ramirez (Marine Sciences, UABCS, La Paz); Diane Gendron (CICIMAR, La Paz); and Gabriela Anaya (Islands of the Gulf of California Protected Area, La Paz).

References

Agardy, T. 1993. "Accommodating Ecotourism in Multiple Use Planning of Coastal and Marine Protected Areas." *Ocean and Coastal Management* 20: 219–39.

Agardy, T. 2000. "Site selection criteria and constraints on MPAs. Paper presented at the 9*th* *International Coral Reef Conference*. October 23-27, 2000. Bali, Indonesia.

Barkin, D. 1996. "Ecotourism: A Tool for Sustainable Development in an Era of International Integration?" *Yale Bulletin Series* 99: 263–72.

Becker, D., and E. Ostrom. 1995. "Human Ecology and Resource Sustainability: The Importance of Institutional Diversity." *Annual Review of Ecological Systems* 26: 113–33.

Bookbinder, M. 1998. "Ecotourism's Support of Biodiversity Conservation." *Conservation Biology* 12: 1399–1404.

Bowman, J. 2006. "Local Projects Seek Borderless Protection for Grey Whales." *TRIO The Newsletter of the North American Commission for Environmental Cooperation* Spring 2003. Accessed at: http://www.cec.org/trio/stories/index.cfm?varlan=english&ed=9 &ID=116; accessed 16 March 2006.

Brandon, K., and M. Wells. 1992. "Planning for People and Parks." *World Development* 20: 557–70.

Brower, B. 1990. "Crisis and Conservation in Sagarmatha National Park." *Society and Natural Resources* 4: 151–63.

Butler, R. 1991. "Tourism, Environment, and Sustainable Development." *Environmental Conservation* 18: 201–9.

Charles, A. 1988. "Fishery Socioeconomics: A Survey." *Land Economics* 64(3): 276–95.

Chien, Y-L. 1994. *Valuing Environmental Amenities with Revealed and Stated Preference Information: An Application to Gray Whales in California*. PhD dissertation. Davis: University of California.

Clark, C.W. 1976. "A Delayed Recruitment Model of Population Dynamics, with an Application to Baleen Whale Populations." *Journal of Mathematical Biology* 3: 381–91.

———. 1990. *Mathematical Bioeconomics*, 2d ed. New York: John Wiley and Sons.

Cocklin, C., M. Craw, and I. McAuley. 1998. "Marine Reserves in New Zealand: Use Rights, Public Attitudes, and Social Impacts." *Coastal Management* 26: 213–31.

CONANP (Comisión Nacional de Areas Naturales Protegidas). 2000. *Programa de Conservación y Manejo de la Reserva de la Biosfera El Vizcaino*. México, D.F.: CONANP [National Commission of Nature Protected Areas].

Conrad, J.M. 1995. "Bioeconomic Models of the Fishery," pp. 405–32. In *Handbook of Environmental Economics*, ed. D. Bromley. Oxford and Cambridge: Blackwell.

Dearden, P. 1991. "Tourism and Sustainable Development in Northern Thailand." *Geographical Review* 1: 400–413.

Dedina, S. 2000. *Saving the Grey Whale: People, Politics, and Conservation in Baja California*. Tucson: University of Arizona Press.

Dedina, S., and E. Young. 1995. *Conservation and development in the gray whale (Eschrichtius robustus) lagoons of Baja California Sur, Mexico*. Washington, DC: Final report to the U.S. Marine Mammal Commission.

Garcia-Martinez, Salvador. 2004. Center for Coastal Studies, School for Field Studies, Puerto San Carlos, Baja California Sur, México. (sgarcia@fieldstudies.org)

Gjerdalen, G. and P. Williams. 2000. "An Evaluation of the Utility of a Whale Watching Code of Conduct." *Tourism Recreation Research* 25(2): 27–37.

Hardin, G. 1968. "The Tragedy of the Commons." *Science* 162: 1243–1248.

Heckel, G. 2001. *The Influence of Whalewatching on the Behaviour of Gray Whales (Eschrichtius robustus) in Todos Santos Bay, Baja California, and Surrounding Waters: Management Plan Proposal.* PhD dissertation. Ensenada, México: Facultad De Ciencias Marinas, Universidad Autónoma De Baja California. (in English)

Hoyt, E. 2000. *Whale Watching 2000: Worldwide Tourism Numbers, Expenditures, and Expanding Socioeconomic Benefits.* Crowborough, U.K: International Fund for Animal Welfare.

Jessen, S. and N. Lerch. 1999. "Baja to Bering Sea Marine Conservation Initiative." *Environments* 27(3): 67–89.

Le Boeuf, B.J., M. Perez-Cortez, R.J., Urban, B.R. Mate, and U. Ollervides. 2001. "High Gray Whale Mortality and Low Recruitment in 1999: Potential Causes and Implications." *Journal of Cetacean Research and Management* 2(2): 85–99.

Loomis, J., and Larson, D. 1994. "Total Economic Values of Increasing Gray Whale Populations: Results from a Contingent Valuation Survey of Visitors and Households." *Marine Resource Economics* 9: 275–86.

Luttinger, N. 1997. "Community-Based Coral Reef Conservation in the Bay Islands of Honduras." *Ocean and Coastal Management* 3(6): 11–22.

Munro, G.R., and A.D. Scott. 1985. "The Economics of Fisheries Management." In *Handbook of Natural Resource and Energy Economics*, eds. A.V. Kneese and J.L. Sweeney. Amsterdam: Elsevier Science.

Ortega-Rubio, A., A. Castellanos-Vera, and D. Lluch-Cota. 1998. "Sustainable Development in a Mexican Biosphere Reserve: Salt Production in Vizcaino, Baja California (Mexico)." *Natural Areas Journal* 18(1): 63–72.

UNESCO. 1999. *Report of the Mission to the Whale Sanctuary of El Vizcaino, Mexico, 23–28 August 1999.* Marakesh, Morocco: United Nations Educational, Scientific and Cultural Organization.

Williams, P.W. 1994. "Frameworks for Assessing Tourism's Environmental Impacts." In *Travel, Tourism and Hospitality Research: A Handbook for Managers and Researchers*, eds. J.R. Ritchie and C.R. Goeldner. 2nd ed. New York: John Wiley.

Young, E. 1999a. "Balancing conservation and development in small scale fisheries: Is ecotourism an empty promise?" *Human Ecology* 27(4): 581-619.

Young, E. 1999b. "Local People and Conservation in Mexico's El Vizcaino Biosphere Reserve." *Geographical Review* 89(3): 364–90.

11

TRANSNATIONAL POLICY ISSUES IN THE ALASKA CRUISE INDUSTRY

John M. Munro and Warren G. Gill

Abstract

The Alaska cruise industry is the world's fourth largest cruise market. The industry produces a service using mainly imported factors of production (ships, crews, supplies), which it then sells to buyers, almost all of whom are from outside the region. Yet certain regional facilities and access to regional environmental capital are necessary to the success of the product. Passengers augment their on-board interests with touristic activities in various Alaskan ports and with similar on-shore travel in British Columbia, Alberta, and Washington State. This international mixture generates a number of interesting transnational policy issues involving shared economic impacts, environmental monitoring and regulation, and national maritime policy.

Introduction

The Alaska cruise industry is the world's fourth largest cruise market. Vancouver is the principal homeport for these cruises, although some ships use Seattle or San Francisco as their southern terminus. The market is seasonal between May and October and is largely configured into one-week segments. About 730,000 passengers were on over twenty-five major cruise ships visiting Alaska in 2003 (producing over 1.3 million embarkations and debarkations). These large vessels and their thousands of passengers have various effects on the local environment, especially the in-port marine environment. Passengers augment their on-board tourism with touristic activities in various Alaska ports and beyond and with similar on-shore travel in British Columbia, Alberta, and Washington State. While over 90 per cent of Alaska cruise passengers are from the United States, crew members represent diverse nationalities, and the ships – almost all built in European shipyards – are owned and operated by large multinational corporations. This international mixture generates a number of interesting transnational policy issues involving shared economic impacts, environmental monitoring and regulation, and national maritime policy.

The cruise industry represents an extreme divergence between localized impact and local policy control. The industry produces a service using mainly imported factors of production (ships, crews, supplies), which it then sells to buyers, almost all of whom are from outside the region. Yet certain regional facilities and access to regional environmental capital are necessary to the success of the product. Moreover, because two regions are involved in two different countries, efforts to balance the incidence of benefits and costs are complex. Resolution of the tensions and conflicts that inevitably arise has involved various national and regional public policy measures, cruise industry organizations, and other tourism interests. This activity occurs against a backdrop of an intensely competitive travel industry where alternatives to cruising abound and there are other competing cruise destinations. Policies that would raise the costs of cruising so that Alaska became an uncompetitive destination for the cruise industry or for individual companies would result in service reductions. So far, judging by the rapid growth of the Alaska cruise industry, this has not happened, but the risk exists.

The development of the Alaska cruise industry over the last thirty-five years and its changing economic relationship with the economies of Alaska, British Columbia, and Washington are also important. The Alaska cruise industry of today grew out of a regional Canadian and U.S. shipping industry that used ships registered in each country and crewed by each country's nationals. While much smaller in size, this pioneer industry had a larger local economic impact per passenger than does today's international cruise industry because it was regionally based. Apparently, its environmental impacts were ignored. On both sides of the border, the recent tremendous growth in the industry has focused attention on economic and environmental issues. Pollution is a major public policy concern in Alaska (and perhaps soon in British Columbia), while Seattle vies for a share of the economic benefits.

There is a substantial literature on the economic impact of tourism on regional economies. This literature (e.g., Dwyer and Forsyth 1998) emphasizes the spending of tourists on accommodation, meals, sightseeing, and other retail goods and services and uses various techniques of economic impact analysis such as multipliers and input-output modelling to assess the impact of tourism. The cruise industry might seem to offer less regional economic impact than shore-based tourism because the main expenditure items, accommodation and meals, are provided on board, not in the local economy. This is more the case for ports of call during cruises than for cities that are terminals for cruise ships. For these places, the potential economic impacts are much larger.

We begin with a brief survey of the contemporary cruise industry with a particular focus on the current characteristics of the Alaska cruise market. Both Canadian and U.S. entrepreneurs and firms played roles in the development of this market, although the context today is multinational. Next, three transnational policy issues are examined: economic impacts, national maritime policy, and environmental problems and regulations. The paper concludes with observations on the prospects for expanding the economic impact of this industry while maintaining an acceptable level of environmental quality.

The Cruise Industry

The North American cruise industry is one of the most dynamic elements of the contemporary leisure market with an average growth rate greater than any other category in the tourism sector (CLIA 2001). While pleasure cruising had long been enjoyed by the more affluent members of western society (Maxtone-Graham 1985; Dawson 2000), the industry today is a more plebeian affair. Mass market cruising is a relatively new activity which originated in 1965 when Seattle entrepreneur Stanley B. McDonald founded Princess Cruises by chartering the Canadian Pacific Alaska cruise ship *Princess Patricia* (1949, 6062 grt) to undertake winter cruises from Los Angeles to Acapulco (Turner 1977; Ward 1999). Today Princess is part of Carnival Corporation which, together with Royal Caribbean International and Star Cruises, dominates the industry, controlling 68 per cent of berths worldwide (Ebersold 2004). These large holding companies are a product of a trend towards consolidation of industry assets over the past fifteen years and each operates a variety of brands (which were once independent companies) oriented to different segments of the market.

The industry offers an 'all inclusive' vacation package with the ship as a seagoing resort travelling to a variety of ports over the course of generally a one-week cruise. The cruise lines have aggressively marketed their product, competing for leisure dollars by pitching the concept that "my cruise vacation is better than your land vacation" (Dickinson and Vladimir 1997: 147). As the leisure market has grown overall, the North American cruise industry has also prospered, growing by an average rate of 8.1 per cent since 1980 (fig. 11.1), slightly faster than the 7.9 per cent increase in berths available for occupancy over this period (CLIA 2004).[1] Industry consolidation and passenger growth has been coupled with dramatically increased capacity in much larger ships. Ship size in the 1970s was typified by the *Pacific Princess* – the original 'Love Boat' (1971, 20,636 grt) – while Carnival Cruises' first newly built ship, *Tropicale* (1982, 36,674 grt), was representative of early 1980s construction. Ship size began to increase dramatically with RCCL's *Sovereign of the Seas* (1988, 73,192 grt) and older tonnage was rapidly discarded in favour of the economies of scale provided by newer floating hotels.

John M. Munro and Warren G. Gill

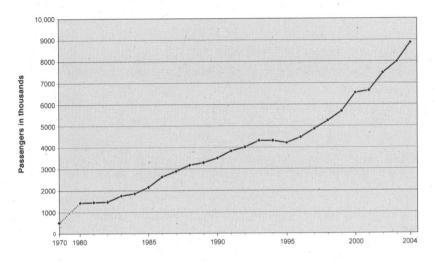

Figure 11.1
North American Cruise Passengers

Figure 11.1 North American cruise passengers (000s). ᵃSource: CLIA
(2004).

Ship size currently peaks with Royal Caribbean's *Voyager of the Seas* class (1999, 137,000 grt) and Cunard's *Queen Mary II* (2003, 150,000 grt).

The Alaska Cruise Market

The Alaska cruise – a seasonal market from May through September – represented about 8 per cent of the North American cruise industry capacity in 2004, as measured in bed-days. This is the fourth largest market after the Caribbean, which remains dominant with 40 per cent of total bed days, the Mediterranean, with 12 per cent, and other European areas, with 10 per cent (CLIA 2004). In season, however, Alaska cruises are a major focus of cruise industry activity, especially for Princess, Holland America (both divisions of Carnival) and Royal

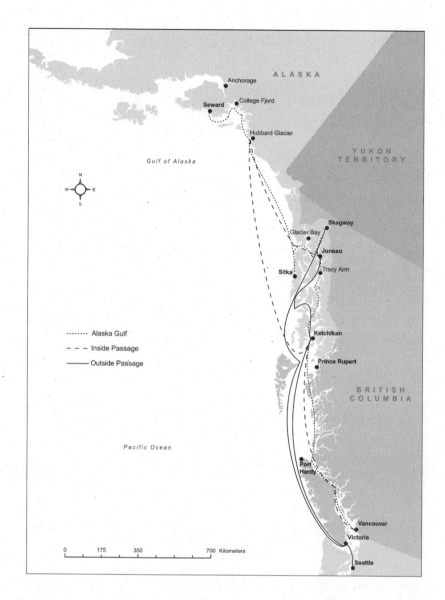

Figure 11.2. The Alaska cruise routes.

John M. Munro and Warren G. Gill

Caribbean/Celebrity, each with six or seven ships engaged in the trade. For Princess Cruises, Alaska represents 20 per cent of annual deployment vs. 34 per cent in the Caribbean (Brown 2001). Unlike sun cruises to the Caribbean, the Alaska experience is focused on scenery, ecotourism and history. For many Americans, Alaska is the 'Last Frontier' and rings with the call of the wild, the rambunctiousness of gold rushes, and the mysteries of native people. Relatively recently settled by Europeans, the Northwest Coast still retains for many a sense of the unexplored. The Inside Passage route, some one thousand miles though British Columbia and the Alaska Panhandle, is largely sheltered and offers a spectacular view of a drowned fjord coast (fig. 11.2).

Vancouver, B.C., is the homeport for most Alaska cruise activity, in part due to the restrictions of the U.S. Passenger Vessel Service Act,[2] first enacted in 1886. This reserves travel between U.S. ports to U.S.-built and -crewed ships. Since almost all contemporary cruise ships are built in Europe and have multinational crews, they must make at least one landing in a foreign port in order to serve U.S. ports. As a result, Seattle, which historically was an important point of departure for Alaska, now plays a lesser, albeit increasing, role. While the legislation is an important factor, Vancouver's location in relation to the Alaska Panhandle also confers an advantage in serving desired ports of call on seven-day cruises. Over time a significant infrastructure has been developed to service the cruise industry; this adds to Vancouver's locational advantage (Marti 1990).

The Contemporary Alaska Cruise

The Alaska cruise has a long and storied history, but the real growth has occurred in the past thirty years with an expansion from 38 sailings for 22,800 revenue passengers in 1970 to 331 sailings for 1,060,383 passengers in 2001 for Vancouver departures (Vancouver Port Authority 2001). This boom paralleled the development of the overall cruise industry over this period. Ships have become much larger and the product more sophisticated. One unique element that

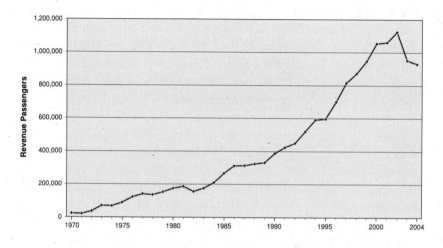

Figure 11.3 Vancouver-Alaska cruise passengers. Source: Vancouver Port
Authority (2004).

has contributed to expansion of the Alaska market has been the focus
on extensive land tour packages to supplement the cruise experience.
While land tours had been included in many early Alaska cruises,
it was the development in the 1960s by Seattle-based Westours of
motor coach and rail tours to the Alaska and Yukon hinterland that
became a key for further growth (Dickinson and Vladimir 1997).
Seeing the prospect offered by this cruise/land excursion combination, a long-established cruise line, Holland America, purchased
Westours in 1970 and entered the Alaska market, moving their head
office to Seattle in 1973. Princess and Peninsular & Oriental (P&O)
began offering cruises to Alaska in the late 1960s (Hacking 1990;
Bannerman 1976) and after their merger in 1974 further developed
their own land tour capability.

Other companies joined the market in the 1970s and 1980s, resulting in tremendous growth in the Alaska cruise business (over tenfold from 1970 to 1985) (fig. 11.3). To meet this demand Vancouver
completed a new cruise terminal in 1986 at Canada Place and later
refurbished a second terminal in 1994.

Passenger growth until 2001 was steady, with large increases
after the Open Skies Agreement of 1995 permitted more U.S. direct

John M. Munro and Warren G. Gill

flights into Vancouver International Airport, thereby reducing the need to bus passengers from nearby U.S. airports. Ship size also grew from 20 major ships of an average size of 26,204 gross registered tons in 1990 to 25 major ships of 61,076 tons in 2001 (*Harbour and Shipping* 1990; 2001). This rapid escalation in numbers of passengers and ship size has not been without problems. Environmental concerns in the 1980s prompted the U.S. National Park Service to restrict cruise ship access to Glacier Bay (a prime sightseeing area) and the number of permits authorized remains a hotly contested issue (Frantz 1999). In addition, the limited capacity of small Alaskan ports-of-call to absorb ever-larger ships and numbers of visitors has raised questions about the environmental and social impacts of the cruise industry on these communities. When combined with terminal capacity restrictions in Vancouver, these issues have forced the cruise lines to expand beyond the preferred Saturday and Sunday departures to almost all days of the week or to place their ships' southern terminus in Seattle. In an attempt to maintain its leading homeport status, Vancouver expanded the Canada Place terminal for the 2002 season to accommodate larger ships and provide for more weekend sailings.

As noted, land tours have become increasingly important (table 11.1). Seven-day "Glacier Route" cruises across the Gulf of Alaska that originate either in Vancouver or Seward, Alaska, with passengers flying the other leg, now comprise over 50 per cent of sailings. These cruises offer greater opportunities to market land packages to Denali National Park and other interior Alaska destinations than does the traditional "Inside Passage" return trip from Vancouver and they have the added benefit of reducing terminal congestion in Vancouver. Competition between cruise lines now focuses on land excursion capacity as well as type and quality of ship. A failed joint venture proposal between P&O Princess and Royal Caribbean International was in part motivated by reducing costs through the joint utilization of Princess's land assets in Alaska (and perhaps gaining more access to Glacier Bay), features where Royal Caribbean is weak (P&O Princess Cruises, 2001).

Table 11.1 Land Excursion Capacity, 2001.

	PRINCESS	HOLLAND AMERICA	ROYAL CARIBBEAN
GUEST ROOMS			
Alaska Interior	1,001	894	
Alaska Southeast		551	
Yukon		585	
Total	1,001	2,030	
RAILCARS			
Cars	10	13	2
Daily Capacity	880	858	160
Motorcoaches	219	192	6
Capital Employed	US $160M	US $200M	US $10M
Balcony Cabins per week	1,824	864	1,845
Glacier Bay Cruises	77	101	

Source: Ball (2001).

The Future Alaska Cruise

After more than a century of evolution, the Alaska cruise has become a significant contributor to the tourism economies of Alaska and British Columbia. For continued growth the challenge will be to develop new ports-of-call as the Alaska ports have become saturated with visitors and many Alaskans are concerned about environmental degradation. Environmental concerns over air and water pollution are significant and are a political issue. So is the U.S. Passenger Vessel Services Act, which encourages use of Vancouver as the principal homeport. This legislation has been reviewed many times (e.g., U.S. House of Representatives 1998) and any significant change could direct more homeport activity to Seattle. In an attempt to create a non-Alaska, Pacific Northwest cruise market, some cruise companies have experimented with pocket cruises of three and four days from Seattle to Victoria and Vancouver on a 'Triangle Route' in the

John M. Munro and Warren G. Gill

shoulder seasons of May and September. Another option for growth, which would also reduce the impact on Alaska, is to develop British Columbia coastal ports, such as Prince Rupert and Port Hardy, as ports-of-call, just as they were in the earlier days of the Alaska service (British Columbia 1988). This will prove challenging, however, as the mainstream American market remains focused on Alaska, with the long journey along British Columbia being just a means to an end.

Economic Impacts

General Economic Impacts

Both the tourism and port impacts of the cruise industry are important in assessing its regional economic impact. The tourism sector consists of industries that sell services and goods to persons who are travelling outside their place of usual residence for business or personal reasons. Since these industries also sell products to business firms such as freight transportation and to local residents in restaurants and local attractions, the spending of particular groups such as Alaska cruise tourists is usually determined by conducting surveys that ask them questions concerning their spending.

On the tourism side, cruise economic impacts are inevitably less than would be generated by the same number of land-based tourists. A cruise is essentially a self-contained, fully prearranged vacation experience; indeed, that feature is one of the most important marketing devices for cruise companies. How much spending stimulus this form of tourism delivers to a regional economy depends on shore spending by passengers before, during, and after the cruise. On the port side, since neither the ships, the cruise companies, nor the crew have any ongoing connection with any of the regional economies, the level of regional spending by cruise companies and crewmembers is necessarily limited. Despite these impact limitations, the magnitude of the Alaska cruise operation and its focus on Vancouver and relatively small Alaskan communities does have the potential for substantial impact on the Alaska and B.C. economies.

There is considerable interest in the economic impact of ports. Port authorities and port-related industries generate most of this, which presumably wish to assure governments and the general public that they are important for local and regional economies. This desire for recognition is likely stimulated by the desire to protect certain benefits and powers conferred on ports such as local tax abatements, local taxing powers, and the ability to borrow against the public credit of the metropolitan area. Port economic impact studies are also used to inform decisions concerning port development and infrastructure investment (Cowan and Brooks 1995).

Cruise ships interface with ports in much the same way as cargo ships. They must be docked, unloaded, supplied and provisioned, repaired, loaded, and undocked. Some of these functions are more or less important for cruise ships than for cargo ships but because cruise ships spend more time in port as a percentage of their annual operation, the port interface is more frequent. Also, cruise ships have far larger crews than cargo ships and crewmembers' personal spending ashore is an important supplement to passenger spending.

As a first step in assessing the magnitude of economic impact and identifying features of the cruise industry that contribute most to regional economic impact, table 11.2 identifies the basic transactions structure of this industry; sales are shown in the rows and purchases in the columns.

John M. Munro and Warren G. Gill

Table 11.2 Cruise Industry Regional Economic Relationships.

SALES/ PURCHASES	CRUISE COMPANIES	PASSENGERS	SHIP SUPPLIERS	TOURISM/ RETAIL	CREW
Cruise Companies	*	Major	*	*	*
Passengers	*	*	*	*	*
Ship Suppliers	Major	*	Small	*	*
Tourism/Retail	Major	Major	*	Small	Small
Crew	Major	Major	*	*	*

* indicates zero purchases or sales; cells in italics are not of great importance to the regional economy.

Table 11.2 only includes the economic relationships that are important in a regional economy where cruise ship operations are seasonal and where crews and ships are nonresident. In the table, cruise companies purchase goods and services from ship suppliers for the operation of ships and tours and transportation from tour and transport companies for resale to their passengers. Passengers purchase their cruise from cruise companies; this transaction is important for the regional economy because it often includes local tours and travel. Passengers also purchase tours and travel directly from local suppliers and passenger shopping impacts the regional economy directly, as does passenger pre- and post-cruise hotels and meals. Sales and purchases within the ship supply and tourism/retail sector are relatively small. Crew expenditures on the retail and tourism sector are much smaller than passenger expenditures.

The regional economic impact of these expenditures is influenced by a number of key parameters:

1. The number of days the average cruise passenger spends in the region is determined by such factors as personal choice, whether a city is the origin and/or destination of the cruise,

and how many regional ports are visited on the cruise and for how long.

2. Average cruise passenger expenditures per day are determined by average passenger income (according to InterVistas [1999], median household income of Alaska cruise passengers is C$65,000; 38 per cent have household incomes over C$80,000), personal tastes and choices, and port arrival/departure travel mode.

3. Average expenditures per crewmember depend on the number of visits to particular ports (for example, seven-day itineraries have twice as many visits to Vancouver as four-teen-day itineraries) and average salary levels of crewmembers. These vary by occupation, by nationality, and by ship.

4. Cruise company expenditures depend on vessel size and characteristics (expenditures per vessel by cruise companies increase as the size of ships increases) and vessel schedule and cruise marketing.

5. Multipliers to extend the economic impact of initial expenditures across the regional economy depend on the interindustry structure of the regional economy and spending stream leakages. For example, a large proportion of the goods sold to Alaska cruise passengers and cruise companies are imported. However, passengers and companies also purchase services and these have a much lower import component and so involve smaller leakages from the regional spending stream.

British Columbia Impact Estimates

A recent study for the Port of Vancouver (InterVistas 2001) estimated 2001 British Columbia tourism spending by Alaska cruise passengers at C$138 million. Crew spending added a further C$41 million. Cruise companies spent an additional C$147 million on supplies and services purchased in British Columbia. This total spending of C$326 million generated 2,970 direct person-years of employment in B.C. and added C$148 million to provincial gross domestic product. Applying western Canada multipliers to account for indirect and induced effects of this spending makes the total B.C. employment impact 6,100 person-years and the total B.C. GDP impact C$277 million.

Alaska Impact Estimates

The typical cruise ship, whether on a seven-day Vancouver-Vancouver round trip or a Vancouver-Seward one-way trip, spends about thirty hours in Alaskan ports (usually three ports). While this is more time than the average ship spends in Vancouver, passengers have no option of extending their time in these ports, except in Vancouver or Seward. Moreover, cruise company spending in Alaskan ports is much lower than in Vancouver or other southern homeports.

There are two recent studies of the economic impact of the cruise industry on Alaska. A study prepared for the International Council of Cruise Lines used initial spending to estimate impact on state economies (ICCL 2003). According to this study, the cruise industry accounted for US$595 million in total purchases in Alaska and employment of 16,455 with wages totalling US$546 million. Another study (McDowell Group 2000), prepared for several southeastern Alaska cities that are important cruise ship ports, was based on spending surveys and did not extend initial spending and resulting employment through the whole economy. For the major port of Juneau (which is included in virtually all itineraries), the study showed spending by passengers, crew, and companies amounting to US$83 million, US$6 million, and US$2 million, respectively. Cruise industry employment effects for all southeastern Alaska ports were estimated at over 2,000 person-years.

National Maritime Policy

U.S. national maritime policy raises an important transnational policy issue for the Alaska cruise industry. As mentioned earlier, the Passenger Vessel Service Act restricts transportation between U.S. ports to ships built, registered, and crewed in the United States. Only two operating deep-sea cruise ships meet these requirements because costs are lower with other arrangements – about 20–25 per cent lower (Buchholz and Cropper 1993). The cruise industry typically builds its ships in Europe, registers them in Liberia, Panama, or the Bahamas, and operates them with diverse international crews, perhaps the most globalized labour force in any industry (Wood 2000).

Consequently, U.S. law means that the international cruise industry must have a Canadian port of call in their Alaska cruise itineraries; geography and port facilities make Vancouver the most suitable port. Companies are permitted to turn their Alaska vessels around in ports such as Seattle and San Francisco, but they must schedule a call somewhere in Canada (usually in Victoria). From Seattle, meeting a seven-day, one-way schedule to and from Seward or a seven-day roundtrip to Skagway is problematic because the voyage to Southeastern Alaska is in outside waters, not the scenic B.C. Inside Passage, and there is little slack in the schedule. From San Francisco, weekly schedules are impossible and ships homeported in San Francisco operate on twelve-day roundtrip schedules to Skagway. These schedules are believed to be less attractive to market.

Cabotage – restricting domestic shipping business to national vessels – is not peculiar to the United States. Other countries, including Canada, also practice cabotage, but it is curious that this constraint has been retained in the U.S. when the domestic deep-sea passenger shipping industry that it was supposed to protect has long since withered away. The explanation is that any loosening of the passenger legislation would be perceived as the first step in weakening the similar protection for intranational freight transportation contained in the Merchant Marine Act of 1920 (well known as the "Jones Act"). That protection is more important and a powerful lobby has so far resisted all moves to rationalize these old protectionist laws.

Change may be slow in coming. Various liberalizing bills have been introduced into both Senate and the House of Representatives in the last few years but the ingrained opposition of U.S. shipping, union, and shipbuilding interests has been strong enough to prevent them from coming to a final vote. In 2000 the U.S. Senate passed the United States Cruise Vessel Act (S. 127) to allow foreign-built ships to be registered in the United States if certain conditions were met. A similar, but not identical bill with the same title was introduced in the House of Representatives in September 2001 (H.R. 2901). However, the conditions set in this legislation were rather onerous (replacement and repairs in U.S. shipyards) and the proposal did not address the higher costs of crewing a ship with U.S. personnel, as would be required under the U.S. flag.

Also, it remains to be seen whether there would be any ship owners who wished to take advantage of the opportunity to enter the U.S. domestic market even under these more favourable conditions. There might be advantages if the proposers' idea that this legislation "would ultimately give consumers greater choice in domestic cruise destinations and allow more Americans to visit our nation's port cities on a cruise vessel" were correct. The immediate effects on the current Alaska cruise arrangements if legislation such as this became law are unclear, but it is possible that over time Vancouver could lose its pre-eminent place as preferred southern terminus.

Environmental Issues

International Regulatory Policy

Environmental and safety regulation of international shipping has evolved over the last fifty years. Shipping in territorial waters has always been subject to national laws but for safety and environmental issues involving high seas navigation a series of international agreements and conventions set up under the International Maritime Organization (IMO) extend this regulation beyond the two-hundred-mile limit. The IMO, a specialized United Nations agency with

159 members, was established in 1948 with a mandate to organize safety and pollution arrangements for international shipping. Over the years the IMO has promoted the adoption of some forty conventions and protocols and has adopted over eight hundred codes and recommendations concerning maritime safety, pollution, and other maritime matters. IMO's major conventions include SOLAS (Safety of Life at Sea), the Oil Pollution Convention, and MARPOL (International Convention for the Prevention of Pollution from Ships). Enforcement of these international regulations and their national counterparts depends on the efforts of countries of vessel registry, ship-owning countries, port countries, and the cooperation of shipping firms and organizations (IMO 2004).

Both vessel safety and environmental standards and performance have equipment and operating aspects. National regulations that apply when vessels are in port or in national waters should be sufficient to ensure that vessels have the equipment to meet appropriate safety and environmental standards but national regulations with respect to operating performance may not be effective beyond the two-hundred-mile limit. As with land-based pollution control, new technologies are not always available or feasible for older ships and so higher pollution standards are typically phased in over time.

Cruise Ships

Cruise ships account for only a small fraction of the world's merchant fleet but these vessels pose special environmental impact concerns. Cruise ships have the same risks of pollution from propulsion fuel and other engine room discharges as nontanker cargo ships, but their risks of other kinds of pollution are vastly higher. The largest cruise ships have almost five thousand passengers and crew on board, compared to far fewer than a hundred on the largest cargo ships. Moreover, cruise ships do more than simply move across the ocean as floating resorts; they must offer a diverse range of activities for their passengers. These activities generate large quantities of waste products, many of which are unknown for cargo vessels. For example, cruise ships take thousands of photographs of their passengers on each cruise. The film is developed on board and significant quantities of toxic waste (one estimate is 150 gallons per day) are produced. Cruise ship itineraries also make them more significant environmental risks than cargo ships of the same size. They spend longer periods of time in port and often travel in shallow, confined coastal waters. In both areas the standards for pollutant discharge must be higher than in the open ocean. The appendix to this paper reports on a hypothetical cruise ship's discharge activities over a twenty-four-hour period.

There is little doubt that the cruise industry is very concerned about its performance and image as a marine polluter. The International Council of Cruise Lines (ICCL), whose member companies include all the major international cruise companies including all those that operate large ships to Alaska, has made the following policy statement (ICCL 2004): "The cruise industry is inextricably linked to the environment. Our business is to bring people to interesting places in the world, over the water. Recognizing the future of the industry depends on a clean and healthy environment, cruise industry senior management is committed to stewardship of the environment and setting industry standards that will make ICCL member cruise ship operators leaders in environmental performance."

This statement nicely captures the corporate self-interest of the cruise industry for a clean environment. However, not all are impressed with the industry's record. Environmental groups such as the Bluewater Network (Schmidt 2004) and West Coast Environmental Law (Nowlan 1999) have reported and lobbied on the cruise ship pollution problem. Various government agencies and political leaders have also begun to pay much more attention to cruise ship pollution in the last few years.

The cruise industry through its various industry associations and the decisions of individual companies has responded to these concerns. (Since, in many cases, they have given rise to new laws and regulations, the industry really had little choice but to respond.) The ICCL adopted detailed waste management standards in 2001 (ICCL 2004). The content of these standards is illustrated in the following excerpt:

> The cruise industry commitment to protecting the environment is demonstrated by the comprehensive spectrum of waste management technologies and procedures employed on its vessels. ICCL members are committed to:

a. Designing, constructing and operating vessels, so as to minimize their impact on the environment

b. Developing improved technologies to exceed current requirements for protection of the environment

c. Implementing a policy goal of zero discharge of MARPOL, Annex V solid waste products by use of more comprehensive waste minimization procedures to significantly reduce shipboard generated waste

d. Expanding waste reduction strategies to include reuse and recycling to the maximum extent possible so as to land ashore even smaller quantities of waste products

e. Improving processes and procedures for collection and transfer of hazardous waste.

Specific requirements for the discharge of "graywater" (waste water from washing) and "blackwater" (sewage) are included.

Graywater will be discharged only while the ship is underway and proceeding at a speed of not less than 6 knots. Graywater will not be discharged in port and will not be discharged within 4 nautical miles from shore or such other distance as agreed to with authorities having jurisdiction or provided for by local law except in an emergency, or where geographically limited. The discharge of graywater will comply with all applicable laws and regulations.

Blackwater will be discharged only while the ship is underway and proceeding at a speed of not less than 6 knots and in accordance with applicable regulations. Treated blackwater will not be discharged in port and will not be discharged within 4 nautical miles from shore or such other distance as agreed to with authorities having jurisdiction or provided for by local law, except in an emergency, or where geographically limited. The discharge of blackwater will comply with all applicable laws and regulations.

Pollution and the Alaska Cruise

Now that Alaska's visible emission standards are largely being met by cruise ships (Alaska 2004), the major concern is water pollution. Most Alaska cruise vessel time is spent in port or in inner coastal waters and so the industry mainly operates in U.S. or Canadian territorial waters. In Canada only federal law applies to this industry. Marine environmental legal requirements for the shipping industry are primarily the responsibility of Transport Canada, which administers the Canada Shipping Act, 2001 (2001, c. 26) as well as the interests of the Department of Fisheries and Oceans. DFO includes the Canadian Coast Guard and is responsible for the Fisheries Act (R.S. 1985, c. F-14). Such marine issues are dealt with through an interdepartmental committee (Canada 2004) (in references see Canada. Statutes for internet source for Canadian legislation). Overall, Canadian laws dealing with cruise ship environmental problems are said to be less stringent than U.S. laws and it has been suggested that standards in Canadian laws be raised to the U.S. level (Nowlan 1999).

U.S. laws that govern cruise industry environmental impact exist at both federal and state levels. Federal law includes the Oil Pollution Act of 1990 (33 U.S.C. 2702 to 2761), the Federal Water Pollution Control Act (Clean Water Act) (33 U.S.C. 1251 to1387), and the Comprehensive Environmental Response, Compensation, and Liability Act (42 U.S.C. 9601–9675) (in references see U.S. Code (U.S.C.) for internet source for U.S. statutes). In 1990 the Alaska congressional delegation succeeded in inserting state-specific amendments to Coast Guard funding authorization legislation that made the graywater and blackwater dumping language later included in the ICCL standards mandatory in Alaskan waters. In Alaska, a joint industry-government program called the Alaska Cruise Ship Initiative has led to improved cooperation between the two parties and apparent improvements in cruise ship practices. The recent Alaska legislation was an outcome of this consultative process.

However, there are differences between cruise ship regulations in different jurisdictions. Nowlan and Kwan (2001) tabulate and compare Canadian, U.S., and Alaska laws regulating cruise ship pollution under seven headings, as shown in table 11.3.

Table 11.3 Comparison of Cruise Ship Pollution Regulations.

	CANADA	U.S.	ALASKA
Blackwater Treatment	Not required	Some required	Some required
Blackwater Discharge	Prohibited in a few small areas+	At 6 knots vessel speed 1 nautical mile from shore if fully treated; otherwise, 3 miles from shore*	Same as U.S.
Graywater Standards	No	No	Yes
Graywater Discharge	No restrictions+	Permitted 1 mile from shore at 6 knots vessel speed	Same as U.S.
Oil Discharge	None, except bilge water with 15 ppm oil	Within 12 miles of shore at 15 ppm oil and beyond at 100 ppm oil	Same as U.S.
Hazardous Waste Discharge	Generally prohibited	Generally prohibited	Generally prohibited
Solid Waste Discharge	Only ground-up food wastes	Some materials prohibited but some dumping beyond 3 miles	No prohibition
Air Emissions	Emission level standards	No standards	Opacity standards
Monitoring and Enforcement	Not specifically required	Monitoring and reporting required	Monitoring and reporting required; sampling program

+ The International Council of Cruise Lines waste management standards discussed above
     would apply.
* Vessels with advanced wastewater treatment systems may be certified for continuous
     wastewater discharge.

John M. Munro and Warren G. Gill

The cruise industry will adhere to whichever applicable regulatory regime is more stringent and so the existence of some higher standards in U.S. laws should tend to bring those higher standards to Canada. This is especially the case when equipment rather than operating procedures are important in mitigating environmental hazards. But if operating practices such as wastewater dumping are permitted under less stringent conditions in Canadian than in Alaska waters, then more dumping may occur in Canadian waters. There is a real need to harmonize regulations affecting cruise ship pollution.

The major cruise lines are undertaking measures to upgrade wastewater treatment and otherwise mitigate pollution from the operation of their ships. According to the North West CruiseShip Association, a quarter of the 2001 cruise ships in Alaska service had installed secondary wastewater treatment to bring discharged waters "near drinking water standards." Also, some companies, such as Holland America, have discharge operating standards that are more stringent than those specified by regulations (2004).

Other Environmental Impacts

A related area of environmental concern stems from a congestion effect created when thousands of passengers descend on a small town or city or a wilderness area. This issue seems to be a growing concern in Alaska entirely apart from the pollution problems created by cruise ships entering these environments. In 2001 a federal court judge ordered the cruise lines to reduce their trips to Glacier Bay National Park and Preserve, arguably the premier scenic attraction on the Alaska cruise itinerary. More recently, the National Park Service has confirmed the limit of two large cruise ships per day allowed to cruise in Glacier Bay and has set other operating constraints associated with whale protection (U.S. National Park Service 2003). This limit means that the majority of cruises to Alaska cannot have itineraries that include Glacier Bay. Congestion is also a concern in the small cities of southeastern Alaska (where the most popular port, Juneau, receives 25–27 cruise ship visits per week during the peak of the cruise season) and in the wilderness areas of central Alaska that are often added to an Alaska cruise trip. Tourism is Alaska's second largest industry in terms of employment (after government) and GDP (after oil and gas) but harmonizing its growth with preserving the attractions that create demand for travel to Alaska will not be easy (National Parks Conservation Association 2003).

Conclusions

The Alaska cruise has been an important historic element in the development of the Port of Vancouver and the economies of British Columbia and Alaska. Its importance to Washington State declined when cruise ship itineraries shifted north to Vancouver but has since rebounded with the development of improved port facilities in Seattle. Since the establishment of a contemporary cruise industry dedicated to tourism in the late 1960s, there has been continued growth in passengers, economic impact, and environmental surveillance. Results from various economic impact studies indicate a significant impact in both GDP and jobs but also suggest substantial potential for greater returns. While Alaska cruises are a relatively small part of B.C. tourism (probably not more than 10 per cent of tourism GDP and employment), this part of the sector has grown more rapidly than total tourism and the potential is there for more growth. Also, there is research (Holmes and Shamsuddin 1997) to support the argument that short exposure to British Columbia touristic attractions leads to return visits.

In Alaska the cruise industry is a larger part of the tourism industry, which is the second largest employer in Alaska and the second largest contributor of value-added to Alaska's gross state product. Overall, the wilderness and scenic attractions of Alaska are more important to the cruise industry than those in British Columbia. Ships are in Alaska longer and the greatest marketing attention is given to various Alaska attractions. Thus, solving the environmental problems of the cruise ship operation is essential if Alaska is to continue to enjoy the economic benefits of this industry.

However, increasing the economic impact of the Alaska cruise industry may prove challenging as some have argued that the Alaska market is probably saturated (Cartwright and Baird 1999) even though the sustained expansion over the past thirty years might seem to belie that assertion. Cruise companies have already shown they can successfully adapt to the limitations of southeast Alaska ports by developing new products, such as Glacier Route cruises and deep interior land excursions. Princess's current marketing strategy is to focus on the 'heart of Alaska' by investing in more land-based facilities in central Alaska (Ball 2001). When combined with ever larger ships – in 2001 Celebrity's Infinity became the first Alaska ship over 90,000 grt and Princess now deploys two large post-Panamax ships, the *Diamond Princess* and the *Sapphire Princess* (113,000 grt) – such strategies auger well for continued passenger growth.

Given the importance of passenger spending in determining economic impact a key strategy is obviously to extend pre- and post-cruise stays in British Columbia and to develop tourist products that encourage higher levels of expenditures. All lines currently have shore packages in Vancouver, with some offering excursions to Victoria, Whistler, and interior points. The task is to make these attractions more central to the Alaska cruise experience.

For British Columbia one of the most important challenges is to ensure that Vancouver remains the principal homeport for Alaska and related cruises. The Port of Seattle has been aggressively pursuing new opportunities but these are inhibited by the restrictions of U.S. national maritime policy. Economic sectors built on trade restrictions do, in the long run, risk both the removal of this protection and the success of measures designed to avoid the restrictions. Overall, the need to balance the costs of higher environmental standards for cruise ships with the pressures of a highly competitive environment inside the cruise industry and in the leisure market overall should be the highest priority in the near term for both Alaska and British Columbia.

Appendix

Twenty-Four Hours in the Life of Cruise Ship Hypothetica

(Note: The *Hypothetica* is fictitious ship. The wastewater generation rates and handling methods are approximations.)

The *Hypothetica*, a 76,000-gross-ton cruise ship with 2,700 passengers and crewmembers on board, moored at Ketchikan City Dock at 6:30 a.m., following a two-day voyage from Vancouver, B.C. The last wastewater discharged had been at 4:30 a.m. when the vessel was in Clarence Strait, approximately twelve miles southwest of Ketchikan. By the time the vessel departed Ketchikan at 2:00 p.m., 5,000 meals had been served, 2,000 showers and baths had been taken, several tons of laundry had been washed, and 115,000 gallons of graywater and treated blackwater from these activities had accumulated in the 300,000-gallon-capacity holding tank. Seven hundred gallons of oily water, primarily from engine maintenance, had accumulated in the bilge. This bilge water was held in a 5,000-gallon tank for eventual processing through an oily water separator. The effluent (<15 ppm oil to water) would be discharged in the Gulf of Alaska, two days later.

Leaving Ketchikan, the *Hypothetica* sailed north through Tongass Narrows, then northwest through Clarence Strait en route to Juneau at an average speed of 19 knots (21.5 mph). On board, wastewater continued to drain to the holding tanks on an average of 7,000 gallons per hour until around 10:00 p.m., after which wastewater production tapered off dramatically. At 3:30 p.m., when the vessel was three miles north of Guard Island, the vessel began to discharge graywater and treated blackwater from the holding tank at 16,000 gallons per hour. As the effluent was pumped through a four-inch overboard discharge port twelve feet below the waterline, it was quickly diluted by the speed of the vessel and water turbulence along the hull. Three seconds after discharge, the effluent was diluted in seawater at a ratio of 1 to 120. Within 400 feet of the discharge port, the effluent had been diluted by a factor of 300 before passing into the prop wash of the ship's propellers where further dilution took place. Wastewater discharge continued until 2:30 a.m. By then the *Hypothetica* was in Stephens Passage, forty-six miles south of Juneau. Overboard discharge ports were secured as the vessel made preparations for a 6:00 a.m. docking in Juneau (Eley 2000).

References

Alaska. 2004. Cruise Ship Fact Sheet. http://www.state.ak.us/dec/water/ cruise_ships/pdfs/cruisefaqs.pdf.

Ball, Charlie. 2001. *Princess Alaska*. Analyst presentation on board Grand Princess, May 12. http://www.poprincesscruises.com/financ.htm.

Brown, Dean. 2001. *U.S. Cruise Market Demand*. Analyst presentation on board Grand Princess, May 12. http://www.poprincesscruises. com/financ.htm.

Bannerman, Gary. 1976. *Cruise Ships: The Inside Story*. Sidney, B.C.: Saltaire.

British Columbia. 1988. *British Columbia Ports and Cruising Destinations*. Report prepared by Don Ference & Associates under the Canada-British Columbia Tourist Industry Development Subsidiary Agreement. Victoria: Province of British Columbia.

Buchholz, Todd G., and Carol M. Cropper. 1993. "All at sea." *Forbes* 152(11): 174.

Canada. Statutes. http://laws.justice.gc.ca/cgi-bin/notice.pl?redirect=/en/C-10.15/index.html.

Canada. 2004. "Memorandum of Understanding between Transport Canada and Fisheries and Oceans Respecting Marine Transportation Safety and Environmental Protection." http://www.tc.gc.ca/MarineSafety/ TP/mou/menu.htm.

Cartwright, Roger, and Carolyn Baird. 1999. *The Development and Growth of the Cruise Industry*. Oxford: Butterworth Heinemann.

Cruise Lines International Association (CLIA). 5 March 2001. Cruise Industry Records 16 Percent Growth in 2000. *Cruise News and Specials*. Cruise Lines International Association. http://www. crusing.org.cvpc/news/news.cfm?NID=69.

———. Spring 2004. *The Overview*. http://staging.cruising.org/press/ overview/ind_overview.cfm.

Cowan, John, and Mary Brooks. 1995. Port Economic Impact Studies: An Examination. *Proceedings, Canadian Transportation Research Forum*, 400–413.

Dawson, Philip. 2000. *Cruise Ships: An Evolution in Design*. London: Conway Maritime Press.

Dickinson, Bob, and Andy Vladimir. 1997. *Selling the Sea: An Inside Look at the Cruise Industry*. New York: Wiley.

Dwyer, Larry, and Peter Forsyth. 1998. Economic Significance of Cruise Tourism. *Annals of Tourism Research* 25: 393–415.

Ebersold, William B. 2004. *Cruise Industry in Figures*. http://www.briefings.com/pdf/858/ACF7B5.pdf.

Eley, W. David. 2000. A Survey of Waste Stream Discharges and Solid Waste Handling Practices of Cruise Ships Operating in Southeast Alaska. *Alaska Cruise Ship Initiative*. Part I, appendix D, Final Report. http://www.state.ak.us/local/akpages/ENV.CONSERV/press/cruise/pdfs/finreportp10808.pdf.

Frantz, Douglas. 29 Nov. 1999. Sovereign Islands – A Question of Regulations: Alaskans Choose Sides in Battle over Cruise Ships. *New York Times*: A1.

Hacking, Norman. 1990. Ship & Shore. *Harbour & Shipping* 73(4): 30–31.

Harbour & Shipping. 1990. Alaska Cruise Ship Issue 73(4): 26.

———. 2001. Annual Alaska Cruise Ship Issue 84(5): 26.

Holland America Line. 2004. Fact Sheet: A Commitment to the Environment. http://www.hollandamerica.com/pdfs/media/factsheets/EnvironmentalCommitment_FactSheet.pdf.

Holmes, Richard A., and Abul F.M. Shamsuddin. 1997. Short- and Long-Term Effects of World Exposition 1986 on U.S. Demand for British Columbia Tourism. *Tourism Economics* 3: 137–60.

International Council of Cruise Lines (ICCL). 2003. *The Contribution of the North American Cruise Industry to the U.S. Economy in 2002*. Exton, PA: Business and Economic Advisors.

———. 2004. Cruise Industry Waste Management Practices and Procedures. http://www.iccl.org/policies/envstd_summary.pdf.

International Maritime Organization (IMO). 2004. About IMO. http://www.imo.org/home.asp.

InterVistas Consulting Inc. 1999. *1999 Vancouver-Alaska Cruise Passenger Study*. Vancouver.

———. 2001. *Port Vancouver Economic Study*. Vancouver.

Marti, Bruce E. 1990. Geography and the Cruise Ship Port Selection Process. *Maritime Policy and Management* 17: 157–64.

Maxtone-Graham, John. 1985. *Liners to the Sun*. New York: Macmillan.

McDowell Group. 2000. *The Economic Impacts of the Cruise Industry in Southeast Alaska*. Juneau.

National Parks Conservation Association. 2003. When the Ships Come In. *Magazine*. http://www.npca.org/magazine/2003/july_august/ships.asp.

Nowlan, Linda. 1999. *Preserving British Columbia's Coast: A Regulatory Review*. Vancouver: West Coast Environmental Law. http://www. wcel.org/wcelpub/1999/12881.html.

Nowlan, Linda, and Ines Kwan. Sept. 2001. *Cruise Control: Regulating Cruise Ship Pollution on the Pacific Coast of Canada*. Vancouver: West Coast Environmental Law. http://www.state.ak.us/local/ akpages/ENV.CONSERV/press/cruise/pdfs/wcelcuiserep.pdf.

P&O Princess Cruises. 27 Dec. 2001. *Proposed DLC Combinations with Royal Caribbean Cruises Ltd*. http://www.poprincesscruises.com/ presframes.htm/RCPcirc.pdf.

Schmidt, Kira 2004. "What Works Best, Regulatory or Non-Regulatory Solutions to Cruise Ship Pollution Prevention? The Environmental Perspective." Bluewater Network. http://bluewaternetwork.org/ reports/rep_ss_cruise_sandiego2.pdf.

Turner, Robert D. 1977. *The Pacific Princesses: An Illustrated History of the Canadian Pacific Railway's Princess Fleet on the Northwest Coast*. Victoria: Sono Nis.

U.S. House of Representatives. 1998. Subcommittee on Coast Guard and Marine Transportation and Infrastructure. Committee on Transportation and Infrastructure. 29 April. *Effect of the Passenger Services Act on the Domestic Cruise Industry*. Washington, D.C. http://commdocs.house.gov/committees/Trans/hpw105-65.000/ hpw105-65_1.htm; accessed: 5 February 2002.

U.S. National Park Service. 2003. Record of Decision: Glacier Bay National Park and Preserve, Alaska – Vessel quotas and Operating Requirements. http://www.glba.ene.com/rod.html.

U.S. Code (U.S.C.). http://www.law.cornell.edu/uscode/.

Vancouver Port Authority. 2001. http://www.portvancouver.com/statistics/ and http://www.portvancouver.com/media/news_2001_11_26.html.

———. 2004. *Statistical Report* . and earlier years

Ward, Douglas. 1999. *Berlitz 2000: Complete Guide to Cruising and Cruise Ships*. Princeton, NJ: Berlitz.

Wood, Robert E. 2000. Caribbean Cruise Tourism: Globalization at Sea. *Annals of Tourism Research* 27: 345–70.

NOTES

1   Note that the companies that comprise CLIA (and are included in CLIA statistics) are defined by their primary focus on the North American market as defined by passenger origin, not cruise destination.

2   46 App. U.S.C. 289. A useful compendium of U.S. shipping statutes is available at http://www.house.gov/transportation/cgmt/compilations/ volume1.html.

12

REACHING ACROSS BORDERS: SUSTAINABILITY INITIATIVES WITHIN AND BEYOND THE RESORT COMMUNITY OF WHISTLER

Hugh O'Reilly and Tina Symko

Abstract

Known worldwide as a leading four-season mountain resort, Whistler provides unique recreational and tourism experiences to millions of visitors each year. Simultaneously, Whistler is home to a small resident community embracing the challenges of moving toward a more sustainable future. In addition to developing significant local initiatives, Whistler is also reaching past its own community to engage in innovative partnership projects across borders to help achieve this movement toward sustainability. This paper discusses the evolution of Whistler's sustainability initiatives with a focus on local, regional, and international collaboration toward common sustainability goals. The 2010 Olympic and Paralympic Winter Games provide a significant opportunity to champion, and act as a catalyst for, sustainability through demonstrated leadership and visionary local and regional partnerships.

Introduction

Throughout thirty years of Olympic bids led by local entrepreneurs, the town of Whistler has grown from a handful of lakeside residences into a world-class destination resort community. While developing as a resort community and pursuing an Olympic dream, a dream which will become a reality in 2010 when Vancouver and Whistler will host the Winter Olympic and Paralympic Winter Games, the community of Whistler has pursued another vision – that of sustainability, of becoming a community that lives within the Earth's limits and that contributes to the overall well-being of the local and global environment.

Whistler recognized early on that the path to sustainability requires collaboration among levels of government, citizens' groups, business and international constituents. In addition to local initiatives, the unique potential of collaborative efforts across borders for promoting economic and social transformations both within and beyond the local region has also been acknowledged. The following provides a summary of Whistler's development and progress toward sustainability within the context of strategic partnerships within and beyond the resort community's boundaries.

Whistler in Context

Whistler is situated in the Coast Mountain Range of British Columbia, 120 kilometres north of Vancouver, Canada's third largest city, and 180 kilometres from Seattle, Washington (fig. 12.1). Incorporating part of the traditional territory of the Squamish and

Lil'wat First Nations, the Whistler Valley remained undeveloped until the early 1960s when a group of Vancouver businessmen formed the Garibaldi Olympic Development Association (GODA). GODA launched a bid for Vancouver/Whistler to host the 1968 Olympic Winter Games. Although the bid was unsuccessful, this period was a turning point in Whistler's history as local visionaries began plans to develop the valley as an international mountain resort. By 1965, a paved road connected Whistler to Vancouver, B.C., and skiing had begun on Whistler Mountain through the operation of the Garibaldi Lift Company. At that time, Whistler had a permanent population of less than four hundred people.

During the 1970s, Whistler underwent a period of rapid development and in 1980 Whistler Village opened for business along with additional ski operations on Whistler and Blackcomb Mountains. Whistler's popularity accelerated, and by 1989, the municipality was named the number one ski resort in North America by *Snow Country Magazine* (Resort Municipality of Whistler 2004). Today, Whistler accommodates nearly ten thousand permanent residents and two million visitors annually (Tourism Whistler 2003). Currently, Whistler contributes approximately 10 per cent of the province's overall tourism revenue each year, making the resort community a powerful tourism and economic driver in the Pacific Northwest (KPMG 2002).

The majority of Whistler's visitors have generally come from the western United States and Canada but in recent years the resort and the broader region are hosting a growing number of visitors from the eastern United States and Canada, as well as international visitors from Asia, the United Kingdom, and continental Europe. The Province of British Columbia hosted over 3.5 million overnight visitors from the United States in 2003, compared to 692,135 from Asia and 401,972 from Europe. While overall visitor numbers for the province were down 7.6 per cent from previous years, the number of Australian visitors increased 6.6 per cent to 121,640, and visitors from the United Kingdom increased 1.4 per cent to 202,396 (Tourism British Columbia 2003). In early 2005, Canada was granted 'Approved Destination Status' by the Chinese Government, which is expected to significantly increase Asian tourism to British Columbia.

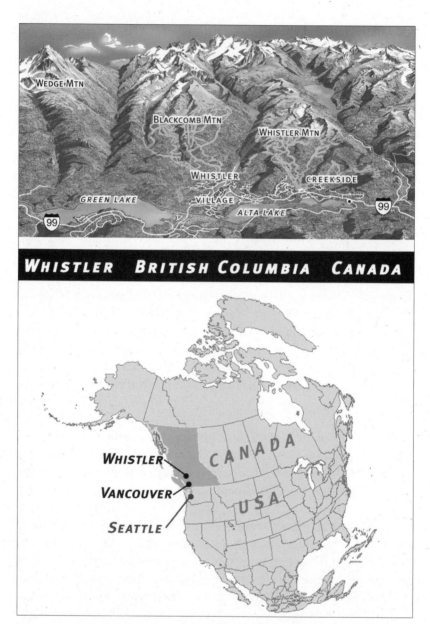

Figure 12.1. Whistler's location in Canada and North America. Source: Z-Point Graphics (2004).

Hugh O'Reilly and Tina Symko

Whistler's Journey toward Sustainability

Due largely to a growing awareness of global environmental issues, sustainability – living within the Earth's limits and ensuring that future generations are able to do the same – has been emerging as a critical focus for an ever-increasing number of organizations, businesses, governments, and communities around the world. Sustainability as a concept, popularized by the World Commission on Environmental Development (WECD) in the 1980s, has attracted international interest as the environmental movement has gained strength. Far different than the traditional concept of conservation, sustainability and sustainable development have come to include the idea that societal well-being depends on both economic and environmental integrity. The WCED, known as the Brundtland Commission, emphasized the necessity of active participation of governments, NGOs, and community members to ensure sustainable outcomes and paid specific attention to the need for economically viable solutions and for the management of natural resources in environmentally sound ways (Dwivedi et al. 2001). In this manner, sustainability offers a framework for integrating environmental strategies with community development.

A sense of sustainability appears to have been part of the Whistler community's DNA from early on, rooted in residents' recreational enjoyment of and appreciation for the outdoors. During Whistler's development in the late 1970s, for example, local design and architecture were aimed at complementing the natural landscape and mountain setting, demonstrating an early collective recognition that the success of the resort community would be inextricably linked to its local environment. Whistler's pedestrian village, the core business and activity centre of the resort community, was itself designed to reflect the form of a river. Flowing walkways lead into public open spaces, which represent pools in a stream where inhabitants can collect and mingle, everything patterned to highlight the natural features and view corridors that make up Whistler's scenic surroundings. Whistler also developed a Valley Trail system for recreation and commuting based on a similar system in Eugene, Oregon, providing nonmotorized (bike/ski/walk) transportation connections between neighbourhoods and village centres.

Whistler experienced rapid growth throughout the late 1980s and 1990s. The town's developed stock increased from 28,000 bed units in 1990 to 46,000 bed units in 2000. "Bed unit" is the term Whistler uses to define the servicing and facility requirements for one person. For example, a single family house is allocated six bed units while a town home is allocated two to four bed units, based on size (Waldron 2003). With this accelerated growth, concern about Whistler's future began to emerge. What would it mean for the community, the local environment, and the overall "Whistler Experience" if such growth were to continue? Did Whistler want to remain a natural place with pockets of development or become a developed place with pockets of nature? It was recognized that the health and beauty of Whistler's natural environment, largely the foundation of the resort community's success as a global tourism destination, could potentially be endangered by continued rapid development. At the same time, awareness was growing of negative environmental trends on a worldwide scale that could potentially affect Whistler. For example, global climate change could have serious consequences for the future of the ski industry. Protecting the environment, and with it Whistler's social and economic health and future, soon became a key focus for the community.

In 1997, the movement toward sustainability began in earnest as the Resort Municipality of Whistler (RMOW) conducted a visioning exercise entitled *Whistler 2002: Charting a Course for the Future*. This process resulted in a five-year vision for Whistler, to be the premier mountain resort community, and highlighted five community priorities and accompanying directions: building a stronger resort community, enhancing the Whistler experience, moving toward environmental sustainability, achieving financial sustainability, and contributing to the success of the region (Resort Municipality of Whistler 1999).

In 1998–99, following the directions of *Whistler 2002*, RMOW developed the *Whistler Environmental Strategy*, a detailed document mapping out environmental values, principles, directions, strategic goals, and tasks. Comprehensive though it was, the *Whistler Environmental Strategy* was complex and difficult to communicate, admittedly lacking an overall compass for moving the resort community toward sustainability.

Through a timely coincidence, Karl-Henrik Robert, a sustainability visionary and founder of The Natural Step, arrived in Whistler with his sons for a snowboarding holiday during the winter of 2000. Accepting a request to speak to the community, Robert introduced Whistler to The Natural Step, an internationally respected framework for sustainability. The Natural Step provided Whistler with a simple yet comprehensive framework, based on accepted scientific principles, which could be used as a clear, effective tool for moving toward sustainability. The Natural Step quickly formed the basis for a common language within Whistler, as local government, businesses, NGOs, and individuals began to function together as a learning community in pursuit of a more sustainable future.

The Natural Step describes four basic science-based system conditions, or minimum requirements, necessary for sustainability. Whistler's ultimate sustainability objectives, agreed upon by key community businesses, organizations, and local government, are stated as eliminating contributions to: 1) progressive build-up in concentrations of waste from the Earth's crust, 2) progressive build-up in concentrations of waste produced by society, 3) the ongoing physical degradation of nature, and 4) the blocking of other people's ability to meet their needs worldwide.

In 2002, as the goals laid out in the *Whistler 2002* process had largely been achieved, Whistler had reached a crossroad. The next task was to establish a plan to maintain Whistler's success as a resort community and to continue moving forward on its plan for achieving sustainability. Whistler embarked on another visioning process in 2002, this time looking ahead to the year 2020. A community-wide planning process, "Whistler 2020," is currently being led by RMOW, which includes a Comprehensive Sustainability Plan (CSP) for Whistler, presented in draft form in 2004. The CSP is a long-term plan to further advance sustainability goals for the resort community. The Natural Step framework has been embedded into the CSP process and draft plan, forming the basis for Whistler's overall sustainability objectives.

Whistler's sustainability efforts to date have met with notable success in several areas:

- *Awareness and Education.* Specialized toolkits were developed and distributed to Whistler households, small businesses, and schools.
- *Materials and Waste.* Significant reduction has been achieved in recent years as part of a zero-waste goal. Eco-friendly landscaping practices have made parks and playgrounds pesticide-free since the early 1990s, also decreasing energy and water use. Excess tipping fees from Whistler's landfill raise $300,000 annually for the community's Environmental Legacy Fund, with interest on this growing fund going toward community environmental projects.
- *Energy.* The RMOW is developing an Integrated Energy, Air Quality and Greenhouse Gas Management Plan, and geothermal heat exchange systems have been installed to heat and cool community and resident housing projects.
- *Transportation.* The development of Whistler's Valley Trail system, a recreation and commuter trail network connecting neighbourhoods, parks, and business and activity areas, has facilitated alternative transportation modes while fostering outdoor recreation values. Whistler's public transportation system serves over 2 million riders per year on twenty-three buses, surpassing the per capita ridership of every other municipality in British Columbia, apart from Greater Vancouver and Victoria (BC Transit 2003). Use of alternative fuel systems is being encouraged. Participation in a regional biodiesel pilot project with five Lower Mainland municipalities (Vancouver, Richmond, Delta, City of North Vancouver, and Burnaby) achieved a 98 per cent success rate, vehicles within the municipal fleet are testing next generation propane technology, and residents are offered shared use of fuel-efficient and hybrid vehicles through the Cooperative Auto Network. Local governments of Whistler, Pemberton, and Squamish are investigating the feasibility of a regional transit service to connect the three municipalities. The Whistler Housing Authority is developing projects to house potentially thousands of local workers, reducing the need for commuter travel.

- *Housing.* The Whistler Housing Authority helps provide affordable accommodation in the form of employee-restricted beds. Currently these total about a third of what is needed, and several projects are in the works to meet projected needs for the 2010 Winter Games.
- *Natural Areas.* In addition to several Watershed Management Plans to protect water resources, Whistler is developing a Protected Areas Network designed to identify and protect through zoning a network of unique and sensitive habitat areas and wildlife corridors within the valley. Wetland and stream protection and rehabilitation by the Whistler Fisheries Stewardship Group is ongoing, including educational initiatives.
- *Built Environment.* Leadership in Energy and Environmental Design (LEED) green building standards are in place for renovation of the Whistler Conference Centre and a new Fire Hall, and green building concepts are being negotiated for incorporation in new construction projects.
- *Growth Management.* To manage rapid growth, the RMOW established a maximum bed unit capacity through the 1993 Comprehensive Development Plan and the 1994 Official Community Plan. The maximum capacity is currently approved at 55,500 market and residential restricted bed units, a level designed to help limit overall expansion of Whistler's developed areas while protecting both the social fabric of the community and remaining natural areas.
- *First Nations Partnerships.* Collaborative initiatives with First Nations include expansion of transit service to Mount Currie, the development of a First Nations trail crew within the RMOW Parks Department, and construction of a First Nations Cultural Centre in Whistler. Through the 2010 Winter Games, First Nations also secured development rights and employment opportunities within Whistler.

Partnering for Success

Strategic partnerships and collaborative efforts can result in far greater successes than acting on one's own, and much of Whistler's success to date in developing sustainability practices has been the result of unique partnerships both within and beyond the community's political boundaries. The following sections detail some of the partnerships that Whistler has engaged in, both within the resort community and externally within the Sea to Sky corridor, the broader Howe Sound and Fraser Basin Regions, and spanning the Canada/U.S. border throughout the Pacific Northwest.

Whistler Community Partnerships

The formation of partnerships within the resort community is proving critical in Whistler's movement toward sustainability. Representatives from key local organizations have come together, effectively creating a collective of community sustainability champions. Below is the story of Whistler's Early Adopters, a group that has become the driving force for promoting and supporting the community's overall plan.

Whistler's Early Adopters of The Natural Step Framework

Soon after Robert's milestone visit to Whistler, a group of key local organizations formed the "Early Adopters of The Natural Step Framework." The Early Adopters, comprised of RMOW (municipal government), Whistler-Blackcomb (ski mountain operator), AWARE (Association of Whistler Area Residents for the Environment – a members-based environmental advocacy and education organization), Tourism Whistler (the marketing organization for the resort), the Fairmont Chateau Whistler (one of Whistler's premier hotels), and Whistler FotoSource (representing small businesses) formed a unique public/private/NGO partnership. This body was created to align approaches and provide support for moving toward sustainability both internally within their individual organizations and collectively as a community.

Together, the Early Adopters developed a common approach to raising awareness about sustainability, resulting in the creation of

Hugh O'Reilly and Tina Symko

a Sustainability Speaker Series featuring presentations by international sustainability experts including Karl-Henrik Robert, Ray Anderson of Interface Inc., author and ethno-botanist Wade Davis, and author, scientist, and media personality David Suzuki, which drew audiences of up to a thousand people. The Early Adopters also established a community-wide education program entitled *Whistler. It's Our Nature*, and implemented a "train the trainers" program based on The Natural Step framework to support and enhance knowledge and skills capacity among participant organizations. Another unique initiative of the Early Adopters was to create the Whistler Centre for Sustainability, an organization that will act as a catalyst for applied sustainability solutions in Whistler and beyond.

Other Community Partnerships

In addition to the Early Adopters group, other partnerships within the resort community are playing significant roles in Whistler's evolution. The Whistler Chamber of Commerce has worked with local businesses and organizations, including local government, to establish a local's Whistler Card program to provide significant discounts on products and services throughout the resort for local employees. The Whistler Card is linked to a project called *Learning Communities* that promotes lifelong learning and supports community initiatives. When locals register for a card, they are asked to respond to an online questionnaire aimed at obtaining feedback on, and improving, service culture, environmental stewardship, First Nations relations, community learning, cultural initiatives, and the overall Whistler experience. Engaging residents and employees to think about and discuss local initiatives helps promote a vibrant community, one that guests appreciate and local businesses benefit from, in addition to helping drive a more sustainable local economy (Whistler Chamber of Commerce 2004).

The Resort Municipality of Whistler has also formed an important relationship with Carney's Waste Systems, a local waste and recycling company. A long-time local waste service provider in the Sea to Sky Corridor, Carney's has played a major role in accelerating waste reduction efforts within Whistler. Working with RMOW, Carney's developed and successfully implemented a comprehensive recycling system for Whistler, including two convenient depot sites and an industrial recycling centre within RMOW. In 2003, Whistler achieved a landfill diversion ratio of 27 per cent, recycling 6,400 tonnes of material, with 17,700 tonnes being sent to the landfill (Resort Municipality of Whistler 2004). Carney's recently opened a centralized composting facility for the Sea to Sky corridor and is facilitating the collection of organic waste from Whistler restaurants, hotels, businesses, and residences, which is expected to result in significant diversion from the landfill waste stream in the future. Carney's also developed numerous education programs for waste reduction and recycling and works with schools, businesses, and local groups to raise awareness and facilitate participation in community waste-reduction and recycling practices. Demonstrating leadership in collaboration with community businesses and organizations toward education and facilitation of best practices around waste management, Carney's has played a significant role thus far in Whistler's move toward sustainability.

Whistler Community Services Society (WCSS) is another organization that has assisted Whistler, working in cooperation with other local businesses and organizations. With the mission of promoting social responsibility and enhancing quality of life for Whistler residents, WCSS provides a network of economic, social, and informational programs including the Whistler Food Bank, community kitchens, counselling services, and numerous youth initiatives, often working in partnership with local government, companies, schools, and organizations. WCSS also runs the Whistler Re-Use-It Centre, a successful operation providing inexpensive items ranging from clothing to furniture and appliances that have been donated or recycled by Whistler businesses, residents, and visitors. While providing affordable goods for residents and visitors, the Re-Use-It Centre also helps to greatly reduce the amount of material entering the Whistler landfill. Working in partnership with WCSS, RMOW has provided both the land and the recently expanded facilities for the Re-Use-It Centre. Proceeds from the sale of items at the centre go toward funding WCSS programs, which benefit the community in a variety of ways that contribute to local sustainability.

Regional Partnerships

In addition to the formation of unique internal community partnerships such as the Early Adopters group described above, Whistler has also engaged in collaborative efforts with partners outside its municipal boundaries. Linking with regional partners in the Sea to Sky corridor – the area spanning from West Vancouver to the Whistler and Pemberton valleys linked by Highway 99 – provides an opportunity for Whistler to promote its sustainability goals and other initiatives on a broader scale and to achieve greater regional successes.

Fraser Basin Council

Whistler participates as a member of the Fraser Basin Council, a nonprofit nongovernmental organization with the mandate of collectively working to protect and advance the Fraser Basin's social, economic, and environmental sustainability into the future. Formed in 1997, Fraser Basin Council partners include representatives from community groups, businesses, and local, provincial, national, and First Nations governments. The FBC's geographic boundary encompasses British Columbia's 240,000 square kilometre Fraser River basin, about one quarter of the entire province. Some of the main issues that the Fraser Basin Council is addressing include urban sprawl, increasing population, air and water quality, aboriginal and nonaboriginal relations, and hosting a sustainable 2010 Olympic Winter Games (Fraser Basin Council 2004).

Sustainability issues can often go unresolved when relevant organizations or agencies work in isolation from each other. The Fraser Basin Council aims to provide a collective forum for addressing environmental issues across political boundaries, recognizing that political jurisdictions often cannot, in isolation, always manage issues effectively at broader spatial scales such as the Fraser River basin. Operating as a collective, the Fraser Basin Council is overseen by a thirty-six-member board of directors including representatives from all levels of government, the private sector, and nongovernmental organizations (Fraser Basin Council 2004).

Whistler's mayor sits on the Fraser Basin Council board as Director of the Greater Vancouver–Squamish–Pemberton Region. Whistler's involvement in the Fraser Basin Council provides opportunities to further the resort community's sustainability initiatives by working with regional partners. By highlighting collaborative means of management and issue resolution that integrate social, economic, and environmental dimensions of sustainability, the Fraser Basin Council helps not only Whistler but every participant community to achieve broader shared objectives working toward a sustainable future for the overall Fraser River basin.

Howe Sound Community Forum

The Resort Municipality of Whistler is a participant in the Howe Sound Community Forum, a collective established in 2000 bringing together representatives from the Howe Sound Region, the branch of the Pacific Ocean that extends from West Vancouver to Squamish, British Columbia. Other participants in the Howe Sound Community Forum include: Greater Vancouver Regional District; District of Squamish; Squamish First Nation; District of West Vancouver; Gambier Island Local Trust Committee; Village of Pemberton; Squamish-Lillooet Regional District; Village of Lions Bay; Sunshine Coast Regional District; and Bowen Island Municipality and the Town of Gibsons (Greater Vancouver Regional District 2003).

The Howe Sound Community Forum operates with the mandate of providing a venue for local and regional governments and First Nations to engage in a cooperative dialogue toward maintaining and improving the economic, social, and environmental well-being of Howe Sound. The forum provides an opportunity for participating communities to share their visions for Howe Sound and to foster harmonized planning where appropriate and possible. Priority topics among participants include environmental, recreational, and industrial issues which frequently span jurisdictional boundaries (Greater Vancouver Regional District 2003).

The Howe Sound Community Forum has provided an opportunity for the Whistler community to engage in a dialogue with regional neighbours on broader transboundary issues such as transportation corridors within the Howe Sound area and the 2010 Olympic Winter Games. Through participation in this forum, as with the Fraser Basin Council, Whistler is able to share and promote sustainable initiatives on a broader regional scale than solely within its municipal boundaries.

The B.C. Hydrogen Highway Project

The British Columbia Hydrogen Highway project represents a tangible example of what progress toward sustainability can look like on the ground. The creation of a "hydrogen highway" between Vancouver, Whistler, and Victoria represents an opportunity to revolutionize fuel infrastructure in North America, powering vehicles with cleaner energy and fuelling the imagination with technological innovation. B.C.'s Hydrogen Highway project is an extensive, coordinated project aimed at accelerating the commercialization of hydrogen for use in fuel cell and internal combustion engines and other technologies, growing a global leading industry and providing economic, social, and environmental benefits not only to British Columbia but across Canada. The goal is to have the hydrogen highway in full operation by the 2010 Olympic Winter Games in Vancouver and Whistler to showcase the feasibility of sustainable transportation options to the world (Canada, Natural Resources Canada 2004).

Currently, the BC Hydrogen Highway consists of seven nodes, each with its own hydrogen fuelling infrastructure for transportation and stationary applications, connecting Vancouver to Whistler and throughout Victoria (Canada, Natural Resources Canada 2004). Whistler has seized the opportunity for involvement in this high-profile project, a natural fit with the resort community's sustainability directions, and plans to develop an "energy mall" offering a number of alternative fuel technologies. Plans for the Whistler energy mall also include a learning centre to facilitate public awareness about global energy issues and the evolution of alternative energy sources. Benefiting from Whistler's status as a premier global resort destination, it is anticipated that the community's participation in the hydrogen highway project will help promote the movement toward more sustainable energy choices on an international scale, in addition to furthering Whistler's own local sustainability objectives.

Demonstrating the power of transboundary collaboration in promoting and facilitating sustainable fuel technology infrastructure, the hydrogen highway initiative brings together partners from local and national government levels within Canada and potentially the United States. For example, the state of California recently implemented legislation to advance public-private partnerships to promote the creation of a hydrogen highway network in that state. Also to be included are technological innovators, sustainability visionaries, and the transportation industry across North America (Fuel Cells Canada 2004). By 2010, the evolution of the hydrogen economy could be well on its way, with Whistler as a significant contributor.

International Collaboration

Reaching beyond regional partnerships within the Sea to Sky corridor and British Columbia, Whistler is engaged in several international collaborations that are proving effective in bringing about positive change across borders. Increased cross-border cooperation in this region is prompted in part by recognition of the potential for increasing cross-border tourism, presumably in the form of visitors from Europe and Asia to tourist destinations in both Canada and the United States. Some of the cross-border projects being considered include a high-speed train from Portland to Vancouver, and a working group to discuss the opportunities available to the cruise ship industry along the Pacific Coast.

Pacific Northwest Economic Region

The Tourism Working Group of the Pacific Northwest Economic Region has created a regional cooperation council to support and invest in collaborative efforts by leveraging the 2010 Winter Games (PNWER 2004). On behalf of the tourism industry in both countries, the Tourism Working Group is also undertaking to ease border security restrictions that have been phased in since 2001, which include the Western Hemisphere Travel Initiative. The security restrictions adopted have had significant detrimental impacts on the tourism industry in Canada and the United States.

Cascadia Mayors Council

Whistler's mayors are members of the Cascadia Mayors Council, an association of mayors from British Columbia, Washington, and Oregon who work together on issues confronting the Cascadia Region. Through a regional approach, the Cascadia Mayors Council aims to coordinate initiatives and maximize opportunities to achieve common sustainability goals. The council has effectively become a forum for information-sharing, networking, and coordinating regional efforts as the mayors work together toward sustainable solutions for transboundary economic development, trade and tourism advancement, transportation planning, natural resource management, livable regions initiatives, and special events (City of Seattle 2004). Whistler seeks to share the resort community's successes and lessons learned, while gaining knowledge from the experiences of other Cascadian communities. Partnering with other mayors to develop regional responses to sustainability and other issues, Whistler is working to extend a message of shared regional values, vision, and leadership. Mayors operate as community champions, and collaboration among such leaders can facilitate sustainable directions within individual communities and, more significantly, on a broader regional scale.

Vancouver 2010 Olympic and Paralympic Winter Games

Whistler was born of an Olympic dream. It was the early 1960s when a group of Vancouver businessmen formed the Garibaldi Olympic Development Association (GODA) and began to promote Whistler as the potential site for a future Olympic Winter Games. Despite two unsuccessful Olympic bids by GODA for the 1968 and 1976 Olympic Winter Games, Whistler continued to evolve with the Olympic dream in mind (Tourism Whistler 2004). By the late 1990s, Whistler had developed into a premier mountain resort destination with the leading ski area in North America, hosting millions of visitors annually.

Despite having become a major tourism success on a global scale, and accommodating a vibrant resident community, Whistler continued to evolve with the Olympic dream in mind. The potential for long-term economic benefits to Vancouver, Whistler, and the surrounding region, primarily in the form of tourism, stimulated the drive to host a Winter Olympic Games. In 1998, Whistler and Vancouver partnered to develop a bid and were selected by the Canadian Olympic Committee as Canada's nominee for the 2010 Olympic and Paralympic Winter Games. While Vancouver would be the official city name for the bid, Whistler would provide the venue for nearly half of the Olympic sporting events (alpine skiing, Nordic skiing, bobsled, luge, and skeleton) and all of the Paralympic sporting events (alpine skiing, Nordic skiing, sledge hockey, and curling).

In 2003, Whistler's Olympic quest became a reality when it was announced from Prague that Vancouver/Whistler would host the 2010 Games. The Olympics story is critical to Whistler's efforts to achieve a more sustainable community and be a model for other resorts attempting similar goals. Beginning early in the bid phase for the 2010 Winter Games, Whistler considered the potential of hosting the Olympic Games as a chance to showcase to the world the community's sustainability initiatives. As a member partner of the Vancouver 2010 Bid Corporation, Whistler played a significant role in developing the content and quality of Vancouver's bid for the 2010 Winter Games. Throughout the bid phase, the Whistler community leveraged its member partner status to ensure consistency between the sustainability values and directions of the resort community and the plans and legacies for the games, effectively fortifying the environmental component of Vancouver's bid.

The Vancouver 2010 bid included a sustainability policy and preliminary strategies addressing a number of important areas. These included environmental stewardship, such as green buildings, clean transportation, zero waste, climate neutral games, leading edge energy management, long-term economic opportunity, and social responsibility related to aboriginal participation, community legacies, education and awareness, inclusivity, affordability, and accessibility (Vancouver 2010 Bid Corporation 2002).

In preparation for 2010, the resort community is working to achieve the maximum sustainability successes possible. With the 2010 Winter Games as a catalyst, Whistler now has a unique opportunity to nurture partnerships and work in collaboration with communities, organizations, and businesses around the world to share and promote sustainability principles and practices.

Two of Whistler's leaders, including the RMOW administrator and the president of Tourism Whistler, sit on the Vancouver Organizing Committee for the 2010 Olympic and Paralympic Winter Games (VANOC) Board of Directors. This arrangement provides an important opportunity to influence the planning and operations of the 2010 Games. The VANOC board also includes representation from the Canadian Olympic Committee, the Government of

Canada, the Province of British Columbia, Squamish and Lil'wat First Nations, the City of Vancouver, the Canadian Paralympic Committee, and VANOC. The board includes no elected officials (Vancouver 2010, 2003). Whistler's sustainability objectives will drive the community's participation in the games, which present an opportunity to promote environmental initiatives through high-profile demonstration projects showcasing leading technology and green facilities, educational programs and messaging, and more. In its vision statement, the Vancouver Organizing Committee for the 2010 Olympic and Paralympic Winter Games articulates a fundamental commitment to sustainability: "A stronger Canada whose spirit is raised by its passion for sport, culture and sustainability."

One example of a partnership project with the 2010 Games as the catalyst is the athletes' Olympic Village planned for Whistler. The Whistler Olympic Village, anticipated to showcase globally leading-edge sustainable site design and buildings, will be accomplished through a strong partnership between VANOC and RMOW. This will leave a legacy of affordable housing complexes for Whistler employees. There is much potential to both incorporate and expand Whistler's ecological initiatives with the 2010 Games, thereby working to improve progress toward local sustainability.

Hosting the 2010 Olympic Winter Games is embraced by Whistler as an opportunity to share the community's sustainability efforts far beyond the town's small boundaries and to help effect positive change on broader regional, national, and international levels. Working in collaboration with Vancouver, British Columbia, Canada, and other countries around the world leading up to and during the 2010 Olympic and Paralympic Winter Games, the community of Whistler will have a global audience, providing the opportunity to potentially inspire and influence other communities to embrace new and more sustainable form of tourism and resort planning.

Lessons Learned and Next Steps

Though there have been several early successes, Whistler's experience has not been without challenges. Cross-boundary collaboration often presents the challenge of differing legislation, particularly across national borders. In such cases, shared values can help uncover creative solutions toward aligning actions and initiatives. Broader successes result from actions based on a common vision for the shared international region, rather than based solely on the agenda of a single player. The Cascadia Mayors Council, for example, has been successful to date in large part due to the common goals shared by the partners, as they work together to accomplish these goals on a regional scale. Similarly, the work of the Pacific Northwest Economic Region in promoting the concept of a "Two Nation Vacation" has focused attention on the value of regional approaches to tourism and environmental well-being. With 4.7 million annual visits by foreign visitors to Whistler in recent years drawn 74 per cent from the United States, 15 per cent from Asia, 9 per cent from Europe, and 3 per cent from Australia, the potential of dividing vacation time between British Columbia and the Pacific Northwest takes on significant economic importance for both countries.

The definition and language of sustainability can often be vague, with varying interpretations obscuring the critical meaning of terms and associated goals. Working with The Natural Step framework has been comparable to learning a new language for Whistler, and it has taken some time for the community to become familiar and comfortable with the dialect. However, as the community becomes more proficient with this new language, Whistler's players are finding themselves able to more effectively communicate and work together toward common goals, transforming theoretical concepts into pragmatic policies. This demonstrates the critical role of a common language of sustainability for shared civic dialogue and learning.

For Whistler, the development of a more sustainable resort and community is constantly tempered by the current reality – that this resort community is not presently sustainable. Acknowledgment of shortcomings has proven to be a critical step in establishing clear goals and a path to achieve them. An understanding of the baseline situation helps reveal the gap between current reality and a vision

Hugh O'Reilly and Tina Symko

for the future, providing direction for the steps needed to bridge this gap.

Whistler is striving to be a net contributor to sustainability in two ways. First, it aims to achieve sustainability in the local context through demonstrable practices. Second, the resort hopes to use its position as a globally recognized tourism and recreation destination to influence other communities in the region, the province, the country, and the world toward comparable changes. As Whistler moves ahead, other communities across Canada may use its Comprehensive Sustainability Plan as a model to achieve similar goals. Green buildings, stakeholder involvement, fiscal responsibility, wise energy choices, innovative policy solutions, and strategic collaboration are all areas in which Whistler aims to lead by example.

References

BC Transit. 2003. *BC Transit 2002–2003 Year End Actuals*. June 10, 2003. Victoria, BC.

Canada. Natural Resources Canada. 2004. *Backgrounder: Hydrogen Highway*. Ottawa. http://www.nrcan-rncan.gc.ca/media/newsreleases/2004/200413a_e.htm.

City of Seattle. 2004. City of Seattle: Cascadia Mayors Council. Seattle, WA. http://www.cityofseattle.net/cascadiamayors/.

Dwivedi, O. P., Patrick Kyba, Peter Stoett, and Rebecca Tiessen. 2001. *Sustainable Development and Canada: National and International Policy Perspectives*. Peterborough, ON: Broadview Press.

Fraser Basin Council. 2004. Fraser Basin Council Homepage: http://www.fraserbasin.bc.ca. Vancouver, BC.

Fuel Cells Canada. 2004. *Fuel Cells Canada Applauds California's Hydrogen Vision*. Vancouver, BC. http://www.fuelcellscanada.ca/Industry%20news/h2highway3.html.

Greater Vancouver Regional District. 2003. Greater Vancouver Regional District: Regional Development – Howe Sound Community Forum. Vancouver, BC. http://www.gvrd.bc.ca/growth/HoweSoundCommunityForum.htm.

KPMG. 2002. *Economic Impact of the Whistler Resort* (Project 01-02534-01). Prepared for One Whistler, Whistler, BC.

PNWER. 2004. *Pacific Northwest Economic Region 14th Annual Summit: Resolutions and Action Points.* Victoria, BC.

Resort Municipality of Whistler. 1999. *Whistler 2002: Charting a Course for the Future.* Whistler, BC.

————. 2004. *The Comprehensive Sustainability Plan.* Draft May 28, 2004. Whistler, BC.

Tourism British Columbia. 2003. *Tourism British Columbia Annual Report 20003/2004.* Victoria, BC.

Tourism Whistler. 2003. *Tourism Whistler's Media Room.* Whistler, BC. http://mediaroom.mywhistler.com/facts_stats/statistics.asp.

————. 2004. *Backgrounder: Whistler Olympic Bid History.* Whistler, BC.

Vancouver 2010 Bid Corporation. 2002. *Vancouver 2010: Accelerating the Journey to a Sustainable Future.* Vancouver, BC.

Vancouver 2010. 2003. *News Release October 28, 2003: Vancouver 2010 Confirms Board Chairman, Announces Next Steps.* Vancouver, BC.

Waldron, D. 2003. *Sustainability and the Resort Community of Whistler.* Prepared for the Resort Municipality of Whistler, Whistler, BC.

Whistler Chamber of Commerce. 2004. *Whistler Chamber of Commerce: The Whistler Card.* Whistler, BC. http://www.whistlerchamber.com/the_whistler_card.php.

Z-Point Graphics. 2004. *Whistler's Location in Canada and North America.* Whistler, BC.

13

ENVIRONMENTAL EDUCATION ON THE U.S.-MEXICO BORDER: CHALLENGES AND OPPORTUNITIES IN TIJUANA/SAN DIEGO

Martin Medina

Abstract

San Diego/Tijuana constitutes the largest urban metropolitan area on the U.S.-Mexico border, and in recent years both cities have been among the fastest growing in their respective countries. Tijuana's population and economic growth has had a particularly deleterious environmental impact that also affects San Diego. Environmental education can play a significant role in minimizing the environmental impact of the region's growth. This paper analyzes the main environmental education activities and programs that exist on both sides of the border. Because of diverging socioeconomic conditions and availability of financial resources, the environmental issues facing Tijuana diverge from those in San Diego, necessitating a different approach to environmental education. In Tijuana, the most urgent need is to educate decision-makers on best practices of urban environmental management that are socially desirable, economically viable, and environmentally sound.

Introduction

The San Diego/Tijuana metropolitan area, with over 3.6 million inhabitants, constitutes the largest binational urban concentration on the U.S.-Mexico border. Both cities are also among the fastest growing in either country. With a growth rate of about 5 per cent a year, Tijuana now has a level of population and economic growth that has serious environmental impacts, including on San Diego to the north. Attracted by one the lowest unemployment rates in the country and the possibility of finding a job, approximately 65,000 individuals from central and southern Mexico move into Tijuana each year. Tijuana's fast population growth implies the enlargement of existing or creation of new urban barrios, or *colonias*. Many of these low-income areas lack sanitation, wastewater treatment, and solid waste management services. The lack of these services translates into air, water, and land pollution, as well as risks to human health and the environment (Medina 1997; Westerhoff 2000).

Providing existing and new colonias with sanitation, wastewater treatment, and solid waste management services would require significant financial resources. The United States has provided its population with sanitation, wastewater treatment, and solid waste management services by making large investments in building sewers, wastewater treatment plants, sanitary landfills, and the necessary equipment and infrastructure. Improvements on the Mexican side, on the other hand, have been much more limited.

This paper analyzes the main environmental education activities currently implemented in the San Diego/Tijuana area which promote more sustainable development in the region. It also addresses the multiple challenges and opportunities seen at present and likely to exist in the near future.

Environmental Issues on the U.S.-Mexico Border

Disparity characterizes the U.S.-Mexico border. According to the World Bank's *World Development Report*, in 1999, the United States economy was nearly twenty times larger than the Mexican economy (ten times at Purchase Power Parity, PPP), while the GNP per capita was seven times greater in the United States than in Mexico (World Bank 2001). This economic disparity and different social conditions between both countries have profound implications for the type of environmental problems faced, for resources available to ameliorate them, as well as for their appropriate solutions. The financial resources available to authorities, for instance, reflect this disparity: Tijuana's current municipal government budget is US$150 million, while the combined budget for the San Diego area governments is US$2.3 billion. In per capita terms, San Diego has ten times more resources than Tijuana for provision of infrastructure and urban services.

If the current rate of population growth continues, the border region population will double in twenty-five years. Such growth will strain the inadequate infrastructure capacity for water, wastewater treatment, and solid waste management. Water has particular importance for the U.S.-Mexico border, given its scarcity as well as its deteriorating quality. However, Mexican authorities devote most investments to increasing supply, whereas reducing demand for water has not been a high priority (Westerhoff 2000).

Wastewater treatment is a serious problem in Mexico: nearly 70 per cent of wastewater generated in the country as a whole does not receive any treatment before being discharged into the environment. Untreated wastewater constitutes a source of pollution as well as a public health problem. Mexican authorities attempt to solve the problem by building wastewater treatment plants. Conventional wastewater treatment facilities, however, tend to be capital intensive, expensive to build and operate, and emphasize disposal over reuse of treated water. Thus, conventional solutions tend to produce socially non-desirable outcomes (Suez Lyonnaise des Eaux 1998).

Solid waste management also constitutes a significant environmental problem for Mexican border towns as well as for the rest of the country. Much of the waste generated in Mexico is never collected. Uncollected waste is often littered on the streets; dumped on public areas or into rivers, lakes, or oceans; or incinerated by residents. And of the wastes collected, only a fraction receives proper disposal. The World Bank (1990) estimates that only 15 per cent of wastes generated in Mexico receive proper disposal in sanitary landfills. Generation of hazardous wastes has also increased with the growth of the maquiladora industry in Mexican border towns. The infrastructure to handle hazardous wastes in Mexico is limited. The inappropriate collection, handling, and disposal of both solid and hazardous wastes present significant risks to human health and the environment (Jacott, Reed, and Villamar 1999; World Bank 1990).

It can be argued, therefore, that the main urban environmental problems facing Mexico and Tijuana are wastewater treatment, sanitation, and solid waste management. Due to the shared watershed and environment, the pollution generated in Tijuana also affects San Diego and its residents. The Tijuana River flows north and west into Imperial Beach, California, and polluted runoff water from Tijuana sometimes reaches the river estuary, in turn affecting the coastline further north.

The next section discusses conventional solutions to water, sanitation, wastewater treatment and solid waste management (WSWSW for short), which characterize the approach followed in Tijuana. Their shortcomings argue for a very different approach, one that includes efforts like the two that are presented below.

Conventional Solutions to WSWSW Problems

Various measures are normally adopted in order to extend water supply, refuse collection, wastewater treatment plants, upgrade disposal facilities, and diminish the risks to human health and the environment associated with WSWSW problems. The solutions that are commonly proposed to meet the WSWSW problems in cities of the developing world often have the following features:

- *Centralized and undiversified*: solutions that do not distinguish the different needs and heterogeneity of neighbourhoods within each city, and between cities;
- *Bureaucratic*: top-down solutions, usually reached with little or no community participation;
- *Capital-intensive approaches*: involving advanced technology and equipment, frequently imported from industrialized countries;
- *Formal*: conventional solutions only consider the formal sector, neglecting the existence and possible contributions of the informal sector that has developed around waste collection and recycling in many cities of developing countries;
- *Emphasis on disposal*: conventional solutions give priority to disposal over the potential recovery of resources that can be reused or recycled.

It can be argued that cities in the developing world require a fundamentally different approach, essentially diametrically opposed to the solutions that are currently proposed. It makes sense for developed countries to use high-tech approaches that minimize labour and are intensive in capital, but often it does not make sense for developing countries to use the same technology to solve their WSWSW problems. Developed countries enjoy a relative abundance of capital and have high labour costs, while the opposite is true in developing countries. Therefore, developing countries need different solutions to WSWSW: they need low-tech, affordable, solutions that create job opportunities – particularly for unskilled labour – that reduce poverty, and that emphasize the recovery of waste materials for reuse and recycling.

Two specific examples of socially desirable solutions for WSWSW problems, discussed below, have been developed in the U.S.-Mexico border area through collaborative efforts which have involved personnel of Colegio de la Frontera Norte (COLEF): Ecoparque, in Tijuana, and the SOSOSEMA scavenger cooperative in Ciudad Juarez. Both provide valuable lessons for possible replication.

Environmental Education in Mexico
and the United States

Environmental education can play an important role in raising awareness and promoting participation of the public and decision-makers for protecting the border environment. The United States and Mexico have both formal and informal environmental education programs and activities, but economic disparities affect the way environmental education is conducted in the two countries. The United States was a pioneer in establishing environmental education (EE) and has included it in curricula since the 1970s (van Matre 1999). A large number of organizations in the United States have informal EE programs, ranging from nature centres to museums. On the U.S.-Mexico border, the Environmental Protection Agency, through its Border XXI, supports environmental education activities on both sides of the border. A website (www.bordereeweb.net in English, www.redeafronteriza.net in Spanish) offers a database listing various resources as well as organizations on the U.S.-Mexico border that work on EE. Some offer EE training to teachers and most offer some kind of EE activities for the general public.

Sharp political differences also affect the way environmental education is carried out in the two countries. In the United States, education is decentralized with a high degree of local and state control in curriculum content. Conversely, Mexico has a highly centralized educational system, where major decisions are made in Mexico City, including curriculum content and textbooks used nationwide.

Some milestones in environmental education at the international level have shaped developments in the U.S.-Mexico border. The United Nations Conference on the Human Environment, held in Stockholm in 1972, recommended the establishment of an international environmental education program. In 1975, UNESCO and the UN Environment Program (UNEP) launched the International Environmental Education Program and sponsored an international EE workshop in Belgrade. The Belgrade Charter, adopted at the conference, established the first principles for the worldwide environmental education movement. In 1977, the first Intergovernmental Conference on Environmental Education was held in Tbilisi, which

Martin Medina

formulated forty-one recommendations for implementing a worldwide EE program. And in 1987, UNESCO and UNEP sponsored the Moscow Congress, which produced the International Strategy for Action in the Field of Environmental Education and Training for the 1990s. The UN Conference on Environment and Development held in Rio de Janeiro in 1992 ("the Rio Summit") in Agenda 21 emphasized the role of environmental education in achieving a sustainable development (van Matre 1999, Cardenas 2000).

Despite the international calls to action, including Mexico's participation in the Stockholm, Belgrade, Tbilisi, Moscow, and Rio conferences, Mexican authorities did not give a high priority to environmental education. Only in the past six years has EE been formally included in the school curriculum. Textbooks for elementary and secondary schools now include topics on environmental issues and sustainable development. Mexico's Program for Training of Teachers ("Programa Nacional de Actualización Permanente") prepared and introduced teaching guides ("Paquete Didáctico de Educacion Ambiental" and the "Guía del Maestro de Secundaria") in the mid-1990s. Mexico has also begun efforts to turn EE teaching into a profession, creating five master's and twelve nondegree programs on environmental education in this period (Sparza 2000).

Informal environmental education in Mexico is also relatively recent. With the support of the North American Association for Environmental Education (NAAEE), five regional networks of environmental educators ("Redes Regionales de Educadores Ambientales") were created in 1992. These networks, composed of approximately six hundred members, were created to exchange information, experiences, and materials, as well as to improve environmental education efforts in their respective regions and nationally (Figueroa 2000). However, some of the networks suffer from poor communication among their members and the fact that the same people tend to occupy the administrative positions over and over again (Chavez 2000).

Following the Mexican tradition of centralization, the federal government created the National Centre for Training in Sustainable Development ("Centro de Educación y Capacitación para el Desarrollo Sustentable," CECADESU) in 1996 to improve formal and informal environmental education in Mexico (Chavez 2000). Based in Mexico City, CECADESU offers training courses on various environmental issues to teachers, government officials, and other interested individuals.

Environmental education in Mexico faces several challenges. Until recently, federal authorities paid little attention to environmental education. Consequently, EE was not a priority in government programs and spending. Being a recent effort, EE programs face a scarcity of trained personnel. Further, EE facilities are scarce. As a result, teachers often limit their EE activities to classroom talks but have no access to outdoor activities to complement their lectures. Thus, students only learn about environmental issues but do not participate in hands-on environmental programs and in developing solutions to problems. This is a serious limitation for the development of EE in Mexico since hands-on activities tend to leave a more lasting impression than classroom instruction alone (Lopez 2000; Barraza 2000).

When environmental education activities are not complemented with the appropriate direct or experiential programs, they may even have unintended negative impacts on students. In Coahuila State, for example, students became frustrated and felt powerless to have an impact due to the lack of corresponding avenues to channel and direct their energy. The students pointed out that it did not make sense for them to pick up litter when there were no wastebaskets, to separate their recyclables at home when there are no recycling collection programs, or to conserve water if they live in areas with no tap water. In many cases, in fact, low-income residents consume very little water to begin with, even less than the per capita use recommended by the UN (Garza 2000).

Individuals teach informal environmental education in Mexico with a wide variation in the type and quality of training they have received. The educators' efforts tend to reflect their educational background and they make use of available resources. However, EE activities have a natural science orientation. Often, EE activities are not evaluated so it is difficult to know the impact of the various programs in solving environmental programs and in promoting more sustainable development (Cisneros 2000).

In conclusion, the Mexican government needs to consider environmental education as a priority in government programs and spending. Educators need better training. Schools need to create programs that complement classroom lectures and that direct their students' energy and creativity, such as composting and recycling programs. Municipal authorities also need to create environmental protection programs and to involve the general public – including students – in the design and operation of such programs. EE can play a significant role in achieving more sustainable development, but its impact among the general public is likely to be felt in the medium and long term (Cardenas 2000; Fuentes 2000; Cisneros 2000). As will be seen below, it can be argued that in addition to environmental education for the general public, educating government officials is at least as urgent a task.

Environmental Education in San Diego and Tijuana

Several U.S. and Mexican organizations have environmental education programs that serve the San Diego/Tijuana area. Table 13.1 shows the main organizations that have EE activities in San Diego/Tijuana, as well as the areas that they address in their programs. Most outdoor, hands-on EE activities take place in San Diego, whereas there have been very few options for outdoor EE in Tijuana. Instead, most EE activities in Tijuana involve teacher-training courses, such as the ones offered by the Bioregional EE Project ("Proyecto Bioregional de Educacion Ambiental," PROBEA).

Table 13.1. Organizations with Environmental Education Activities in San Diego/Tijuana.

ORGANIZATION	FOCUS OF ACTIVITIES	EE AREA OF WORK
Grassroots Educators	San Diego, Tijuana	Various issues
Los Ninos	Tijuana	Community gardens
Daedalus Alliance for EE	San Diego, Tijuana	Various issues
Olas Limpias	San Diego, Tijuana	Marine pollution prevention
Parque Morelos	Tijuana	Various issues
Proyecto Fronterizo de EE	Tijuana, Tecate, Ensenada, Baja California Sur	Various issues
Pro Esteros	Baja California Norte and Baja California Sur	Estuaries conservation
San Diego Water Authority	San Diego	Water conservation, pollution
San Diego Natural History Museum	San Diego, Tijuana	Biodiversity, conservation
Sistema Educativo Estatal de Baja California	Baja California	Various issues
Sistemas Bilingues Especializados	San Diego, Tijuana	Various issues
Tijuana River National Estuarine Reserve	San Ysidro	Estuarine conservation
Proyecto Bioregional de EE	Tijuana, Tecate, Ensenada, Baja California Sur	Various issues
San Diego County Parks	San Diego	Various issues
San Diego Zoo / Wild Animal Park	San Diego	Biodiversity conservation
Sea World	San Diego	Marine issues
Scripps Aquarium	San Diego	Marine issues
Ecoparque	Tijuana	• Wastewater treatment and reuse • Composting • Recycling • Appropriate technologies

Environmental education in San Diego/Tijuana clearly reflects the socioeconomic, political, and cultural differences between the United States and Mexico. San Diego residents have access to a wide variety of informal EE activities at parks, museums, and educational institutions. They can learn marine environmental issues at Scripps, desert ecology at the Anza Borrego State Park, mountain forests at Cuyamaca State Park, riparian habitats at the Mission Trails Regional Park, coastal sage scrub communities at the Torrey Pines State Reserve, and estuaries at the Border Field State Park. Tijuana has very limited opportunities to learn about the local environment and needs to develop more facilities for hands-on EE activities.

The main environmental problems that Tijuana faces are water issues, sanitation, wastewater treatment, and solid waste management. However, EE directed to the general public and to decision-makers does not always give priority to solving those problems. A notable exception is the Ecoparque program, administered by El Colegio de la Frontera Norte, which focuses on hand-on EE activities directed to Tijuana students.

Ecoparque

Ecoparque was created as an alternative solution to wastewater treatment in low-income communities. Wastewater treatment is a serious problem in cities of the developing world, and one of the most intractable in Mexico. Only about 30 per cent of the wastewater generated in Mexico receives any kind of treatment. Many low-income neighbourhoods lack sewers and wastewater treatment facilities. Untreated sewage constitutes a source of pollution and a breeding ground for communicable diseases.

Most people who immigrate into Tijuana are poor and cannot afford to purchase a home. Many of them are forced to live in slums and shantytowns, which have proliferated so rapidly that local authorities have lacked resources to provide urban infrastructure. Wastewater treatment was a serious problem throughout most of the second half of the twentieth century. As a result of population growth and the absence of treatment facilities, in the early 1980s as much as 5 million gallons of untreated sewage a day flowed through the Tijuana River and then north into California and the Pacific Ocean. The Tijuana River estuary constitutes an environmentally sensitive area, designated as the Tijuana River National Estuarine Reserve in California. In the past, untreated sewage from Tijuana polluted this reserve and the beaches of southern San Diego. Such pollution caused protests from U.S. residents and environmental organizations, yet untreated sewage sometimes still flows from Tijuana neighbourhoods into the United States.

Considering Tijuana's limited wastewater treatment facilities, in 1965 the City of San Diego started treating part of Tijuana's sewage at its Point Loma treatment facility through an 'emergency connection.' This arrangement between Tijuana and San Diego was to expire in 1985. The United States and Mexico deemed unacceptable an indefinite reliance on this emergency connection, and other options began to be considered. In 1983, the City of San Diego and the EPA proposed the construction of a binational wastewater treatment facility, but it was rejected by Mexico because of its high cost. A more affordable solution had to be found. In the mid-1980s, the California Coastal Conservancy provided funds for the design of the facility and other U.S. and Mexican organizations provided financial and in-kind contributions.

In order to provide a location for a model wastewater treatment plant, COLEF secured twenty-three acres from the Mexican federal government. The plant has three basic components: 1) a static stainless steel hydrasieve (fine screen) widely used in various industries to separate solids; 2) a plastic biological filter arranged in a cross-flow configuration, made of corrugated PVC sheets that form self-stacking blocks with 95 per cent voids; and 3) a fiberglass settling basin (clarifier) designed by the project team and made in Tijuana. The unit has a forty-five-degree hopper that allows solids to be collected without using mechanical scrapers.

In order to contribute to raising public awareness of the most pressing environmental issues facing the city and region, COLEF started an EE program in 1997. Ecoparque offers tours of the facility and park, as well as talks on various environmental issues, such as water efficiency, water reuse, and recycling of solid wastes. Groups of students from all educational levels are invited to the tours and talks. Activities are tailored to the age of the students and include identifying particular species of plants or birds in the park, colouring of figures, and workshops on how to make recycled paper. In 2003, Ecoparque offered over a hundred EE activities to over ten thousand visitors making it the most active EE program in Tijuana. Ecoparque received a finalist's award from the 2001 Bremen Partnership to recognize its activities in promoting a more sustainable urban development. This award is supported by the United Nations Environment Program, the United Nations Center for Human Settlements, and other international organizations and private companies.

The SOCOSEMA Scavenger Cooperative

A different approach to the management of solid wastes has been developed in Ciudad Juarez, across the border from El Paso, Texas, where solid waste is as serious a problem as it is in Tijuana. Like Ecoparque, this case can inform us about another model with considerable promise. As in Tijuana, the City of Juarez does not collect the totality of wastes generated, and of those collected only a fraction receive proper final disposal. Uncollected wastes and the disposal of wastes at open dumps constitute a source of pollution and pose risks to human health and the environment. Juarez does not have a municipal recycling program.

Instead, recycling of municipal solid wastes relies largely on the informal recovery of materials carried out by human scavengers. Scavengers' low incomes can often be explained by the low prices paid by middlemen. In some cases, middlemen in monopsonistic markets grossly exploit scavengers. A monopsony exists where there is only one buyer, as opposed to a monopoly, where there is only one seller. Dumpsite scavenging, in particular, is susceptible to the development of monopsonistic markets, due to the relative isolation of many dumps, which makes it nearly impossible for scavengers to transport materials to the nearest town. Another factor that encourages the formation of monopsonistic markets is the awarding of concessions for the recovery of recyclables (Medina 1997).

Until 1975, dumpsite scavengers at the Juarez dump were exploited by middlemen. Mexican cities usually require that anyone wishing to recover materials from dumps/landfills obtain a concession. Scavenger leaders colluded with middlemen to obtain concessions. Such concessions in actuality legitimize monopsonistic markets at disposal sites, and in some cases, the exploitation of scavengers. In this case, a middleman had a concession to recover recyclables at the local dump. The middleman, operating in a monopsony, paid low prices for the materials recovered by scavengers and dictated which materials he would buy. As a result, scavengers had very low incomes. They could have been considered poor and had harsh living and working conditions. Thus, opportunities exist for the improvement in scavengers' living and working conditions by circumventing the middlemen (Medina 1997).

In 1975, the middleman announced that he would buy only paper from then on, and at a lower price. Scavengers protested immediately. With the assistance of a college professor – Guillermina Villalba, who later became a professor at COLEF – supported financially by a local businessman and a sympathetic mayor, a co-op was formed. That year, local authorities awarded a concession to the co-op for the recovery of recyclables contained in the wastes arriving at the dump. The co-op was named Sociedad Cooperativa de Seleccionadores de Materiales (SOCOSEMA). The impact of the creation of SOCOSEMA was impressive: within a few months after its creation, and the displacement of the middleman, the incomes of scavenger members increased tenfold (Medina 1998).

Today SOCOSEMA constitutes one of the most successful scavenger co-ops in Mexico. Scavenger members recover nearly 5 per cent of the wastes arriving at the municipal dump: 150 tons of paper, cardboard, glass, rubber, plastics, animal bones, organic material, and metals per day (Medina 1998). The co-op also receives donations of recyclable materials – largely paper and scrap metal – from the border assembly plants popularly known as 'maquiladoras.' SOCOSEMA members provide cleaning services to these plants as well for a fee. Co-op members now enjoy higher incomes, participate in training courses and formal education programs sponsored by the co-op, and have access to health care and to legal protection. SOCOSEMA has developed good relations with industry, despite initial reluctance to do business with the co-op. Industrial demand for recyclables in Mexico is strong, and the co-op often buys materials from independent scavengers in order to satisfy the demand (Medina 1998).

Conclusions

Environmental education in San Diego/Tijuana reflects the economic disparity as well as the social, political, and cultural differences between Mexico and the United States. The main environmental problems facing Tijuana are water issues, sanitation, wastewater treatment, and solid waste management. Tijuana's environmental problems also affect the quality of the environment in San Diego. There are efforts to improve environmental education in Tijuana, including a binational program directed at teachers. Most EE efforts, however, focus on teacher training and on instruction to the general public.

Decision-makers have a major impact on the Tijuana environment through the plans and programs they adopt. They often tend to favour conventional, high-tech solutions to water issues, sanitation, wastewater treatment, and solid waste management. This paper argues that low-tech approaches can be economically viable, socially desirable, and environmentally sound, as illustrated by the Ecoparque program in Tijuana and the SOCOSEMA scavenger cooperative in Juarez. The most urgent task in EE is to educate decision-makers so that they make more informed decisions. Such EE efforts should be based on an analysis of best practices in urban environmental management of successful programs throughout the developing world. It is crucially important to start offering training courses to Tijuana government officials and community leaders on sustainable development topics and urban environmental management. Such education should emphasize approaches that are low cost, create jobs, reduce poverty, conserve resources, prevent pollution, and improve economic competitiveness. In this way, the impact would be felt in the short term and would contribute towards achieving long-term sustainable development in the area.

References

Barraza, L. 2000. "Educar para el Futuro: En Busca de un Nuevo Enfoque de Investigacion en Educacion Ambiental." In *Memoria Foro Nacional de Educacion Ambiental.* Mexico City: Secretaria de Medio Ambiente, Recursos naturales y Pesca (SEMARNAP).

Cardenas, L. 2000. "Hacia un Nuevo Paradigma de la Educacion Ambiental Formal." In *Memoria Foro Nacional de Educacion Ambiental.* Mexico City: SEMARNAP.

Chavez, C. 2000. "Redes de Educadores Ambientales: El Proceso de Cambio y Estrategias de Permanencia, el Caso de la Red Centro." In *Memoria Foro Nacional de Educacion Ambiental.* Mexico City: SEMARNAP.

Cisneros, J. 2000. "La UICN y la Educacion Ambiental: Enfoques y Perspectivas." In *Memoria Foro Nacional de Educacion Ambiental.* Mexico City: SEMARNAP.

Figueroa, A. 2000. "Dandole sobre lo mismo: Redes de Educadores Ambientales de Mexico." In *Memoria Foro Nacional de Educacion Ambiental.* Mexico City: SEMARNAP.

Fuentes, S. 2000. "Hacia la Construccion de una Nueva Identidad: la Investigacion Educativa en el Campo de la Educacion Ambiental en Mexico." In *Memoria Foro Nacional de Educacion Ambiental.* Mexico City: SEMARNAP.

Garza, R. 2000. "La Educacion Ambiental como parte de la Gestion Ambiental del Estado." In *Memoria Foro Nacional de Educacion Ambiental.* Mexico City: SEMARNAP.

Jacott, M., C. Reed, and A. Villamar. 1999. *Hazardous Waste Management in the United States-Mexico Border Region: More Questions than Answers.* Austin: Texas Center for Policy Studies.

Lopez, R. 2000. "Educacion Ambiental en una Concepcion Amplia a partir de una Experiencia de 17 años en Comunidades Indigenas en Oaxaca." In *Memoria Foro Nacional de Educacion Ambiental.* Mexico City: SEMARNAP.

Medina, M. 1997. *Scavenging on the Border: A Study of Informal Recycling in Laredo, Texas and Nuevo Laredo, Mexico.* Ph.D. dissertation. New Haven, CT: Yale University.

———. June 1998. Scavenger Cooperatives in Developing Countries. *BioCycle.*

Secretaria de Medio Ambiente, Recursos naturales y Pesca. 2000. *Memoria Foro Nacional de Educacion Ambiental.* Mexico City: SEMARNAP.

Sparza, O. 2000. "Metodologia de la Educacion Ambiental: Las mismas bases otras Necesidades." In *Memoria Foro Nacional de Educacion Ambiental*. Mexico City: SEMARNAP.

Suez Lyonnaise des Eaux. 1998. *Alternative Solutions for Water Supply and Sanitation in Areas with Limited Financial Resources*. Nanterre, France: Suez Lyonnaise des Eaux.

Van Matre, S. 1999. *Earth Education: A New Beginning*. Greenville, WV: Institute for Earth Education.

Westerhoff, P., ed. 2000. *The U.S.-Mexican Border Environment: Water Issues along the U.S.-Mexican Border*. San Diego: San Diego State University Press.

World Bank. 1990. *Assessment of Municipal Solid Waste Services in Latin America*. Washington: The World Bank.

———. 2001. *World Development Report 2000/2001: Attacking Poverty*. New York: Oxford University Press.

14

ENVIRONMENTAL
EDUCATION IN CASCADIA

John C. Miles

Abstract

Environmental education is a vital tool for environmental management. Although field education has been widely adopted in the Cascadia Region, it remains on the margins of formal education even in
such an environmentally aware area. Noteworthy is the near absence
of shared environmental educational activities across the boundary,
even though the region's ecosystems crisscross the borderlands and
the work of many NGOs and journalists deals with common environmental issues. This paper compares environmental education
activities on both sides of the international boundary and explores
reasons underlying the current "blockade" of binational educational collaboration. It also profiles one example of international
cooperation in environmental education, the Skagit Environmental
Endowment Commission. One of its education initiatives is to bring
together people from both sides of the international boundary not
only to foster appreciation for the environment, but also to address

actions to support the commission's goal of fostering transboundary cooperation so the watershed is managed as a unified, natural system. The paper concludes with an examination of the need and potential for more transboundary environmental education.

Introduction

The population of the Cascadia region is considered to be more environmentally aware and concerned than the population in other parts of the United States and Canada (Pierce et al. 2000). The environment is a part of the Cascadian culture with people commonly stating the "quality of life" associated with a beautiful, diverse, and healthy natural setting as a reason for moving to the region and for staying there. Outdoor recreation of all types is highly popular. The quality of the natural environment is featured in much of the literature of the region. There is considerable environmental education activity both north and south of the international boundary. Yet while there is a "culture of the environment" that exists in the region and transcends the boundary, there is very little exchange and interaction in the environmental education arena across that boundary. The intent here is to describe and analyze this situation and to suggest potentials for more transboundary environmental education.

The need for transboundary activity on environmental matters is well established. Salmon travel through U.S. territorial waters and into the Fraser River. Waste generated by the large urban centres in the region move through the waters of the Salish Sea. Air pollution flows back and forth across the boundary. Fauna traverse it. And increasingly land managers recognize the need to manage watersheds and ecosystems, which do not adhere to political boundaries. Protection of threatened and endangered species like the grizzly bear in the North Cascades mountain region requires such transboundary management.

The human population of the Cascadia region is large and growing, with nearly 7 million residents in 2000. Slightly less than 4 million of these people live in the United States, and about 3 million live in Canada, with projections of growth to 9 million by 2020 (Georgia Basin Ecosystem Initiative 2002). Studies of environmental quality in the region have shown improvement in some indicators, stability or decline in others. Air quality has improved, waste generation has been stable with increased recycling, pollution of marine organisms continues to be a problem, and many species are at risk often as a consequence of habitat loss due to development associated with human population growth. The prospect of continued growth and development of the human community indicates a continuing challenge to meet human needs and wants to maintain environmental quality.

A simplified way to describe the effort to manage for environmental quality in this region, as elsewhere, is to consider it a three-pronged effort. One approach is regulatory, with government coercing citizens into practising environmentally responsible behaviour. A second is to offer incentives for good environmental behaviour. The third is education, wherein people are informed and educated about their dependence on nature, their impact on it, and what behaviours relative to that environment are or are not in their best interest. Of these approaches, the focus here is upon education.

Environmental Education

The term "environmental education" is used very broadly here, referring to the learning process by which people of all ages become aware of, knowledgeable about, and concerned for the environment in which they live. It involves, as United Nations conferences in the 1970s established, elements of knowledge, attitude, motivation, commitment, and skills (UNESCO 1978). The aim is to empower and motivate people to seek and find solutions to environmental problems at home and in the larger world. It takes many forms, such as formal classes, field study, outdoor school and learning centre programs, even television programs, books and educational tourism. The public, nonprofit organizations and the private sector sponsor it. While some communities embrace it, others find it controversial.

All of these forms and qualities of environmental education may be found in the Cascadia border region.

Environmental education is practised, both north and south of the international boundary, on the educational "fringe." It is not systematically incorporated into the public school curriculum but depends primarily on the motivation of individual teachers and educational entrepreneurs. Despite its marginal importance in the formal educational scheme of things, a dedicated if small corps of educators has promoted and developed environmental education programming in both British Columbia and Washington State for over three decades. A historical treatment of this is beyond the scope of this paper, but in general the history has been parallel in both parts of the Cascadia border region. Support for environmental education has waxed and waned during this period as the politics of the environment have shifted. When public support for environmental initiatives has been strong, so has support for – and activity in – environmental education. When public interest in the environment has been less, as it was in the United States in the late 1990s, support for environmental education was down. Despite this, the general trend line for environmental education activity throughout the region has been slowly upward over the past three decades.

A brief description of environmental education activity in a community of 7 million is difficult. While the level of effort overall in environmental education is relatively small when compared with the overall educational enterprise in the region, there is still a lot happening. Environmental education effort can be categorized in many ways. Some of it, for instance, is governmental. In Washington there is an EE mandate in K-12 education, but it is not enforced (or perhaps even enforceable), yet it has stimulated considerable effort in public school districts. Some schools do more than others. A similar situation seems to exist in British Columbia, though there the Ministry of Education barely recognizes the field. The EE effort is primarily nongovernmental in British Columbia, with a large array of organizations seeking to address the need to educate about the environment. Among these are Eco Education BC, which seeks to foster care for the environment by providing educational resources and programs, the North Vancouver Outdoor School, which provides an outdoor classroom for many students, and River Works, a Vancouver Aquarium Marine Science Centre initiative that aims to use education, among other tools, to inspire stewardship of aquatic habitats. Environmental educators have come together in the state of Washington to form the Environmental Education Association of Washington as a means of building communication and community among practitioners. In British Columbia, the Environmental Educators Provincial Specialist Association serves this need. Organizations on both sides of the border have targeted specific problem areas and developed curriculum and learning materials to address them. The British Columbia Conservation Foundation aims its efforts at reducing conflicts between people and bears. In Washington State, a major effort has been launched to teach people how their activities affect the welfare of the salmon, a regional environmental icon.

Environmental education may also be divided into formal approaches, where an institution such as a school controls the objectives and the means of learning, and nonformal approaches, where the learner controls the objectives but not the means to attain them (Heimlich 1993; United States. Environmental Protection Agency 1996). A safe generalization is that the majority of programs in the region are of the latter nature, usually provided by private nonprofit groups of one sort or another. Programs may also be distinguished by the levels of the learners involved, as in the distinctions between primary, secondary, and postsecondary education. Much EE effort is aimed at primary level learners on the presumption that they are forming their perceptions of their environment and relationships to it, and thus are a critical target group. The most common targeted level is the upper elementary fifth- and sixth-grade student since cognitive faculties are sufficient at this age for students to grasp complex ideas, yet they have not advanced into the fragmented curriculum of middle and high school where integrated, interdisciplinary programs are more difficult to implement. Postsecondary environmental education is also present with programs at the University of Victoria, the University of British Columbia, Simon Fraser University, and Western Washington University.

The situation of environmental education in the region may be summarized as significant and more than is present in most other regions of Canada and the United States, even though it is far from the level that environmental educators themselves think necessary. Victor Elderton, principal of the North Vancouver Outdoor School, observed recently that, even though there is no popular recognition of the importance of EE, no recognition of it from the provincial government, and little or no coverage of it in the press, interest in it among educators is strong. Many teachers take the initiative to teach EE because they recognize how important it is. They also see the power of integrated, interdisciplinary, problem-oriented, and experiential learning. Environmentally oriented learning is about the world of the learners, and this is powerful motivation that moves many students to new levels of learning and achievement. So, throughout the region, despite lack of "official" support and systematic organization and support, environmental education is happening (Elderton 2003).

Boundary as Blockade

While the situation of environmental education north and south of the international boundary in Cascadia is similar – more happening south of the border than north but similar initiatives and challenges – there is little to no exchange across the border. Since the Canada–United States border is one of the most open in the world, why does it have this blockading effect in environmental education? This is a question worthy of research that has not been done, so only speculation is possible at this time, but several reasons come to mind.

Nationalism. In general, Americans are so focused on their own national problems and identity that they are hardly aware of what is happening in Canada, even in a region like Cascadia, where Canada is right next door. In general, Canadians wish to tend to their own affairs with no help or hindrance from their southern neighbours. Doing so is a matter of pride for them, and thus they tend to their environmental education business, as to much of their business, with the goal of finding their own path and avoiding domination by the powerful neighbour.

Full agendas. Each community of educators has enough challenges on their "home" ground without extending themselves to another country. There is simply so much to do in one's own community that there is not time, energy, or will, to think about what is happening, even in a narrowly specialized field like environmental education, beyond the boundary.

Different histories and different problems. While there are many similarities in the environmental situation of the two countries, there are also many differences. For instance, public land in the United States and Crown land in Canada are very different, with a much more centralized approach to land conservation in America than in Canada. The history of forest conservation is very different in the two countries, and this translates into a National Forest System and a National Wilderness Preservation System in the United States, neither of which is present in Canada. Thus, curriculum focused on forests is different in detail, if not in general concept, in the two countries.

Two governments. Education in general is considered a responsibility of government. Washington State has adopted environmental education guidelines for its public education system. One could hardly expect the government of British Columbia to adopt the same guidelines. Thus, to whatever degree the state and provincial governments are involved in facilitating, or hindering, environmental education, there will be two paths. The paths may be parallel, but they will be distinct.

Distinct organizational systems. British Columbia has the Environmental Educators Provincial Specialist Association, while similarly both Washington and Oregon have their own environmental education associations. Organization is structured according to political boundaries, and thus professionals in the EE field tend to meet together in their respective jurisdictions. Communication occurs among these separate groups, with limited reach beyond. There is also a North American Association for Environmental Education (NAAEE), which includes Canadian and Mexican members. Consequently some communication occurs among environmental educators in the Americas, though U.S. educators dominate the NAAEE. There is a *Journal of Environmental Education* published in the United States, and a *Canadian Journal of Environmental Education.* While research in these periodicals informs environmental education everywhere, each draws more from its home community and informs that community.

The simple fact is that in environmental education, as in most activities within the Cascadia region, people are occupied with concerns that affect them directly; on their "home ground," and that ground is in no small part defined by the nation in which they live. Thus the international boundary through Cascadia blocks interchange around environmental education.

The Skagit Environmental Endowment Commission

The Skagit Environmental Endowment Commission (SEEC) is an exception to this rule. SEEC was not established specifically to facilitate cross-border environmental education, but it has done so. Its story suggests potential for more such cross-border effort. The City of Seattle, Washington, has, since the 1920s, generated a significant portion of its electrical energy with the Skagit Hydroelectric Project on the Skagit River of British Columbia and Washington. The upper part of the Skagit watershed covers 1,380 square miles, of which 400 square miles are in British Columbia. Seattle completed construction of its third Skagit dam in 1940, then raised it twice, thereby creating twenty-four-mile long Ross Lake, which extends one mile into British Columbia at full pool. A financial settlement between the City of Seattle and the provincial government allowed this incursion of an American project into Canada.

Between 1942 and 1983 there were extensive discussions between the two countries over a fourth stage of the Ross Dam project. Controversy erupted because raising the dam an additional 125 feet would flood 5,000 acres of prime recreational and wildlife habitat lands in British Columbia. After many years of political battle and negotiation, an agreement between the City of Seattle and the Province of British Columbia stipulated that Seattle would not raise the dam for eighty years in exchange for power purchased at rates that would be equivalent to what would have resulted from raising the dam. This settlement became a formal treaty between the United States and Canada in 1984 (Solomon and Howell 1998: 3).

The treaty created the Skagit Environmental Endowment Commission and funded it with $5 million contributed by Seattle and the Province of British Columbia. The endowment was to be used to "enhance recreational opportunities" in the upper Skagit watershed and "conserve and protect wilderness and wildlife habitat (Treaty with Canada 1984). An eight-member commission, with four Canadian and four U.S. members, would administer the endowment with the intent of "continuing international cooperation" within the watershed, and it has done so since 1984. Much of the land within the area served by SEEC is managed by governmental agencies. On the Canadian side are the Skagit Provincial Park, E.C. Manning Provincial Park, Skagit Provincial Forest, Dewdney Provincial Forest, and the Cascade Provincial Recreation Area. Public lands on the United States side include the Okanogan and Mount Baker – Snoqualmie National Forests, North Cascades National Park, and the Ross Lake National Recreation Area. There is little settlement within the upper watershed, but it is important for recreation and wildlife habitat.

Initially the commission defined its mission narrowly. During its first decade, 56 per cent of its projects "enhanced recreation opportunities" in the Skagit watershed, and 27 per cent addressed the goal of protecting and preserving wildlife. The commission began to recognize education as a means to address its goals late in this first decade. It saw interpretation and other educational efforts as a way of increasing public understanding of the cross-boundary ecosystem of the Upper Skagit, and it saw that understanding as important in the long run to achievement of the goal "to conserve and protect wilderness and wildlife habitat" stated in the treaty. In 1993 it stated one of its goals to be "Education – Increase understanding of and support for ecological cultural values of the Skagit watershed upstream of Ross Dam" (Solomon and Howell 1994: 11). Other goals involved recreation, research, stewardship, and collaboration. This last was stated as "Foster trans-boundary cooperation to ensure that the watershed is managed as one ecosystem."

The goal of education was addressed in several ways. One approach was to raise awareness of, and appreciation for, the natural history of the area. This effort was directed at the general public, recreational visitors, school-age children, and teachers. SEEC-funded programs directed at awareness and appreciation include a website describing glaciers in the area and changes occurring in them, overnight camping field trips for students from schools on both sides of the boundary to introduce them to natural systems, and programs called "Mountain School" and "Skagit Watershed Education Project," conducted by an educational nonprofit, the North Cascades Institute, in cooperation with school districts in the watershed. SEEC provided a portion of the funding of these programs to the Institute that, in turn, offered a subsidy to schools that participated. Financial assistance to schools is necessary, particularly for transportation to off-school sites, and the SEEC grant contributed to this assistance. In addition, interpretive programs, signage, and other educational initiatives by British Columbia Parks and the U.S. National Park Service have been directed at recreational visitors to the area. These and other projects offered exposure to, and information about, the natural systems of the area. They helped people young and old understand the natural environment of the Upper Skagit.

A second educational approach supported by SEEC grants, which logically follows the raising of awareness, is introduction of these populations to the notion of "stewardship" of public lands and of nature in general. The values of any natural area must be actively maintained to avoid human-induced change that might degrade those values. Thus managers and others interested in preserving environmental quality respond to a need to explain the nature of and need for active stewardship of resource values. This involves explaining how stewardship is the responsibility of all who use the area and the hope that people will act to minimize their impact on it. Examples of SEEC-funded projects directed at this goal include: brochures and signage about camping impacts on vegetation and restoration efforts being undertaken by the U.S. National Park Service; a Canada-U.S. Youth Conservation Crew recruited by the Student Conservation Association (an American NGO that places young people as interns and volunteers with public land management agencies) which works in summer on various projects on both sides of the boundary; an issue of a student magazine about the area that was researched, written, published and distributed regionally by students at Western Washington University; and development of a "mountain curriculum" that includes descriptions of problems and issues in resource management, many of them present in the Upper Skagit watershed, which impart the principles of minimum impact recreational use. These and other projects have been attempts to move people beyond appreciation to action for maintenance of resource quality.

A third part of the SEEC effort has been to support educational programs that will bring together people from both sides of the international boundary not only to foster appreciation of, and action for, the environment, but also to address the commission's goal of fostering transboundary cooperation so that the watershed will be managed as one, unified, natural system. This has been less successful than the other approaches due to the difficulty of recruiting and coordinating such programs. Until recently the commission was not actively promoting one approach over another and simply waited for responses to its requests for proposals. There were few proposals to tackle the difficulties of bringing transboundary groups together. Nonetheless, there are some examples, including a conference convened to explore economic, cultural, biological, and managerial dimensions of transboundary management in the Skagit Watershed and the Greater North Cascades Ecosystem (National Parks and Conservation Association 1994). In addition, a Canada-U.S. International Youth Program brought a select group of students together to experience and study the watershed and examine the shared nature of managing a watershed split by an international boundary. Another Canada-U.S. Youth Conservation crew not only completed work projects, but also allowed extended interaction of young people from both countries around the topic of stewardship of natural resources.

These efforts have encouraged understanding by participants from both countries of the fact that a boundary drawn by humans across a watershed or any other natural system is a cultural construct of which nature is not "aware." Animals travel back and forth, actions on one side have implications for the others, and so on. Most people have given this reality no thought, and educational programs at least introduce people to the fact that, as the international conference was titled, "Nature has no borders." These programs have demonstrated the potential for bringing together people from both sides of the boundary to work on environmental stewardship issues shared across that boundary.

Environmental Education as Mitigation

A unique opportunity for environmental education appeared in the region in the late 1980s when negotiations began for relicensing of the Skagit Hydroelectric Project mentioned earlier. The re-licensing process involved stakeholders in the Skagit River watershed negotiating with the public utility – Seattle City Light – about how the environmental impact of the project over the life of the licence might be mitigated. Such mitigation was required under the *Federal Power Act* according to the rules of the United States Federal Energy Regulatory Commission. The legal interveners in the negotiations were the United States National Park Service, the United States Forest Service, the Upper Skagit and Sauk-Suiattle tribes, the Swinomish Tribal Community, and the North Cascades Conservation Council (NCCC). NCCC was the intervener representing the conservation community and it argued that environmental education be considered a mitigative strategy. Eventually this idea was accepted and North Cascades Environmental Learning Center sited in the North Cascades National Park Complex was proposed. This would be a residential facility accommodating sixty students and staff located on federal land. Construction of the facility and partial endowment of its operation over the life of the licence would be funded by Seattle City Light. Educational programming at the site would be created and delivered by the North Cascades Institute, a nonprofit environmental education organization operating in the area since 1986. As mentioned earlier, some of the institute's programs had been supported by SEEC. The North Cascades Environmental Learning Center (NCELC) is located approximately thirty miles from the international boundary, on the impounded Skagit River shore of Diablo Lake. The Memorandum of Agreement in the relicensing agreement called it the "centrepiece" of the agreement on recreation and aesthetics. The centre is to provide "vital support to a management philosophy for the North Cascades as an ecosystem." The agreement states that the City of Seattle "accepts this action [construction of the NCELC] as appropriate to increasing the depth and breadth of public appreciation for the North Cascades ecosystem" (Skagit River Hydroelectric Project, No. 553, MOA concerning NCELC 25). The proposal that education serve as part of the mitigation package was approved by the Federal Energy Licensing Commission, and the facility has been constructed.

The agreement is significant in several ways. First, the United States federal government and the municipal government of Seattle have accepted environmental education as a way to mitigate some of the impact of a regionally important environment-altering project. Second, and related to the first, the power and importance of education as an environmental management tool has been accepted. Third, because of its location close to the international boundary and the long-standing relationship between the NCELC centre's operator and SEEC, there is potential for educational programming out of the centre involving transboundary-learning objectives. At this early stage of centre development, this potential has yet to be realized, but it is on the minds of the educational programmers. Finally, as stated in the MOA, NCELC is to address the North Cascades as an ecosystem. The range extends north beyond the international boundary, and thus the charge to the NCELC, if met, should enhance educational programming about the whole range – the ecosystem – not just the part of it lying below the forty-ninth parallel.

Prospects

What does all of this suggest about the prospects for environmental education in the Cascadia border corridor? The Skagit Environmental Endowment Commission example is a unique, fortuitous opportunity that has supported environmental education and suggested possibilities for more collaborative efforts of all sorts aimed at good environmental stewardship. It suggests that when enough people care about a transboundary environmental issue and become engaged with it, sustained action can be the consequence. Perhaps international treaties involving environmental disputes can become a vehicle for encouraging and even funding international collaboration to solve environmental problems, with education recognized as one potent tool in that effort. When the treaty establishing SEEC was written, education as a means of achieving treaty goals was not on anyone's mind; but as the years passed the potential of education as a complement to research and infrastructure development was gradually recognized. Since the early 1980s, environmental education has matured as a part of environmental stewardship and will continue to do so. Educators were able to convince commissioners that education could contribute to treaty goals and thus garnered commission support for their work.

Education as environmental mitigation, as recognized in the case of the NCELC, suggests a potent new possibility for supporting environmental education in many settings. It certainly has that potential in the North Cascades setting. While not a substitute for ecological restoration, scientific study of damaged natural systems, and other important elements of mitigation, education of the population which enjoys the benefits and bears the costs of projects like the Skagit Hydroelectric Project can yield many benefits to resource managers and the general public. The case of the NCELC will be an interesting one to ascertain how significant a contribution to mitigation education can make.

As population in the Cascadia border corridor increases, with consequent increased stresses on the environment, and as knowledge of how those stressed can be minimized grows, Canadian-American partnerships to educate the populace should increase. But this will not happen spontaneously. It will require initiative and effort. It will require inventory of the environmental education resources and needs in the region. There is little doubt that a critical mass of interest and activity is present to achieve a successful transboundary effort in the region, but catalysts will be necessary for anything substantial to happen. A joint meeting of the Environmental Educators Provincial Specialists Association and the Environmental Education Association of Washington would be a good first step. This would allow recognition of shared concerns and a sharing of ideas and approaches. The focus of such a meeting should be on the transboundary nature of many environmental challenges and how collaborative Canadian-American educational efforts might help address those challenges. The experience of the SEEC educational efforts could be examined and might suggest models useable in other watersheds. All of this would occur in a nongovernmental setting, separating the effort somewhat from the vagaries of governmental environmental politics.

However it occurs, the need for such sharing and collaboration across the boundary in clear. Nature truly has no borders, and this is abundantly evident in the Cascadia region. If environmental problems in the region are to be addressed, the shackles of nationalism and provincialism must be shaken off and differences transcended. There is little doubt that this can happen when the will to do so emerges.

References

"A Treaty with Canada Relating to the Skagit River and Ross Lake in the State of Washington, and the Seven Mile Reservoir on the Pend d'OReille River in the Province of British Columbia," 2 April 1984. *Treaties and Other International Acts Series* 11088; 1469 UNTS 309.

Elderton, Victor. Nov. 2003. Interview with Rory Crowley, Principal, North Vancouver Outdoor School.

Georgia Basin Ecosystem Initiative. 2002. *Georgia Basin-Puget Sound Ecosystem Indicators Report*. Vancouver: Environment Canada.

Heimlich, J.E. 1993. "Nonformal Environmental Education: Towards a Working Definition." ERIC Clearinghouse for Science, Mathematics, and Environmental Education Bulletin 93-3. Accessed online www.stemworks.org/Bulletins/SEB93-3.

National Parks and Conservation Association. 1994. *Nature Has No Borders: A Conference on the Protection and Management of the Northern Cascades Ecosystem*. Washington, D.C.

Pierce, John C., Nicholas P. Lovrich, Brent S. Steel, Mary Ann E. Steger, and John Tennert. 2000. *Political Culture and Public Policy in Canada and the United States: Only a Border Apart*. Lewiston, NY: Edwin Mellen Press.

Solomon, A., and J. Howell. 1998. Report to the Skagit Environmental Endowment Commission on Strategic Planning. Seattle: Northwest Renewable Resources Center and Cedar River Associates.

United Nations Educational, Scientific and Cultural Organization. 1978. "Framework for Environmental Education," pp. 23–29. *Intergovernmental Conference on Environmental Education.* Final Report ED/MD/49. Paris: UNESCO.

United States. Department of Interior. Skagit River Hydroelectric Project, No. 553. 1991. "Settlement Agreement on Recreation and Aesthetics Between the City of Seattle and the U.S. Department of the Interior, National Park Service; U.S. Department of Agriculture, Forest Service; Upper Skagit Tribe, Sauk-Suiattle Tribe, and Swinomish Indian Tribal Community; and North Cascades Conservation Council." April.

United States. Environmental Protection Agency. Environmental Education Division. 1996. *Report Assessing Environmental Education in the United States and the Implementation of the National Environmental Education Act of 1990.* Washington, D.C.

15

Contributors

DONALD K. ALPER is Professor of Political Science and Director of the Center for Canadian-American Studies and the Border Policy Research Institute at Western Washington University, in Bellingham. Donald.Alper@wwu.edu

K.S. CALBICK is a Ph.D. candidate at the School of Resource and Environmental Management at Simon Fraser University, in Burnaby, British Columbia. ksc@sfu.ca

JOSE LUIS CASTRO-RUIZ is Professor of Planning and Researcher at El Colegio de la Frontera Norte (COLEF), in Tijuana. jlcastro@colef.mx

J.C. DAY is Professor Emeritus at Simon Fraser University, in Burnaby, British Columbia. jday@sfu.ca

ALEJANDRO DÍAZ-BAUTISTA is Professor of Economics and Researcher at El Colegio de la Frontera Norte (COLEF), in Tijuana. adiazbau@hotmail.com

DAVID A. FRASER is Senior Advisor, International and Intergovernmental Affairs, of Environment Canada, Pacific and Yukon Region, in Vancouver. david.fraser@ec.gc.ca

SALVADOR GARCIA-MARTINEZ is Researcher at the Center for Coastal Studies, School for Field Studies, in Puerto San Carlos, Baja California Sur. sgarcia@fieldstudies.or

WARREN G. GILL is Professor of Geography at Simon Fraser University, in Burnaby, British Columbia. gill@sfu.ca

DUNCAN KNOWLER is Assistant Professor at the School of Resource and Environmental Management, at Simon Fraser University. djk@sfu.ca

JAMES LOUCKY is Professor of Anthropology at Western Washington University, in Bellingham. James.Loucky@wwu.edu

KRISTA MARTINEZ is a Master of Arts student in Political Science at Western Washington University, in Bellingham. Krista.Martinez@wwu.edu

MARTIN MEDINA is Professor and Researcher at El Colegio de la Frontera Norte (COLEF), in Tijuana. Medina2525@aol.com

JEAN O. MELIOUS is Associate Professor in the Department of Environmental Studies, Huxley College of the Environment, Western Washington University, in Bellingham. Jean.Melious@wwu.edu

CRISTÓBAL MENDOZA is Professor in the Department of Sociology, Universidad Autónoma Metropolitana-Iztapalapa, in Mexico City. cristobalm endozaperez@yahoo.com.mx

JOHN MILES is Professor in the Department of Environmental Studies, Huxley College of the Environment, Western Washington University, in Bellingham. John.Miles@wwu.edu

JOHN M. MUNRO is Professor of Economics, at Simon Fraser University, in Burnaby, British Columbia. jmunro@sfu.edu

HUGH O'REILLY was Mayor of Whistler, British Columbia, 1996–2005

VICENTE SANCHEZ-MUNGUIA is Professor and Researcher of Planning at El Colegio de la Frontera Norte (COLEF), in Tijuana. vsanchez@colef.mx

PRESTON SCHILLER is Adjunct Professor at the Center for Canadian-American Studies and the Department of Environmental Studies, Huxley College of the Environment, Western Washington University, in Bellingham. Preston.Schiller@wwu.edu

EMMA SPENNER NORMAN is a Ph.D. candidate in geography at the University of British Columbia, in Vancouver. enorman@interchange.ubc.ca

TINA SYMKO is the Information Centre Manager, Whistler Vancouver Organizing Committee for the 2010 Olympic Winter Games. Tina_ symko@vancouver2010.com

PETER WILLIAMS is Professor, School of Resource and Environmental Management, at Simon Fraser University, in Burnaby, British Columbia. peterw@sfu.ca

INDEX